STAR

*Vintage Movie Posters
from Classic Hollywood*

IRA M. RESNICK

Foreword by

MARTIN SCORSESE

STRUCK

Abbeville Press Publishers | New York | London

PAGES 1–7
Jezebel
Detail
(See fig. 254 on p. 229)

FRONT JACKET
No Man of Her Own
Detail
(See fig. 283 on p. 259)

BACK JACKET
Sherlock Holmes
Detail
(See fig. 63 on p. 72)

First published in the United States of America in 2010 by
Abbeville Press, 137 Varick Street, New York, NY 10013

Editor: Michaelann Millrood
Copyeditor: Miranda Ottewell
Designer: Misha Beletsky
Production manager: Louise Kurtz

First edition
10   9   8   7   6   5   4   3   2

Library of Congress Cataloging-in-Publication Data

Resnick, Ira M.
  Starstruck : vintage movie posters from classic Hollywood /
by Ira M. Resnick. — 1st ed.
  p. cm.
  ISBN 978-0-7892-1019-7 (hardcover : alk. paper)
  1. Film posters, American. I. Title.
  PN1995.9.P5R47 2009
  791.43'750973—dc22
                                              2009009337

For bulk and premium sales and for text adoption proce-
dures, write to Customer Service Manager, Abbeville Press,
137 Varick Street, New York, NY 10013, or call
1-800-ARTBOOK.

Visit Abbeville Press online at www.abbeville.com.

CONTENTS

JEZE...

with

HENRY FONDA GE...
MARGARET LINDSAY DONAL...

RICHARD CROMWELL HENRY O'NEILL

A WILLIAM WYLE...

SCREEN PLAY BY CLEMENTS RIPLEY, ABEM FINKEL & JOHN HUSTON FROM TH...

A WARNER BRO...

BEL

EORGE BRENT

D CRISP FAY BAINTER

PRING BYINGTON   JOHN LITEL

R PRODUCTION

PLAY BY OWEN DAVIS, SR. MUSIC BY MAX STEINER

OS. PICTURE

To my wife Paula and my children, Jack and Samantha, who fill my life with the love and reality that puts my movie passion in a more appropriate perspective.

There NEVER was a woman like Gilda!
COLUMBIA PICTURES presents
Rita HAYWORTH
as
Gilda
with
Glenn FORD

Foreword

By Martin Scorsese

Gilda
Detail
(see fig. 205
on p. 186)

For me, and for anyone who grew up before a certain time—sometime in the 1980s, I'd say— posters were a key part of the moviegoing experience. You'd walk through the lobby, and you'd look at the poster, usually accompanied by lobby cards and often by stills and promotional language, of the film you were about to see, and the one that was coming next. You'd hold and absorb the image in your mind's eye. Part of the excitement then was in watching the actual film and comparing it with the *possible* or *likely* film you'd conjured up during the few seconds you'd looked at the poster.

The poster was meant to embody the film, but you always knew that it was somehow *outside* the film, too. It had to give you some sense of the picture, but it also carried its own mystery and romance. That's why there are people like Ira Resnick, and myself, who have devoted a lot of time and money to building our own collections of movie posters. That's what this glorious book is all about.

For instance, take the poster for *Gilda* (fig. 205). It's one of the most iconic images in American movies: Rita Hayworth standing in a long, form-fitting, strapless blue satin dress, a wrap dangling from one hand and a lit cigarette held in the other, her head cocked back in something like disdain, carelessness, and maybe superiority. It's her character, it's the movie, but it's also something else. She's standing against a dark background, on a wash of white and purplish blue over a lighter blue. In other words, she's a goddess standing on a cloud. There's some standard promotional language ("There NEVER was a woman like Gilda!") positioned over her head in an arc, and the white letters (only "Gilda!" is red) suggest stars. The imagery is in line with the general idea of *movie star*, but it's beyond that. It suggests a kind of enchanted celestial life, far above us. It was entrancing when I was a kid, and it's just as entrancing now. And it's quite distinct from the movie. Now, the poster for *Gilda* seems wonderfully complementary to the movie *Gilda*.

Take the three-sheet for *My Darling Clementine* (fig. 188)—a low-angle medium shot of Henry Fonda pointing his pistol positioned against a close-up of Victor Mature and Linda Darnell cheek to cheek. Fonda stands on a dark

ridge against the suggestion of a sunrise, and the ridge is crossed with a brown wash suggesting the desert. Mature and Darnell are set against a delicate range of colors, so that the yellow of Fonda's sunrise is also the yellow of the otherworldly backdrop. It's not quite the movie—the poster is much more garish—but it's exciting on its own because it has that odd, floating quality, like an emanation from a higher world.

Posters carry the DNA of their era, and that's also exciting. The art deco blindfolded, disembodied men's heads forming a triangle at the top of Stroheim's *Blind Husbands* (fig. 225) poster *is* the 1920s. The iconic image of James Dean in a cowboy hat and jeans stretched out on a wagon against a big sky and a western mansion in the distance, from *Giant* (fig. 207), *is* the 1950s. You look, and you either remember what it was like to be alive then, or you imagine what it *must have been* like. The poster for *Spitfire* (fig. 110)—a painting of Katharine Hepburn sitting on the top of a mountain, leaning back on her hands and staring up at the heavens, the shafts of sunlight breaking into the title—would be unthinkable now, or in the 1920s or '50s. It could only have come from the early '30s. Design changes, techniques and styles change, the sense of romance changes, along with a million other subtler, more fleeting common notions, practices, and shared emotions—and you're confronted with an image that is speaking directly of, and from, its time. And it's often speaking beautifully and gracefully, because that's the visual language of movie posters at their best.

As I said, I share Ira Resnick's passion for collecting movie posters. And you may very well begin to share that passion after you look through *Starstruck* and are caught by stunning reproductions of, for example, a lobby card for *Orphans of the Storm* (fig. 223), a German poster for Pabst's *Diary of a Lost Girl* (fig. 25), a window card for *Bringing Up Baby* (fig. 242), or stunning posters for pictures you may not even know of like *Private Detective 62* (fig. 164) with William Powell or *Daphne and the Pirate* (fig. 46) with Lillian Gish.

Welcome to the bewitching otherworld of the movie poster.

Stage

KATHARINE
HEPBURN
ME

WITH
GAIL PATRICK CON

SAMUEL S. HINDS · LUCILLE

DIRECTED BY GREGORY LA CAVA

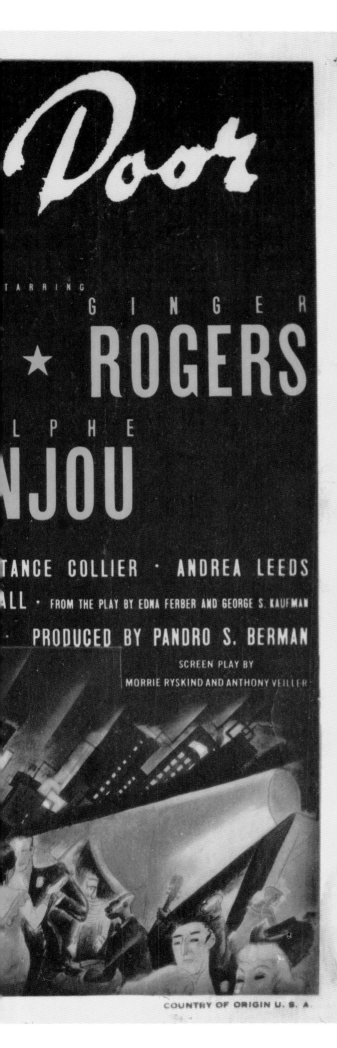

INTRODUCTION

I bought my first film posters forty years ago, and I still have all three. I found them at Cinemabilia, a now-legendary movie bookstore on Cornelia Street in Greenwich Village. I paid $50—a heavy price at the time—for a title lobby card from *Stage Door* (fig. 1), and $35 each for one-sheets promoting *Love Before Breakfast* (fig. 3) and *The Awful Truth* (fig. 7). This was the modest beginning of a collection of posters and stills, spanning the years 1912 to 1962, which now numbers in the thousands. Initially I was attracted to them because they appealed to my visual sense and reinforced the pleasure I had recently discovered in the world of classic movies, and then, as the collection grew, because they gave me access to a vivid slice of American history. In time I came to feel that I had a responsibility to preserve these artifacts, once taken for granted and considered ephemeral, now increasingly rare and precious as representatives of a lost era. When all is said and done, though, I fell in love with film posters because they let me cut myself a slice of movie magic, because they provided me with a special and almost visceral connection to the movies I loved, and to the actors and actresses who brought them to life.

Bottom line, I was starstruck.

Back in the golden age of Hollywood, long before television and the Internet, posters were the principal means used by the movie studios to alert the public to current and upcoming releases. The artwork for them was produced by studio publicity departments, and poster exchanges around the country provided theater owners with a constant stream of material designed to fit display cases in several different standard sizes, ranging from the half-

11

ABOVE

2. *The Virginian*
U.S. (1929)
Paramount
Title card
11 × 14 in.
(27.9 × 35.6 cm)

OPPOSITE

3. *Love Before Breakfast*
U.S. (1936)
Universal
One-sheet
41 × 27 in.
(104.1 × 68.6 cm)

sheets and one-sheets found inside lobbies, to the larger three-sheets and six-sheets typically found at theater entrances, right up to gigantic twenty-four-sheet billboard-sized posters. There were also window cards, distributed to local merchants for exhibition in their storefronts, and—a key category for collectors—lobby cards, issued in sets of eight consisting of a title card—generally similar to the poster art and showing the credits—along with seven others illustrating key scenes from the movie. Theater owners would select cards and posters from a press book and rent them for a nominal fee. In theory they were supposed to return them to the exchange when the promotion was over, but this didn't always happen. Some were simply thrown

out, and many of those that were dutifully returned were pulped, often as the result of World War II paper drives. Luckily a few were taken home and saved by movie-loving projectionists or theater ushers—fans of all stripes—while others sat for years in storage rooms, attracting no attention until an old theater was threatened by the bulldozers. The posters that survive today are valuable because they escaped the normal process of attrition. All of them are rare. A few are rarer than paintings by Vermeer.

To build my collection, I haunted flea markets and stores that cater to the desires and needs of the movie-smitten; I scoured country salesrooms and bid at auctions at Sotheby's and Christie's; I jumped on airplanes to follow

CARL LAEMMLE presents

Carole Lombard

Faith Baldwin's

LOVE BEFORE BREAKFAST

With **PRESTON FOSTER**

CESAR ROMERO · JANET BEECHER
FROM THE NOVEL "SPINSTER DINNER"
DIRECTED BY WALTER LANG · AN EDMUND GRAINGER PROD.

A universal picture

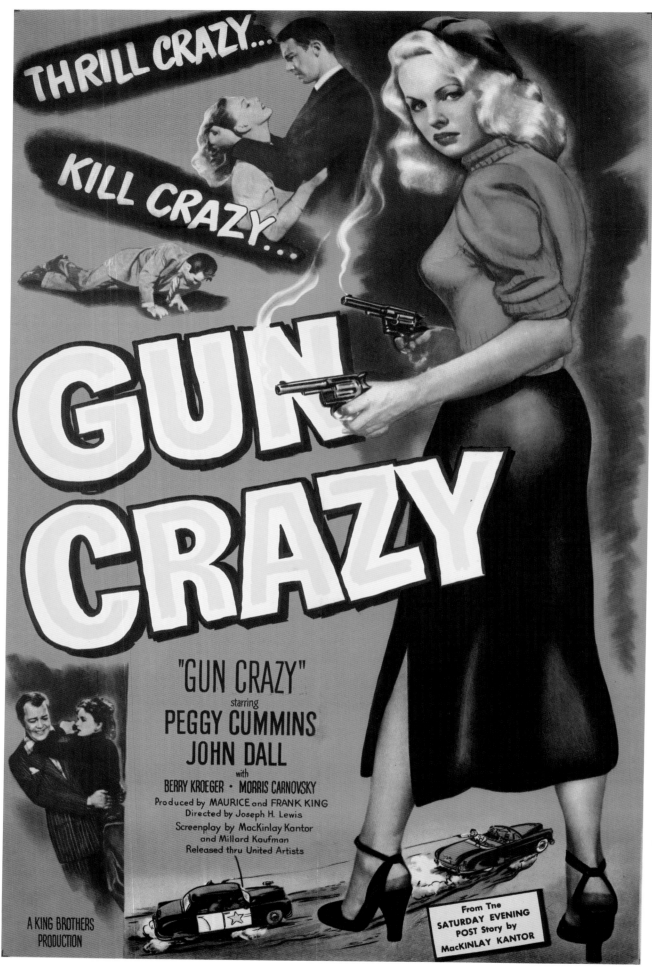

4. *Gun Crazy*
Also known as:
Deadly Is the Female
U.S. (1950)
United Artists
One-sheet
41 × 27 in.
(104.1 × 68.6 cm)

5. *Hallelujah!*
U.S. (1929)
MGM
Title card
11 × 14 in.
(27.9 × 35.6 cm)

promising leads, and bargained with collectors who would tease year after year with tantalizing glimpses of some gem from Paramount or Columbia. I developed a network, and finally opened my own gallery, which enabled me to see a lot of material I might not otherwise have had access to, and to expand my collection, the cream of which is represented on these pages.

I do not wish to pretend that my collection should be taken as historically comprehensive. Only a museum could aspire to completeness. I think, though, I can claim a broad knowledge of the history of cinema—especially of the varied and wonderful movies that came out of Hollywood between the heyday of silent films and the demise of the studio system in the 1950s—and I believe that my collection encapsulates significant parts of that history; but I'm happy to admit that ultimately it's a reflection of my own taste and preferences.

Collecting these beautiful artifacts, over the past forty years, has allowed me to preserve the sense of what particular movies meant to me. Surrounding myself with images that evoke the mood of a favorite comedy or musical has

LEFT

7. *The Awful Truth*
U.S. (1937)
Columbia
One-sheet
41 × 27 in.
(104.1 × 68.6 cm)

BELOW

6. *Ziegfeld Follies*
U.S. (1946)
MGM
One-sheet
41 × 27 in.
(104.1 × 68.6 cm)

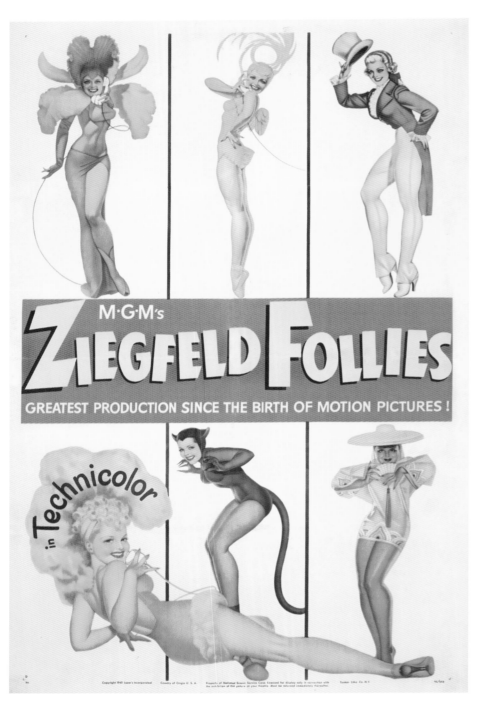

RIGHT

8. *Her Husband's Trademark*
U.S. (1922)
Famous Players–
Lasky/Paramount
One-sheet
41 × 27 in.
(104.1 × 68.6 cm)

16

9. *A Midsummer
Night's Dream*
U.S. (1935)
Warner Bros.
Title card
11 × 14 in.
(27.9 × 35.6 cm)

meant that the party didn't have to end when the film
was over. They conjure up a world peopled with actors
and actresses who for me possess the same kind of magic
I associate with the fairy-tale characters of my earliest
memories. I've been bewitched by these fabulous performers, and I hope that as you turn these pages, you too will
experience some of that enchantment.

1

*The Education
of a
Collector*

PAGES 18–19
In a Lonely Place
Detail
(See fig. 22 on p. 31)

BELOW
10. *Yankee Doodle Dandy*
U.S. (1942)
Warner Bros.
Midget window card
14 × 8 in.
(35.6 × 20.3 cm)

OPPOSITE
11. *Dodge City*
U.S. (1939)
Warner Bros.
Title card
11 × 14 in.
(27.9 × 35.6 cm)

I grew up in New Rochelle, New York, the town celebrated by George M. Cohan in his musical *Forty-five Minutes from Broadway.* That was the show that introduced the songs "Mary Is a Grand Old Name" and "So Long Mary," revived by the great James Cagney when he played Cohan in *Yankee Doodle Dandy* (fig. 10). Coincidentally, New Rochelle is also the location for much of Cagney's last film, *Ragtime.* Back to Cohan—his musical's title derived from the fact that New Rochelle was thirty-five minutes from Grand Central Station on the New Haven Line, and a ten-minute walk would take you from the arrival platform to the bright lights of Broadway. Despite the brevity of the journey, the two places could not be farther apart, and that was the point made explicit in lyrics that read, "They've got whiskers like hay / And imagine Broadway / Only forty-five minutes from here." By my time, whiskers had become rarities in New Rochelle, and the town was known to millions as the home of Rob and Laura Petrie on *The Dick Van Dyke Show;* but it was still only forty-five minutes from the excitement of the Great White Way.

One day in the fall of 1954, my mother took me into the city, and we made our way to West Fiftieth Street and Seventh Avenue in the heart of the Broadway theater district. I was about to see my first movie, and my initiation would take place in a theater that was as far from today's multiplexes as can be imagined. The movie was *Brigadoon,* with Gene Kelly and Cyd Charisse, and I would experience it in glorious CinemaScope and stereophonic sound from the vast auditorium of the Roxy, a movie palace rivaled only by Radio City Music Hall and known in its day as the Cathedral of the Motion Picture. With more than 6,000 seats and its lavish pseudo-Andalusian decor, the Roxy was awesome. Launched in 1927 by the innovative impresario

Starstruck

Samuel L. "Roxy" Rothafel, it was famous for its spectacular stage shows, its three pipe organs, its 110-piece symphony orchestra, and the glamorous Roxyettes, precursors of Radio City's Rockettes. Astonishingly, much of this survived into the 1950s in a kind of glorious time warp. When you went to see a movie at the Roxy, you also got showgirls and singers, comedians and acrobats, and maybe Tchaikovsky's *1812 Overture* or a snatch of Beethoven's Fifth. Years later, my mother would tell me I didn't see too much of that 1954 performance because she had to take me to the bathroom ten times, but I do recall the sense of awe I felt. The Roxy was a living embodiment of the glorious Hollywood heyday that, as an adult, I would try to recapture through my poster collection.

Except for a cousin who was in the chorus of *My Fair Lady*, we were anything but a show-business family. My mother was an immigrant from Russia. My father was a hardworking real estate developer, born in Harlem of Yiddish-speaking parents. Certainly they enjoyed movies—my mother's favorite star was Dick Powell—but money was tight when they first got together, and they probably didn't go to a picture show as often as they would have liked. In any case, they belonged to a generation that knew how to let its imagination run wild in books like *The Count of Monte Cristo*, my father's great favorite.

By contrast, I belonged to the first generation to grow up with television, conditioned to value images over words. There were more visits to movie theaters—I remember seeing Kirk Douglas in *The Vikings* and being shaken up by the violence—but at first it was the small screen that

GRAND THEATER | MONDAY MARCH 18TH.

JULIUS STEGER PRESENTS

Evelyn Nesbit

AND HER SON RUSSELL THAW

IN A PHOTO-PLAY FROM LIFE

"REDEMPTION"

DIRECTED BY JULIUS STEGER AND JOSEPH A. GOLDEN

Movie." Monday through Friday it would show the same film twice a night, and maybe half a dozen times on the weekend. One week, when I was still very young, the featured movie was *Yankee Doodle Dandy*. After I saw it once, I was hooked, and I think I watched it every time it was broadcast for the rest of the week. The film was made in 1942, but with its patriotism, its energetic singing and dancing, its uncomplicated treatments of love and loss, youth and aging, it seemed to embody all of the values instilled in us, growing up in the Eisenhower years. I couldn't have put it into words back then, but it was as if that movie opened a window to my soul and provided an outlet for the sensitive side of my being. My fanatic passion for movies was beginning to take root.

In 1956, Topps issued a set of eighty Davy Crockett cards that came packaged with one-cent and five-cent packages of bubble gum. As proud of my coonskin hat as the next kid, I naturally wanted to have the entire set. This was my introduction to collecting, but Davy was soon supplanted by a passion for baseball cards, itself an offshoot of my enthusiasm for the New York Yankees, and especially Mickey Mantle, a real-life hero to match any movie star.

dominated my viewing. I was hypnotized by those early kids' shows—*Miss Frances' Ding Dong School*, *Howdy Doody*, and *Kookla, Fran and Ollie*—and it was mostly by way of television that I was first exposed to the panorama of Hollywood movies. In those days, the networks bid against one another for the rights to show recent theatrical releases, then afterward the films would go into syndication, which meant that they showed up frequently in the living room, as did the classic movies that I came to love. The fact that many of the older films were in black and white didn't matter because television was black and white too. I have a clear memory of seeing *Shane* on television early on, and while I was never a big fan of the Disney animated movies, I was very taken with some of their live-action films, like *Tonka* and *Old Yeller*, which made me cry.

James Cagney was one of the first stars I identified with. Channel 9 in New York had a feature called "Million Dollar

CARY GRANT ☆ DORIS DAY "That Touch of Mink" *A Eastman COLOR FRANSCOPE* Adult Sophisticated Comedy!

GIG YOUNG • AUDREY MEADOWS

In my case the impetus to collect—and of course to deal—was heightened by the fact that I was an accomplished "flipper" of cards who on one memorable occasion won a pot of five thousand cards in a knock-down-the-leaner tournament played in front of a large and noisy crowd at summer camp. That was a lot of capital to have available for trading. I recall once trading a thousand cards for Topps number 503—Jim Owens, a so-so right-handed pitcher for the Phillies—which I needed to complete my set.

The way I collected baseball cards anticipated the way I would collect movie posters. I wanted desperately to identify with "The Mick" and other great players like Roberto Clemente, Willie Mays, Hank Aaron, and Duke Snider. I loved those cards. I kept them neatly organized in albums,

with shoeboxes filled with duplicates and spares. Years later, when I came home from college, I discovered that the collection was missing, and my mother informed me that while cleaning and reorganizing, she had given it away to my cousin Jeffrey. I was furious. My mother called Jeffrey's mother to broker a return, and was told that the entire collection had been lost during a move. From that time on I vowed that any collection I formed would remain under my supervision and control. This was because of my passion as a collector rather than because of the possible monetary value of the lost collection, which in the case of those Topps cards would not be much today, because serious baseball card collectors demand cards in pristine condition and very few of mine would have matched that

15. *42nd Street*
U.S. (1933)
Warner Bros.
Midget window
card
14 × 8 in.
(35.6 × 20.3 cm)

description (which, I must say, makes me feel a little better about having lost them).

In high school, I started collecting vintage postcards. The golden age of postcards lasted roughly from 1900 to World War I. With my friend Charlie, I would head for shows organized by the Metropolitan Postcard Club at various hotels around Manhattan. I would go from booth to booth hunting for fantasy cards, ranging from the sort that would show a railroad truck loaded with a single orange or a single watermelon the size of a crosstown bus to the trick photography kind that might portray an old man lost in contemplation in front of a fire, its smoke morphing into the shape of a beautiful young girl, perhaps his long-lost love. The latter might be captioned simply "Ashes." I also collected New York City cards, and those with views of my hometown. New Rochelle had had a vibrant turn-of-the-century culture, and a little later became home to celebrities ranging from Norman Rockwell to Lou Gehrig. I was proud of that heritage and wanted to own a part of it.

What all these cards had in common was that they evoked nostalgia for a past I had never known. I wanted to lose myself in a romantic vision of that lost world, a notion that my mother found hard to understand. She had lived through some hard times after arriving in America and knew that the old days weren't always like a Fred Astaire–Ginger Rogers movie. Still, I persisted, and it was thanks to this romantic vision that I became involved with the notion of collecting tokens of stardom, especially female stardom, of which I first became enamored in the person of Evelyn Nesbit. Remembered as "The Girl on the Red Velvet Swing," Evelyn Nesbit was the darling of Edwardian postcard publishers, as famous in her time as Madonna is today. A great beauty—originally an artists' model and a "Floradora Girl"—her fame was due to the fact that in 1906 her husband, Harry Kendall Thaw, heir to a Pittsburgh coal and railroad fortune, murdered the distinguished architect Stanford White—who had seduced Nesbit when she was just sixteen—on the famous Madison Square Garden roof. The newspapers dubbed it "The Trial of the Century," and Nesbit's performance on the witness stand at the subsequent trial is said to have been worthy of Sarah Bernhardt. In fact Nesbit went on to make stage appearances and silent movies, and I have a striking poster for one of the latter. More than half a century after the scandal had died down, I became infatuated with her as a symbol of the lost era I found so fascinating.

Around the same time, I began to look out for photographic movie star cards. These were issued by postcard companies from all over the world who licensed the images from Hollywood studios and their European equivalents. My favorites were produced in Germany in the 1920s and 1930s, and I remember in particular the "real photo" cards that came from the Berlin publisher Ross Verlag, some sexy,

some sentimental, some illustrating scenes from films like *Ben-Hur* and *Grand Hotel* (fig. 122). And so my collecting fervor had taken me from Yankee Stadium to the back lots of Hollywood, at least in my imagination.

During my postcard period, we moved from New Rochelle into Manhattan, and there my moviegoing habits began to take shape. With friends, and on dates, I would get to know the full range of New York movie theaters, from Radio City, to all-night Forty-second Street houses, to Cinema Village on East Twelfth Street near Strand Books. My favorite was the Trans-Lux 85th Street Theatre—now sadly gone—which was a block from the family apartment on Madison Avenue. Opened in the 1930s as a newsreel theater—part of a chain launched by Percy Norman Furber, inventor of the rear projection screen—in my day the Trans-Lux showed a lively mix of first-run features, second-run features, and foreign movies, with kids' programming on weekends. (For the latter, there was actually a matron in attendance!) What made the place special was the fact that the interior had been designed to resemble a small French town, complete with bistro tables where you could enjoy coffee and sweets, which made it a very romantic place to take girls, or so I thought at the time.

A large part of my film education was still coming by way of television (which had acquired color by then). In those years I liked to watch *The Early Show* and *The Late Show* on CBS Channel 2. There was also *The Late Late Show*, which would start at around three in the morning and would often program 1930s MGM movies. These fueled my nascent interest in old Hollywood, and around 1967 my infatuation with the cinema was given fresh impetus. This was a tense time for young men of my generation. The Vietnam War was at its height, and the military draft was a fact of life that could not be ignored. I enrolled at Boston University that year, very much aware that staying in college would keep me out of the war. Beyond that, however, I was looking for ways of escaping the frightening realities of the Nixon years, and I turned on the one hand to rock music, and on the other to movies, both current and vintage. Sometimes the two obsessions overlapped. I loved the Beatles and must have seen *Help!* thirty times or more. I discovered the Exeter Street Theatre in Boston, a gaunt, ecclesiastical-looking building, and the Brattle in Cambridge. Both screened a mix of old films, foreign films, and American independent films. Viola Berlin, the manager and booker of the Exeter Street Theatre, had a particular penchant for British movies and even ran British newsreels along with them. The Brattle had a tradition of showing Humphrey Bogart movies, especially during Harvard finals week.

It was in Boston too that I saw *The Graduate*, which for me, as for many others of my generation, was a defining moment. Like everyone else, I fell madly in love with Katharine Ross.

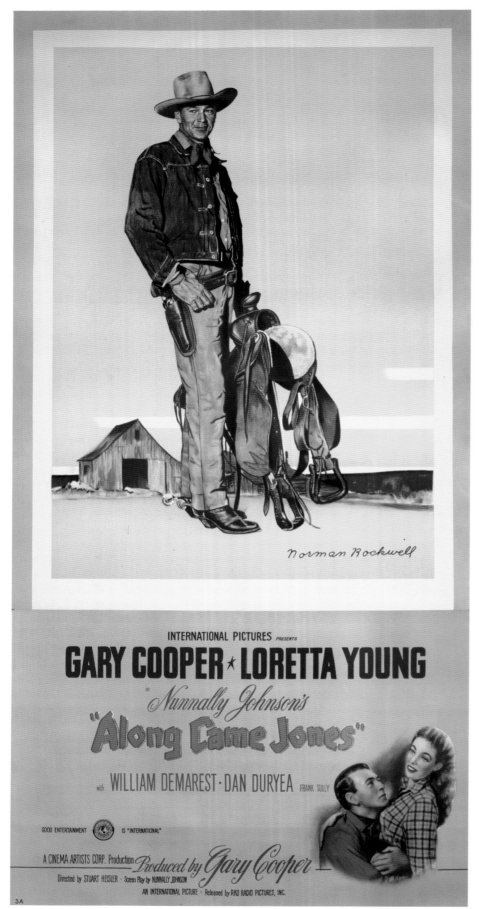

16. *Along Came Jones*
U.S. (1945)
Cinema/International/RKO
Three-sheet
81 × 41 in. (205.7 × 104.1 cm)

After two years, I returned to New York, enrolling at NYU Film School and renting an apartment in Greenwich Village, which I promptly made mine by affixing a poster of Jean-Paul Belmondo—Gauloise dangling from his lips—to the wall. This was a period during which my friends and I lived and breathed cinema, which served as a great buffer against the chaos of a crazy, changing world, and helped ease us into adulthood. There were no videos or DVDs, so if you wanted to see interesting films, you had to go out and find them, combing the pages of the *Village Voice* and the entertainment section of *The New York Times* to discover which half-forgotten gems were playing where. We'd haunt revival houses like the Elgin, Theater 80 St. Marks, the New Yorker, and the Thalia. Once my friend Jamie and I saw seven movies in a single day, a record I do not expect to beat.

Film school itself was exciting and creative. The directorial problems class taught by Martin Scorsese was one of the highlights, and the wonderful film history courses provided me with a solid foundation for all of my future explorations of Hollywood's past glories.

It was during this period that I bought those first three posters. The original Cinemabilia was on Cornelia Street near Café Cino, and it was not the kind of store that believed in the creed "The customer is always right." Ernest Burns, the owner, was a sullen character whose contempt for casual shoppers misguided enough to wander in off the street was matched and sometimes exceeded by that of his minions. (The level of civility to be expected at Cinemabilia can be judged by the fact that later employees included punk rockers like Tom Verlaine, Richard Hell, Robert Quine, and Terry Ork.) If you didn't know what you were looking for, you were shown the door. Most people didn't wait that long—they took the hint and left without being asked. I spent money there on a regular basis, so I was largely immune to the rudeness. Years later—his shop long closed—Ernest, needing money, would come to my gallery to sell me posters.

(The $35 I paid Ernest for that *Love Before Breakfast* one-sheet [fig. 3], on my first Cinemabilia visit, seemed like a lot of money at the time. Forty years later, in conjunction with another dealer, I sold at auction another copy of that same poster for $47,000. Had I started collecting a few years earlier, I've been told, I could have bought almost anything for less than $10.)

Another destination when I began my quest—and not a salubrious one—was the Memory Shop, run by a man called Mark Ritchie along with his partner. In the back they had file drawers, but nobody seemed to know what was in them—bugs, I imagine. I was always told that the good stuff was kept in a warehouse somewhere, and they would habitually respond to inquiries by saying, "If you come back . . ." The fact is, they always seemed too busy hanging out to deal with their customers. When you did get their attention, it sometimes came with extracurricular trimmings you were not expecting. I have a clear memory of looking at stills on the counter while the pair of them ate roast beef sandwiches. The Russian dressing dripped onto eight-by-ten glossies of John Barrymore and Greta Garbo. Mark and his partner were unperturbed. Hopefully these prints were reissues, because the tissues that they nonchalantly used to clean up the mess simply served to smudge the images. This was a *very* laissez-faire operation, but the cavalier attitude at least taught me respect for the materials.

Along with James Cagney, the first stars I liked were John Barrymore, Katharine Hepburn, Carole Lombard, and the Marx Brothers, but as my knowledge of film history grew I began to look beyond this core group, and the way my collection grew related directly to the movies I saw and liked. If the Thalia had a Busby Berkeley series, that would give me the impetus to search for items related to stars like Ruby Keeler and Dick Powell, or titles such as *42nd Street* (fig. 15) and *Footlight Parade* (fig. 14). If W. C. Fields was being featured at the Elgin, I would hunt for material from *It's a Gift* (figs. 19 and 183) or *The Bank Dick*. My collection grew in direct response to my exposure to, and knowledge of, an ever wider range of films.

It was at this time I bought from Harry N. Abrams, the noted art book publisher, one of the rarest pieces in my collection—unique, in fact—the original painting of Gary Cooper made in 1946 by Norman Rockwell for the poster publicizing the film *Along Came Jones*. This large canvas embodied both my love of film and my love of art, and later I acquired a three-sheet of the *Along Came Jones* poster (fig. 16).

As film school came to an end, I began to think about what I was going to do with my life. My father had built a successful business, and had signaled his intentions for my future by naming it Jack Resnick & Sons. This was the rebellious 1970s, however, and, while I was not as radically antiestablishment as some of my contemporaries, I did not see myself spending the rest of my life in real estate. In the summer of 1972 I worked on the film *Badlands*, starring Sissy Spacek and Martin Sheen, but dreams of being a moviemaker did not pan out. That same year, I had a fling as a Broadway angel, coproducing a version of Aristophanes's *Lysistrata*, starring Melina Mercouri. The show's antiwar theme was timely, but the production was poorly conceived for an American audience and the show received bad reviews, closing after just eight performances.

I decided to become a freelance photographer. Classic American photography was something I had discovered at the same time I discovered classic American cinema, and one of my heroes was Edward Weston. I admired his photographs—ranging from exquisite nudes in landscapes to near-abstract still lifes—and I was taken with the passionate and committed way in which he had lived and loved while pursuing his art, as set down in the "daybooks" he began to keep in 1923 when, his marriage on the rocks, he moved to Mexico. An entry might, for instance, describe something as simple as going to an outdoor market to buy a pepper, bringing it home, photographing it, then eating it for lunch. The lifestyle he described seemed pure and unpretentious, yet at the same time erotic and poignant. It jelled with the mood of a period when many of my contemporaries were choosing to live outside society, joining communes or heading for Nepal to find themselves. I guess I wanted to find myself too, so I packed the two volumes of Weston's daybooks in my car, along with my cameras, and set off across Canada with Alaska as my destination.

While looking for myself, I didn't forget about my poster collection. I knew about a poster exchange in Calgary, Alberta, so I stopped off there and found several choice items, which I shipped back to New York. Had I only known, I could have had a major coup in Calgary because the Royal Theater there contained a roomful of rolled vintage posters in near-mint condition. These would not be discovered—or rediscovered—until a decade later, when they set off a storm in the poster-collecting world. Instead, I went on my way, and after five months on the road, and exposing innumerable rolls of film, I reached the Alaska Highway. It was Thanksgiving. Winter was coming on, and I'd had my fill of gas stations and diners for the time being, so I headed south and ended up in Mill Valley, California—just across the Golden Gate from San Francisco—where I settled for the next three years.

Like Boston and New York, the San Francisco Bay Area is a mecca for those of us who love old movies, home to revival houses and dealers in cinema collectibles of all kinds. One of the people I met during this period was a man named Jose Carpio, who ran a café and poster gallery called Cinemonde on Polk Street in San Francisco. His store became an important source of material for me, and later—when I opened my own dealership—he became an important ally. Meanwhile, I was working for a magazine called the *Collector's Voice*, a job that involved photographing collections and collectors ranging from a Satanist who lived in a spooky Charles Addams–style Gothic house in Bolinas to Rock Hudson. For the latter story, the editor and I traveled down to Los Angeles to the star's home on Mulholland Drive, which was filled with sculptures of naked young men by a Mexican artist, the significance of which emerged later. Working for the *Collector's Voice* was a good gig and left me plenty of time to search for posters, and for photographs, which by then I was also collecting avidly.

At that time San Francisco was a hotbed of rock music, much of it promoted under the banner of Bill Graham, of Fillmore fame, who in the mid-1970s was operating another venue, Winterland, and organizing concerts and band tours.

LEFT

17. *Sunset Boulevard*
U.S. (1950)
Paramount
Insert
36 × 14 in.
(91.4 × 35.6 cm)

ABOVE

18. Yvonne de Carlo
and Howard Duff
U.S. (1948)
Universal
Publicity still
14 × 11 in.
(35.6 × 27.9 cm)

OPPOSITE

19. *It's a Gift*
U.S. (1934)
Paramount
Insert
36 × 14 in.
(91.4 × 35.6 cm)

As a photographer I had access to many of the rock events
of that period and began making an extensive visual record
of the West Coast music scene.

In 1977 I finally made the move to Hollywood, settling
into a house in the Hollywood Hills. I opened a photography
studio in a lovely little cottage above the house, and there
I shot romance covers and actor and actress portfolios,
as well as my own personal work. I also worked for Globe
Photos and was a stringer for Media Press International,
a European syndicate, and I continued shooting rock con-

certs. (Today I'm curating these music photographs as historical artifacts.)

And now I was in Hollywood, and the world I had fallen in love with through films and posters was all around me. There were the studios themselves, of course. If you drove past Paramount, Warner Bros., or MGM, the lots still looked much as they must have in the 1930s or '40s, with their rows of humpback sound stages visible through elaborate gateways, their water towers emblazoned with company logos. Hollywood was still peppered with restaurants and bars with names that were familiar from movie magazines and gossip columns: Dan Tana's, Le Dome, Musso & Frank Grill, Trader Vic's, Chasen's, Scandia. The Vine Street Brown Derby was crowded at lunchtime, and the daddy of them all, Perino's, was still in business. Each of these places had its own character. At Musso's—still happily with us—you were more likely to encounter writers and directors. At Chasen's you might catch glimpses of movie stars, past and present, being ushered to their booths by the attentive maître d'. But then again you were quite likely to run into instantly recognizable faces—though the names might sometimes escape you—at Hamburger Hamlet, or the newsstand on Las Palmas Avenue, or the checkout line at the all-night Ralph's on Sunset. I remember going to a garage sale at Yvonne de Carlo's house. She was absolutely charming and was nice enough to sign a few things I had bought at the sale (fig. 18).

For me, though, there was much more to it than famous faces and restaurants with legendary names. It was the whole atmosphere of the place. Living in the Hollywood Hills, with its Tuscan villas and Monterey cottages, was a constant reminder of the Hollywood that had been: not necessarily the playground of the stars but the world of makeup artists, and camera operators, and second unit directors, and struggling screenwriters, and aspiring actors and actresses—the Hollywood that caught the jaundiced eye of Nathanael West in *Day of the Locust*, and the knowing attention of F. Scott Fitzgerald in his Pat Hobby stories. I knew people who lived in bungalows just like the one Humphrey Bogart occupies in *In a Lonely Place* (fig. 22)—Nicholas Ray's brilliant 1950 exercise in film noir, a great favorite of mine. ("The Bogart suspense picture," the poster announces, "with the surprise finish!") Then there was the actual apartment building that Judy Garland called home in the early scenes of *A Star Is Born*, or the bungalow court near Vermont Avenue that had once housed the writing department of a major studio. Reminders of cinema's golden age were everywhere. I would drive to the Strip to locate the former locations of Ciro's and the Café Trocadero, or out to Santa Monica to peruse the beachfront Millionaire's Row, where Louis B. Mayer, Marion Davies, and Darryl Zanuck had built lavish homes.

All the time, of course, I was collecting as avidly as ever.

Right below my house, on Hollywood Boulevard and the side streets that crossed it, were many used bookstores, several of which also dealt in movie posters. Perhaps the best known was Larry Edmunds, which sold new and old books about the cinema, vintage *Variety* yearbooks, press kits from the 1930s and '40s, bound copies of old fan magazines like *Photoplay* and *Modern Screen*, and contemporary fanzines and movie magazines from all over the world such as *Cahiers du cinéma*, as well as film stills and posters. Also on Hollywood Boulevard, in an old building not far from Grauman's Chinese Theatre, was Bennett's Book Store (later the name was changed to Collectors Book Store), a cavernous space with a lofty antique tin ceiling that was a place of pilgrimage for both movie buffs and science fiction fans. The movie material was in the front of the store, where the walls were hung with posters. There were tables loaded with boxes of stills (the good ones were behind the counter and had to be requested) and discarded shooting scripts. For me the primary attractions were the posters and stills, and it was here that I found many wonderful images of forgotten and half-forgotten silent movie stars. Typically I could buy a gorgeous poster from some little-known silent movie for around $75.

There were other similar places in different parts of the city, such as Eddie Brandt's in the Valley, not to mention flea markets and junk stores where you could get lucky. By then my collecting was becoming more systematic. I would look for specific stars and specific movies, my taste and interests always widening as I continued to expand my knowledge through visits to theaters such as Laurence Austin's Silent Movie Theater on Fairfax Avenue. (Austin—who had the embalmed look of a character from a James Whale horror film—was later brutally murdered in his theater in what turned out to have been a hit planned by his projectionist/boyfriend James Van Sickle: a story straight out of a B movie.)

In those days there was a weekly phone auction that I often participated in, once buying a wonderful poster for the 1922 movie *Beyond the Rocks* (fig. 21) starring Gloria

Starstruck

Swanson and Rodolph Valentino (which is how his name was spelled at the beginning of his career). My winning bid was $3,000. Today it would fetch at least ten times as much. There was also the Berry Auction Company, where I netted a *Twentieth Century* half-sheet and many other choice items. I would also frequent a shop off Santa Monica Boulevard called the Hollywood Poster Exchange, run by a man named Bob Colman who had bought a cache of posters found in the Cozy Theater, a tiny, now-demolished movie house in downtown Los Angeles, across Broadway from the Million Dollar Theater. It's the dream of every poster collector to stumble upon a priceless cache in a locked room in some movie palace that has survived the decades (though in the case of the Cozy it had been more of a movie cottage). I've already mentioned the Calgary hoard that I missed, and I've never had that great stroke of luck, but I don't regret it at all because it has forced me to hunt down the prizes I really wanted, which has made collecting more of a challenge. In any case, I enjoyed schmoozing

with people like Bob Colman, a necessary prelude to being allowed access to the stacks in the back of the store where the prize would be something I wanted to buy that Bob was willing to part with. You had to be patient and sift through masses of material, but the rewards made it all worthwhile, and my collection still includes many lobby cards with "Cozy Theater" stamped on the back. In the Cozy stock, I found Warner Bros. cards on beaded paper produced to promote late-1930s Errol Flynn classics like *The Adventures of Robin Hood* (fig. 20) and *Dodge City* (figs. 11 and 165). It was in Bob's backroom that I began to be interested in Ida Lupino, just because there were so many good examples there of posters featuring her. (Sometimes it was posters that led me to particular movies or stars rather than vice versa.) What I learned at the Hollywood Poster Exchange and places like it was, Pick the best you can from any given situation. Every piece doesn't have to be A plus material, so don't always go for the home run. Be happy with a bunt single or a sacrifice fly if it brings home the goods.

The Education of a Collector

Another strong memory of the period is the Mary Pickford auction at which, although I bought no posters, I got photographs, furniture, and notepaper from Pickfair—items of personal nature that allowed me to feel close to that privileged circle where stars like Pickford and Chaplin hobnobbed with visiting celebrities from very different worlds, such as H. G. Wells and George Bernard Shaw. The best piece was a wonderful silver art deco bowl that was presented to Mary and Doug Fairbanks by Baron Nishi, a Japanese nobleman who was an equestrian gold medalist at the 1932 Los Angeles Olympics, and who at that time was enthusiastically welcomed into the Pickford-Fairbanks social circle. A tank commander in World War II, Baron Nishi was killed at Iwo Jima but lives on as a major character in Clint Eastwood's *Letters from Iwo Jima.*

One disappointment of my Hollywood period came at Paramount Studios one day, where I was visiting my friend Robert Klein, who was working there. As I wandered around the lot, I noticed a bungalow with Katharine Hepburn's name on the door. Naturally this aroused my interest, so I hung around and after a while, sure enough, Hepburn arrived, accompanied by a man who turned out to be her hairdresser, and they disappeared into the bungalow. As it happened, I had come from Bennett's, where I had bought some choice stills, including one from *Quality Street* (fig. 23) with plenty of room at one side of the image for an autograph. I went back to my car to retrieve the photograph and knocked on the bungalow door, knowing full well that Hepburn was notorious for not signing autographs but still daring to hope that she might be in an accommodating mood that particular day, and, who knows, perhaps invite me in for tea. Nothing ventured, after all. Needless to say, she was not pining for my company. When the hairdresser answered the door, I handed him the still and made my request, saying that I was a big fan. He returned promptly and returned the unsigned still. "Miss Hepburn only signs for friends," he told me, before politely asking me to leave.

As the 1970s gave way to the '80s, New York began to beckon me home. I was returning to the East Coast with a plan, however. My collection by then was becoming quite extensive and had real substance, consisting of prime material diligently researched and sought out. These posters and stills, all associated with original releases, allowed me to feel that I could possess part of the movies themselves, since in fact the promotional campaigns for a Hollywood film were integral parts of the production package. A gorgeous contemporary lithograph encapsulated—even embodied—a movie in a way nothing else could, and a set of lobby cards brought back the events of a film in précis form. If this had begun as a hobby, I was now an addict, and I wanted more—I wanted the best collection imaginable, and I realized that the only way I could do this was by

"QUALITY STREET" — An RKO Radio Picture

PERMISSION IS HEREBY GRANTED TO NEWSPAPERS, MAGAZINES AND OTHER PERIODICALS TO REPRODUCE THIS PHOTOGRAPH. Printed in U. S. A. Copyright 1937. RKO Radio Pictures, Inc. Property of RKO Radio Pictures, Inc. Loaned for restricted use only; must be returned to RKO Radio Pictures, Inc. and must not be sold, leased or given away by any other party.

ABOVE

23. Katharine Hepburn
in *Quality Street*
U.S. (1937)
RKO
Still
10 × 8 in.
(25.4 × 20.3 cm)

OPPOSITE

24. Motion Picture
Arts Gallery
U.S. (1984)
32 × 24 in.
(81.3 × 61 cm)

becoming a dealer. That would give me access to otherwise inaccessible riches, and it would allow me to trade my way to perfection, or something that approximated it. The boy who had determinedly swapped his way to a complete set of Topps baseball cards was now a grown man still driven by the same instinct.

What I didn't want was a street-level store with a counter, like Cinemabilia, or the Memory Shop, or Bennett's, or the Hollywood Poster Exchange. I wanted to avoid the sense of a barrier between my clients and the art, so I took a space in midtown Manhattan, on the tenth floor of an office building on East Fifty-eighth Street, and set it up in a style that might be described as part living room, part boardroom, with music from the movies playing quietly on the stereo, sofas, comfortable chairs, and a big table on which work could be displayed and studied. It was to be a nest of Hollywood memories just around the corner from Bloomingdale's. The walls, of course, were hung with framed posters—some of my best—and on December 7, 1982, a gala party celebrated the launch of the Motion Picture Arts Gallery.

Falling in Love Again (and Again):
The Development
of a Collection

. . . . as Booth Tarking
loveliest heroine!

ALICE
ADAMS

This Novel
BEST

My friend Patricia used to say, "You fall in love with dead actresses."

I guess she was right. From the beginning of my collecting career I was a little bit in love with actresses like Carole Lombard and, as my knowledge of movies grew, I found more and more of them to fall in love with. You'll have gathered by now that I have a passion for silent movies— densely layered films that unfold at a leisurely pace, allowing the camera to linger hungrily on exquisite female stars, and on brooding alpha males like Rudolph Valentino, all captured in the subtly graded tones of black and white that cinematographers of the period knew how to provide. To watch a silent film like *Sunrise* (figs. 126 and 229) or *Greed*, with orchestral accompaniment, in one of the movie palaces of the era, like the Roxy or Grauman's Egyptian, must have been an amazing experience. I could only approximate it, but that did not stop me falling in love with Lillian Gish, Mary Pickford, Gloria Swanson, and Louise Brooks. That was what was supposed to happen, after all. The stars were up there on-screen to sweep you away into another world where some kind of ideal passion was possible. The studios planned the movies and their promotion campaigns around that idea, and for it to work the stars had to be able to project a special poignancy and eroticism along with a unique personality. (Katharine Hepburn famously said, "Show me an actress who's not a personality and I'll show you an actress who's not a star.")

I was perhaps unusual in that, although I was as susceptible as anyone to contemporary stars like Katharine Ross, I was even more so to the female stars of another era, one that I had made myself completely at home in—though perhaps I should admit it was an idealized version of that era. Nor did it come to an end with the revolution wrought by *The Jazz Singer* (fig. 77), since I was just as infatuated with stars of the talkies: Barbara Stanwyck, Irene Dunne, Mary Astor, Myrna Loy, and, of course, Lombard and Hepburn from the 1930s, continuing through the early 1940s with Veronica Lake and Ida Lupino, then the dark heroines of film noir, and on as far as the early 1960s with Audrey Hepburn, Marilyn Monroe, and Grace Kelly. It was not necessarily the most famous stars that I fell most strongly for. Inevitably Garbo features prominently in my collection— her stature is impossible to ignore—but the sense of distance she projects was a barrier for me, and I liked her better in her silent films, though *Ninotchka* (fig. 131) is a wonderful exception among her talkies. Similarly I like Marlene Dietrich best in her earliest films, but find that she lost her much of her attraction in later movies. Nor is it necessarily the most beautiful women that I'm drawn to. Rita Hayworth, for example, seems almost too beautiful, her figure too perfect, but she's wonderful in a few films.

Typically the kind of stars I'm attracted to are beautiful in a somewhat idiosyncratic way—each one very much her own person rather than the embodiment of some stereotype—and they project wit and intelligence, often combined with a sassiness that can range from Stanwyck's street-smart cynicism to Myrna Loy's understated irony. All of them can mix it with the boys, hold their own in the toughest of circumstances. I found them irresistible. I could imagine running into Louise Brooks or Carole Lombard at a

25. *Das Tagebuch
    einer Verlorenen*
    U.S. title: *Diary
    of a Lost Girl*
    Germany (1929)
    Poster for German
    release
    Pabst-Film
    56 × 37.5 in.
    (142.2 × 95.2 cm)

party and striking up a conversation, feeling an immediate rapport. I had my fair share of flesh-and-blood girlfriends, but for a long time these Hollywood goddesses complicated my love life as they offered an ideal that was impossible for anyone to live up to. It didn't help that I knew that, off-screen, many of them had had less than satisfactory personal lives, tragic in some cases. What mattered to me was what they were able to project when the auditorium lights were lowered and the screen came alive. Just the sight of a favorite's name on the title card was enough to excite my anticipation.

I had favorite male stars too—John Barrymore, Gary Cooper, Cary Grant, Errol Flynn, and William Powell (all of whom often partnered my female favorites), and the great comedians, including the Marx Brothers, W. C. Fields, Charles Chaplin, Buster Keaton, and my absolute favorite, Harold Lloyd. As a cinema historian, I had also developed a special interest in the work of certain great directors, including Erich von Stroheim, Josef von Sternberg, Ernst

Lubitsch, Howard Hawks, William Wyler, Frank Capra, Orson Welles, Preston Sturges, and Billy Wilder. Taken together, these favorites—both stars and behind-the-camera talents—provided the armature around which my collection has been built. Beyond that, I would look for material associated with specific films that I felt best embodied the talents of the people on my list. But I don't want to give the impression that I was totally rigid as a collector. I would buy great examples that fell outside my normal interest, but that were irresistible. I do not collect animation, for example, but I have some fine material from Walt Disney's *Snow White and the Seven Dwarfs* (fig. 26). I am always on the lookout for posters from half-forgotten films with barely remembered stars, so long as they feature high-quality graphics. These posters may not belong in the ultimate pantheon, but they still have their place in my collection, which, I would like to think, is a record of the evolution of a vital popular art form.

Once I had my own gallery, it did not mean that I just sat

on a sofa schmoozing with fellow enthusiasts. There was always the excitement of the hunt, and sometimes it meant jumping in a plane to make sure no one else got there first. On one occasion I heard from two elderly ladies in Fairmont, Alabama, whose father had left them a suitcase full of posters. Until you see for yourself, firsthand, you're never quite sure what you're going to find, but I was intrigued enough by the possibilities that I rushed down and took Air Florida's last flight out of West Palm Beach to Pensacola, a stomach-churning trip through squalls and thunderstorms.

From Pensacola I drove a rented car to Fairmont, where I met the two ladies, whose father had once run a theater, and finally set eyes on the suitcase. Among other things, it contained 1925 posters for movies starring Harold Lloyd and Rudolph Valentino—priceless stuff—and I'll never forget the elation I felt as I spread them out on the floor in the local library. That flight from West Palm Beach to Pensacola had been a nightmare, but it was more than worthwhile.

Another time, I flew to Memphis to visit an old-time dealer there. I was familiar with his holdings by way of a mimeographed monthly sheet that he sent out. Now he needed money for a down payment on a house, and my intuition told me it would be worth it to make a trip down there. He collected Jean Harlow, and also had material relating to a variety of top film titles, but at first his asking price seemed high. After seeing the lobby card albums he was offering, though, I realized they were amazing. We had lunch and negotiated a deal, and I put the albums in my

OPPOSITE
26. *Snow White and the Seven Dwarfs*
U.S. (1937)
Disney/RKO
Half-sheet
22 × 28 in. (55.8 × 71.1 cm)

BELOW
27. *A Social Celebrity*
U.S. (1926)
Famous Players–Lasky/ Paramount
Lobby card
11 × 14 in.
(27.9 × 35.6 cm)

MARLENE DIETRICH in "BLONDE VENUS" with Herbert Marshall and Cary Grant A Josef Von Sternberg Production
COPYRIGHTED 1932 — PARAMOUNT PUBLIX CORP. MADE IN U.S.A.   COPYRIGHT WAIVED for NEWSPAPERS

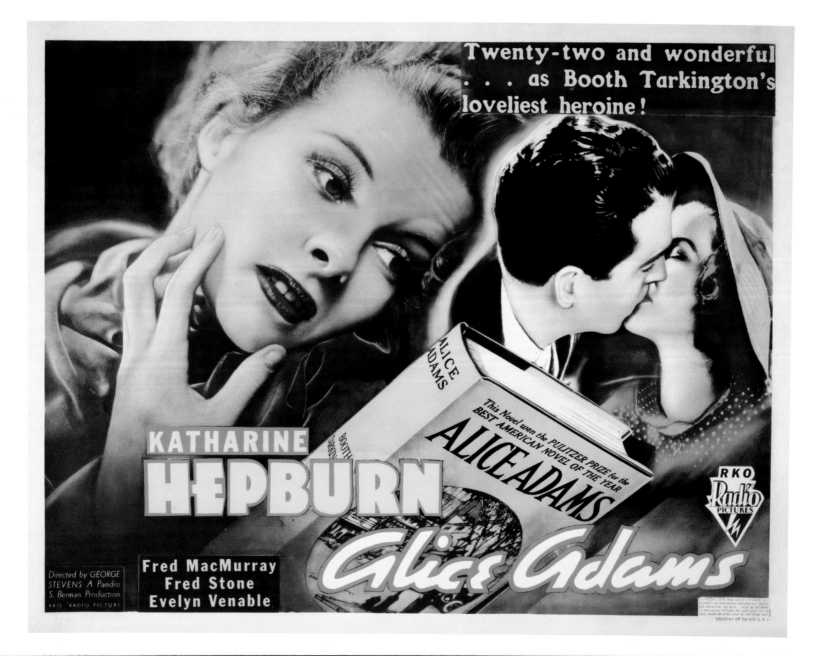

To Don
From Louise
1955

55

NERO-FILM

shoulder bags a[...]
the best buys I ever [...]
the time to visit Gracela[...] with m[...]
Jamie from that seven-films-in-one-day marathon, mentioned earlier).

Sometimes there were disappointments. Once I got a call from a lady in Asbury Park, New Jersey. She said she had a one-sheet from D. W. Griffith's *The Birth of a Nation*, a tantalizing piece of information that certainly caught my attention. I drove down there and met two lovely sisters, who reminded me irresistibly of the Brewster sisters in Frank Capra's *Arsenic and Old Lace*. If this had been a one-sheet from the original release, it would have been worth a small fortune. In fact it turned out to be a poster from a late 1920s rerelease of the picture with no image whatsoever, just the words "*Birth of a Nation*, with Sound." I bought it anyway, for a little more than it was worth, but drove home feeling deflated. But that's an inevitable part of the collecting experience. You have to take your chances and hope for the best, always relying on your knowledge and your eye to make good decisions. Sometimes I would find myself going into very depressing situations—collectors down on their luck, for example—and discover wonderful pieces in less-than-wonderful condition. Then I would have to make a decision as to whether or not to buy them and have them restored.

Restoration is very much a matter of taste and judgment. Sometimes you'll see posters that have been, to my mind, over-restored, so that at first glance they seem to be in mint condition. Not long ago, for example, a poster for the famous 1932 production of *The Mummy*, starring Boris Karloff, was offered at auction. Through my contacts in the business, I heard that most of the image had been repainted, but such is the demand for great horror film posters that it still ended up going for hundreds of thousands of dollars.

Ultimately conservancy is a matter of taste. In general, I prefer as much as possible of the original to remain visible, even if evidence of handling and the passage of time is apparent. I have an odd-sized photo of Humphrey Bogart and Ida Lupino from *High Sierra* (fig. 31) that is in terrible condition. I keep it in a plastic sleeve and value it because it's a great image that captures my feeling about the film, and I'll hold on to it unless perhaps I get lucky and find a mint copy of the same image.

What constitutes mint condition? The grading system—which defines posters as "good," "very fine," "near mint," and so on—varies wildly and is prone to the subjective judgments of dealers and auction houses. The term *mint condition* should properly be applied only to items such as a rolled one-sheet or a complete set of lobby cards still in the paper they were packed in, which implies that they were never used. Needless to say, such finds are rare, and my

31. Humphrey Bogart and Ida Lupino in *High Sierra*
Photographer: Bert Six
U.S. (1941)
Warner Bros.
Still
14 × 11 in.
(35.6 × 27.9 cm)

rule of thumb is that you try to find the best example available that illustrates your favorite image from the film.

Becoming a dealer, of course, changed the game for me. While it gave me access to things I might not otherwise have seen, it also meant that I sometimes had to part with items that were very dear to my heart. One of my all-time favorite actresses is Louise Brooks, for me the sexiest of the silent move stars, the epitome of the Jazz Age, the ultimate flapper. I became captivated with her after reading Kenneth Tynan's wonderful profile—"The Girl in the Black Helmet," published in the *New Yorker* in 1979—in which he described her as "the most seductive image of woman ever committed to celluloid."

Enchanted as men were with her beauty, Louise Brooks was never enchanted with the film industry, and after starring in classics such as G. W. Pabst's *Pandora's Box* (fig. 30), she simply walked away from it all, which made her that much more enigmatic and intriguing. For a while she was reduced to working as a sales clerk at Saks Fifth Avenue. Later still, she was rescued from obscurity and alcoholism by James Card, curator of the Eastman House film collection in Rochester, New York, and a major figure in film restoration, who persuaded Brooks to settle in Rochester where many of her films were preserved, and encouraged her to pursue a writing career. James Card was himself a fascinating and flamboyant individual, and when I received a call from him, inviting me to visit his home in Naples, New York, I did not need to be asked twice. That visit resulted in me acquiring a number of first-rate stills and posters from his personal collection, including what became the core of my Brooks collection. The focus of that collection was a large Austrian poster for Pabst's *Diary of a Lost Girl* (fig. 32)—*Das Tagebuch einer Velorenen*—which I had bought in California. It featured a blatantly erotic image showing Louise with her archetypal bobbed hair—the "black helmet" of Tynan's title—her body seductively wrapped in a tight, sarong-like dress pulled down around her high breasts so that the dark areolas of her nipples show. (A still from the movie shows

LEFT

32. *Das Tagebuch einer Verlorenen*
U.S. title:
Diary of a Lost Girl
Germany (1929)
Poster for Austrian release
Pabst-Film
75 × 50 in.
(190.5 × 127 cm)

ABOVE

33. *The Freshman*
U.S. (1925)
Harold Lloyd/Pathé
One-sheet
41 × 27 in.
(104.1 × 68.6 cm)

that the dress was designed to be worn over one shoulder.) Her pose is confrontational and submissive at the same time, and the draftsmanship that captures it is exceptionally firm and assured, somewhat in the Viennese Secessionist style made famous by artists like Gustav Klimt and Egon Schiele.

For years this was the centerpiece of my collection, the first thing that a visitor would see upon entering the gallery. It was one of my most precious possessions, yet, as a dealer, I had to put a price on it. I started it at $50,000, which was unheard of at the time, and as prices climbed I raised it to $100,000. I employed a publicist, and we made use of that poster—and that price—in many newspaper and magazine articles. One day, after about ten years, I received a visit from an art buyer representing a famous media magnate who told me that his client had seen the poster reproduced in one of these articles and wanted to buy it. I was reluctant to let it go, but I had had years of pleasure and publicity out of it, and finally we settled on a price of $80,000, which made it the most expensive piece I ever sold at the gallery.

Not long after, another great Louise Brooks poster—this one from the campaign for *The Canary Murder Case* (fig. 53)—came up at a Christie's auction. I bid on it to my limit and beyond, but didn't get it. Coming up second best at an auction is always a letdown, but on this occasion my disappointment was mitigated when, after the sale, someone came up to me and told me that he knew where there was another copy of the poster. I was able to purchase it for about $5,000 less than I would have had to pay at Christie's. It now occupies a proud place in my collection and has gone some way toward replacing the *Diary of a Lost Girl* poster.

In 2004, the Motion Picture Arts Gallery moved to East Rutherford, New Jersey, where day-to-day operations are now in the very able hands of my longtime associate Joe Burtis, the gallery's knowledgeable director. This has allowed me more time to concentrate on my primary passion, collecting for its own sake.

When I receive an auction catalog these days, 90 percent of the lots will be posters that I'm familiar with, but I still experience an adrenaline rush because there's always the possibility that there will be something there that I've been searching for for years, or maybe something I've never even seen before. The thrill of the hunt is never diluted. There is always the same blend of anticipation and apprehension, and there's still a real excitement when I'm waiting for an item that I've bought to be delivered. As I write, I'm eagerly awaiting a half-sheet from *Alice Adams* (fig. 29) with a great picture of Katharine Hepburn, which I bought at the last Heritage auction in Dallas, and a marvelous one-sheet for Harold's Lloyd's 1925 movie *The Freshman* (fig. 33) with the star's head framed against a football.

Inevitably there are gaps in the collection that I regret. One is in the area of horror film titles, which have always been heavily sought-after items. Early in my collecting career I would come across choice *Dracula* (fig. 264) and *Frankenstein* (figs. 265 and 266) material that seemed too expensive at the time, so that I passed on a number of first-rate examples. Bad decision. Horror posters have soared in value.

I am primarily a collector of Hollywood posters, but that does not mean I'm indifferent to fine European examples (such as the Austrian Louise Brooks poster already mentioned). I have a classic poster for Ingmar Bergman's *Seventh Seal*, and I would always find room for posters from the remarkable movies produced by UFA, the famous German studio of the 1920s and '30s. These would include titles such as F. W. Murnau's film *The Last Laugh*—which featured Emil Jannings in perhaps his greatest role—and *The Golem*. The ultimate, in that field, would be an example of the magnificent *Metropolis* (fig. 39) poster that hangs in the Museum of Modern Art.

Even today, it's not impossible that items like that will turn up somewhere, and it's the knowledge that posters still remain to be discovered that keeps someone like me going. I'm always looking for fine-quality one-sheets of beautiful silent-era actresses like Lillian Gish and Corinne Griffith, and I never despair of finding one. The same goes for lobby cards and stills. Recently I found a still of Marlene Dietrich from *Blonde Venus* (fig. 28), a shot from the scene where she does the "Hot Voodoo" number, wearing what I can only describe as a blond Afro wig. It's an image that would have been ideal for a portrait card. Similarly, I came across a still from John Ford's classic 1939 western *Stagecoach*, showing the first scene in which we encounter John Wayne in the role of the Ringo Kid. In the movie, a tracking shot moves in on this young, handsome cowboy, his saddle slung over his shoulder. It says everything you need to know about the character, and the still I have captures that moment perfectly. I've always felt that this was the image they should have used on the one-sheet, but—perhaps because Wayne was not yet the blockbuster star this film would help make him—the United Artists publicity department decided to go with a dramatic rendition of the stagecoach itself, and the posters that feature variations on that image are in fact highly sought after.

Collectors are a strange lot. The reason they spend so many precious hours seeking out and finding comfort in the artistry of people who are long dead cannot be entirely explained by logic, but in that respect collecting film posters is no different from becoming lost in the works of Charles Dickens, or devoting oneself to studying Victorian paintings or restoring an old house. Wanting to possess examples of such artistry is what makes a collector a

34. *Holiday*
U.S. (1938)
Columbia
One-sheet
41 × 27 in.
(104.1 × 68.6 cm)

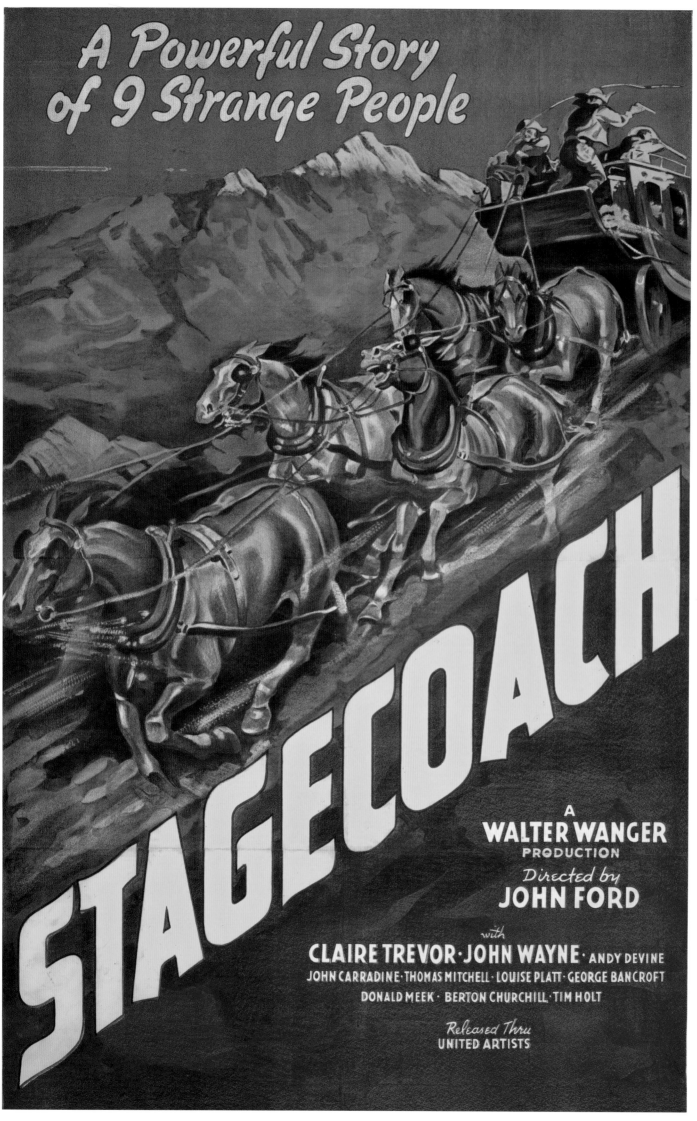

35. *Stagecoach*
U.S. (1939)
Wanger/United
Artists
One-sheet
41 × 27 in.
(104.1 × 68.6 cm)

Starstruck

collector. I recognize that as the owners of these mementos of another age, we are just caretakers, preserving them for another generation to enjoy.

Conservation is one of my passions. In addition to the posters and photographs in my own collection, I find great satisfaction in supporting various film preservation projects. The golden age of Hollywood may be long past, but I think of the movies of the silent era, and the early talkies, as being still-vital art forms that, thanks to the magic of film (not to mention television and DVDs), can be conjured back to life. These old posters and stills would have much less meaning if we could not see the films that inspired them. This is one reason why, for the past twenty years, I have served as a trustee of the Film Society of Lincoln Center, and from 1999 to 2005 I had the honor to be chairman of the board. In particular I am a supporter of the society's Golden Silents series, which screens examples of the astonishing movies made in the cinema's early years, attempting to capture the experience of moviegoing in that era by providing orchestral accompaniment.

My connection to this august institution has made it possible for me to meet some of my heroes, including Audrey Hepburn, Gregory Peck, Mel Brooks, Bette Davis, James Stewart, and others. I am not much of an autograph collector, but on these occasions, like any other fan, I make sure I have a still or some other memento available for the star to sign.

In *Hannah and Her Sisters*, Mickey Sachs, the neurotic and hypochondriacal character played by Woody Allen, bounces from religion to religion searching for the meaning of existence. When he's at the end of his rope, he happens into the old Metro Theater, which is screening the Marx Brothers' *Duck Soup* (figs. 36, 149, and 185)—a film he has probably seen fifty times—and is reminded by the antics of Groucho, Chico, and Harpo why life is worth living. I can identify with that. It's laughter and loving that keep you going through the hard times, and appreciating beauty that makes it all worthwhile.

For me, old movies and old movie posters combine art and entertainment, and that's one reason I'll keep watching those films and searching out those one-sheets and lobby cards. Finding them and caring for them is like putting together photo albums of my family and friends. Some people cannot understand how I could watch a film like *Holiday* (figs. 34 and 162) over and over again. To me, movies of that quality and entertainment value are dependable companions—lovely and reassuring—and the same goes for the posters that embody them.

3

The Silents,
1912–1929

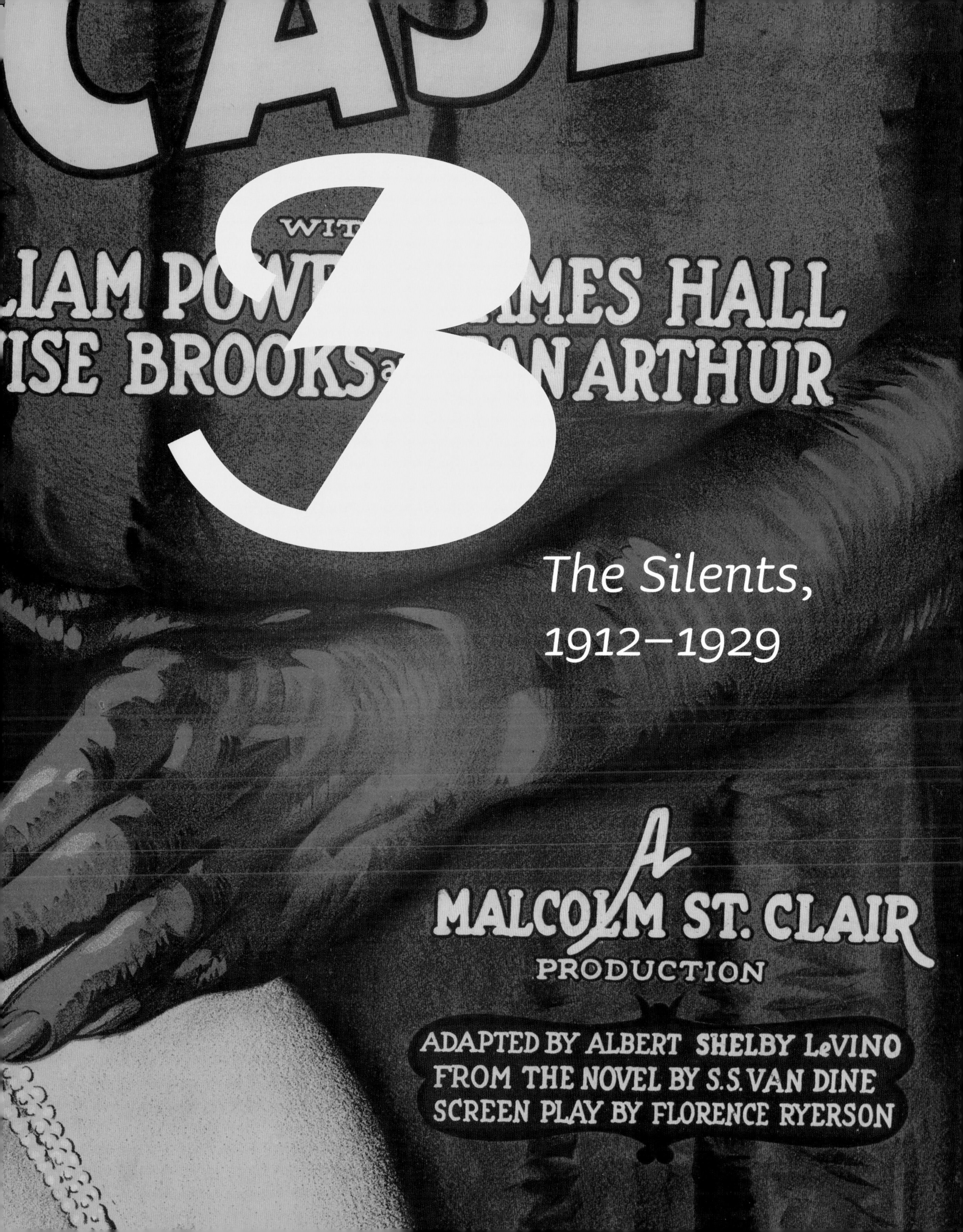

PAGES 48–49
*The Canary
Murder Case*
Detail
(See fig. 53 on p. 64)

37. *The Lily and
the Rose*
U.S. (1915)
Fine Arts/
Triangle
Lobby card
11 × 14 in.
(27.9 × 35.6 cm)

THE LILY AND THE ROSE FEATURING LILLIAN GISH, ROZSIKA, DOLLY AND WILFRED LUCAS—FINE ARTS PRODUCTION

It would be hard to overstate the significance of the silent cinema, or the pleasures to be found if one takes the trouble to explore that endlessly rich world, even though it lasted for just a little more than a quarter of a century. This was the birth of a totally new art form, and simultaneously a new industry. It was the beginning of the technologically driven media revolution, and a social and cultural bombshell that transformed the way people perceived the world. Immigrants in New York, Philadelphia, and Detroit taught themselves English by reading the on-screen title cards, and their sons and daughters migrated to California to make their fortunes in the foothills of the Santa Monica Mountains. In the earliest days, there were studios in Manhattan and Queens and Chicago, but it was Hollywood that overnight became synonymous with entertainment and glamour. Nor were the movies purely an American phenomenon. Since there was no spoken dialogue, silent movies presented a truly international language, with studios big and small springing up in Europe and around the world, and distinct traditions becoming quickly established in places like Germany, France, Scandinavia, Japan, and the Soviet Union. And in all these places, the cinema attracted brilliant young talents—writers, directors, actors, and actresses—who would shape the future of the medium, and in many cases were still active thirty and forty years later, when it had been totally transformed by one technical innovation after another.

None of these innovations—sound, color, or panoramic screens—could improve on the magical beauty of the silent cinema. In the pioneering days of the nickelodeons,

audiences were so spellbound that they would applaud the image of waves breaking on the shore, and duck for cover when a speeding locomotive seemed about to burst out of the screen. They soon became much more sophisticated, and so did the cinematographers, who learned to orchestrate luscious tones when using orthochromatic film stock to create images so exquisite they could melt stone. Then there was the star system. There were stars before the cinema—Lily Langtree and Sarah Bernhardt, for example—but it was the pioneering film studios that developed the star system, though at first they did so reluctantly. Since the production companies did not want to give performers too much power, they kept the stars anonymous. Even the great Mary Pickford, at the beginning of her career, was known simply as "The Biograph Girl," or "The Girl with the Golden Locks." What the studios hadn't counted on, however, was the fact that audiences—predominantly working class in those days—identified with the actors and actresses they saw regularly on-screen and wanted to know who they were. Fledgling publicity departments were inundated with postcards and letters demanding to know the names of their favorites.

In 1909, in response to this demand, the Kalem company, home to stars like Alice Joyce, began the practice of supplying theaters with postcards and posters that featured the names of cast members. Later that year, *Moving Picture World* published a feature devoted to Ben Turpin and titled "The Life of a Moving Picture Comedian," the first time a film performer had ever been accorded such treatment. In 1910, Carl Laemmle, then head of the Independent Motion

Picture Company (IMP), came up with the idea of a publicity stunt to promote the name and talents of Florence Lawrence, who he had just been hired away from Biograph, where she had preceded Mary Pickford as "The Biograph Girl." First Laemmle placed a newspaper story that "Flo Lo" (as she would become known) had been killed in a streetcar accident in Saint Louis, where she was scheduled to make an appearance at a premiere. He then took out full-page ads in the papers denying the story, implying that it was a fabrication devised by a rival studio that wanted to discredit him and his star. This whipped up a frenzy of interest, and when "Flo Lo" arrived at the premiere, with a prominent escort of bodyguards, she was greeted by pandemonium as her newly minted fans—most of whom had not known her name twenty-four hours earlier—caused a near riot.

The age of the star system had arrived, and with it the golden age of the movie poster. The studios now realized that stars were their greatest assets and treated them accordingly. They still attempted to keep them under control by trying to tie them to long-term contracts, but they rewarded them with astronomical salaries, and they devised elaborate publicity campaigns that could transform a shopgirl into a princess overnight—or something better than a princess, because part of her remained in the everyday world, allowing moviegoers to think of her as the girl next door.

In the emerging arena of improbable stunts, planted stories, and lavishly stage-managed events, posters remained perhaps the soberest form of publicity around. They placed an emphasis on the stars—which is why I love them—but they also tended to reflect the character of the film they were promoting. Deriving from the great French poster tradition at the turn of the century, as well as from the Anglo-American theatrical poster tradition, Hollywood posters were from the outset inventive and sometimes spectacular, the studios employing first-class illustrators in an age when schools like the Art Students League in New York and the Art Institute in Chicago were turning out a steady stream of highly competent academically trained artists. And from the beginning no expense was spared in making these posters as beautiful as possible. They were printed in high-quality lithography on good grades of paper or card, and—while the films they advertised were made in black and white—the posters often made extravagant use of color.

38. *Salomé*
U.S. (1923)
Nazimova/Allied
Lobby card
11 × 14 in.
(27.9 × 35.6 cm)

METROPO

Directed by FRITZ LANG

AN UFA PRODUCTION

Ada

a P

My introduction to silent films came by way of old television shows with excessively cute names like *Fractured Flickers* and *Silents Please*. Typically shows like these would present Keystone Cops one-reelers or Fatty Arbuckle shorts deliberately projected at the wrong speed (or perhaps the producers didn't know what they were doing) so that everything was speeded up even more than had been done on purpose at the Mack Sennett Studios.

While at college I first began to appreciate the special qualities of silent movies. In film school, I was exposed to some of the early Hollywood classics such as Griffith's *The Birth of a Nation* (fig. 221) and Erich von Stroheim's *Greed*, as well as masterpieces of the European silent cinema such as Fritz Lang's *Metropolis* (fig. 39) and Sergei Eisenstein's *Battleship Potemkin*. It was relatively easy to see silent comedies, and to become familiar with the oeuvres of Charlie Chaplin, Buster Keaton, Harold Lloyd, and their contemporaries, but it was much harder to get a sense of the achievement of the silent cinema as a whole. By attending revival houses and museum film programs, I was gradually able to broaden my knowledge of the films of the period, and as I did so, my love of the silent screen grew. As silly as some of the stories were, I found myself mesmerized by the fairy-tale quality of many of these movies, by the larger-than-life presence of actors like Douglas Fairbanks, Rudolph Valentino, and John Barrymore, and especially by sublime female apparitions such as Lillian Gish, Mary Pickford, Gloria Swanson, and Louise Brooks.

LEFT

39. *Metropolis*
U.S. (1927)
UFA/Paramount
Lobby card
11 × 14 in.
(27.9 × 35.6 cm)

BELOW

40. *Октябрь*
U.S. title: *Ten Days That Shook the World*
Soviet Union (1928)
Poster for Soviet release
Sovkino
28.3 × 60.5 in.
(71.8 × 153.8 cm)

The WIND

Starring

LILLIAN GISH

with

LARS HANSON

A

VICTOR SEASTROM

PRODUCTION

Scenario by Frances Marion · From the novel by Dorothy
Scarborough · Titles by John Colton · Directed by
Victor Seastrom.

Terror
seized her

"The cyclone!
The cyclone!"

A Metro-Goldwyn-Mayer Picture.

THE **WIND** *starring* **LILLIAN GISH** *with* **LARS HANSON**

A Metro-Goldwyn-Mayer PICTURE

"I hated you, but now—"

MADE IN U. S. A.

OPPOSITE

41. *The Wind*
U.S. (1928)
MGM
One-sheet
41 × 27 in.
(104.1 × 68.6 cm)

ABOVE

42. *The Wind*
U.S. (1928)
MGM
Lobby card
11 × 14 in.
(27.9 × 35.6 cm)

Lillian Gish

Lillian Gish virtually invented screen acting. She and her talented sister Dorothy had appeared in touring stage shows before D. W. Griffith cast them both in his 1912 film *Unseen Enemy*. Gish was nineteen at the time, rather old for a screen actress of that era to make her debut. The cameramen of the period did not have the filters that could soften a complexion, and the film stocks of the day tended to exaggerate flaws, so that filmmakers sought out very young actresses with perfect skin. This was not a problem for Gish, who always photographed beautifully—as in my signed 1915 poster *The Lily and the Rose* (fig. 37)—she was the most ethereal of actresses. Her emotional range was remarkable too, a fact that did not escape Griffith, who became the great champion of both her and Dorothy.

Gish is unforgettable in Griffith movies such as *The Birth of a Nation*, *Intolerance*, *Way Down East*, *Broken Blossoms* (fig. 224), and *Orphans of the Storm* (fig. 223), though my personal favorite is Victor Sjöström's 1928 masterpiece *The Wind*, which is represented in my collection by a striking, largely monochrome one-sheet (fig. 41), as well as by a tinted lobby card (fig. 42). The title refers to the fact that the Gish character, Letty Mason, is driven to madness by the unrelenting winds of West Texas. She spends much of the movie battling fierce dust storms, a degree of discomfort that might have deterred other actresses, but then Gish was famous for the almost masochistic lengths to which she would go for the sake of making a role seem authentic. Another special Gish poster in my collection is one for *Daphne and the Pirate* (fig. 46), from 1916. This very early film has been lost, but finding a full-colored one-sheet like this is always an exciting event.

I have other fine posters, lobby cards, and stills of Gish in my collection, and she exemplifies the stars for whom I never despair of finding more and still finer examples. This is equally true of Mary Pickford material. If Lillian Gish invented motion picture acting, Pickford—another Griffith discovery (and an old friend of the Gish sisters) and a fine actress herself when given the opportunity—was the first superstar, and also a shrewd businesswoman who understood the power that her talent and public image had vested in her.

Mary Pickford

Mary Pickford may not have matched Lillian's Gish's dramatic range and power, but what she did, she did supremely well, as is evident in films like *Pollyanna* (1920), in which, as so often, she played a character much younger than she really was—a pretense that audiences willingly went along with. I have strong posters from the 1912 Griffith short for Biograph, *The Informer* (fig. 44), and for William Desmond Taylor's *Johanna Enlists* (fig. 45)—a World War I comedy in which boy-starved farm girl Johanna Rensaller, played by Little Mary (to use another of her names), is unexpectedly confronted with a surfeit of eligible young men when an army unit sets up camp nearby. Given that Pickford was so popular and made so many movies—fifty-one in 1909 alone—you would think that more material would have survived, but top-quality posters of her are very rare. This is perhaps because silent movies were eclipsed so suddenly by sound pictures, and the backstage areas of many of the theaters where posters might have been stored were ripped apart to accommodate the cumbersome new sound equipment. Mary Pickford herself at one point decreed that all of her films should be destroyed after her death, apparently believing that no one would be interested in watching them. Happily she was talked out of this, and verbally

bequeathed her collection of stills and other memorabilia to the Academy of Motion Picture Arts and Sciences (an organization she had helped found). Thanks to her second husband, Buddy Rogers, most of this material did find its way to the academy's library, though hundreds of items were diverted to unscrupulous dealers.

ABOVE
43. *The Fatal Marriage*
Also known as:
Enoch Arden
U.S. (1915)
Majestic
Lobby card
11 × 14 in.
(27.9 × 35.6 cm)

OPPOSITE
44. *The Informer*
U.S (1912)
Biograph/General
One-sheet
41 × 27 in.
(104.1 × 68.6 cm)

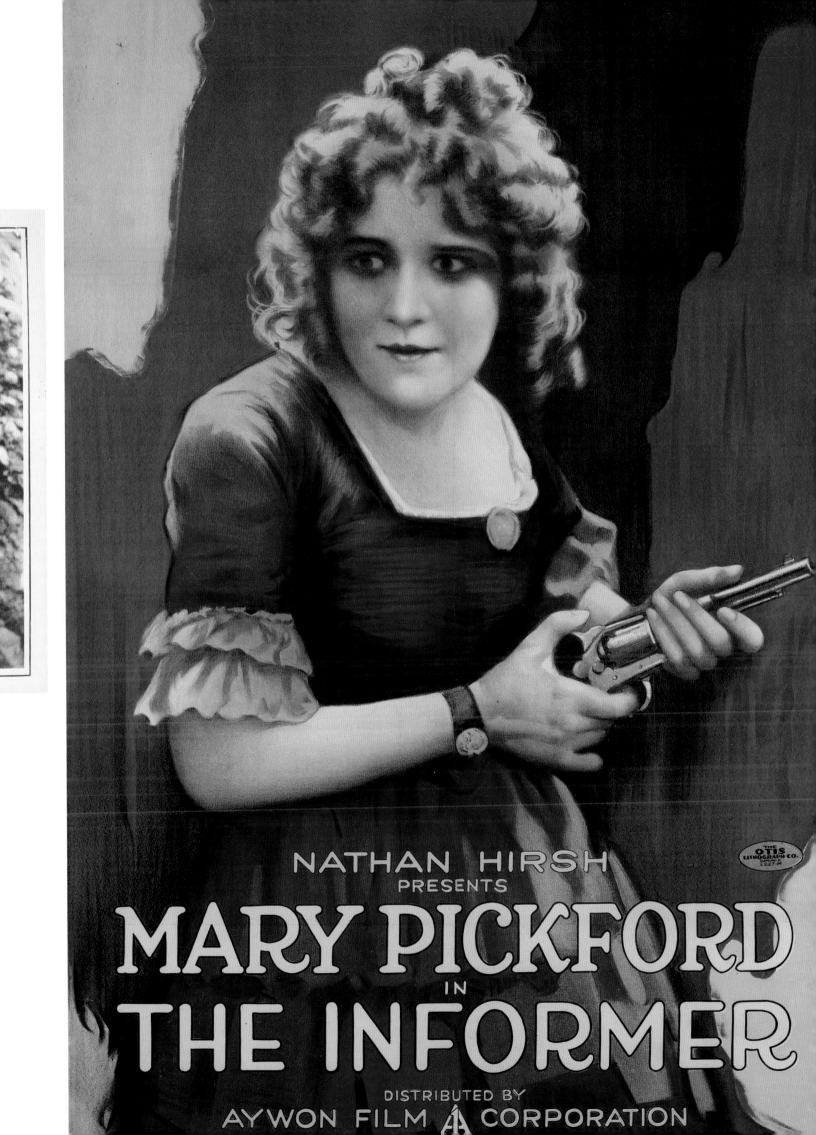

NATHAN HIRSH
PRESENTS
MARY PICKFORD
IN
THE INFORMER
DISTRIBUTED BY
AYWON FILM CORPORATION

45. *Johanna Enlists*
    U.S. (1918)
    Pickford/Artcraft
    One-sheet
    41 × 27 in.
    (104.1 × 68.6 cm)

Starstruck

Gloria Swanson

Gloria Swanson is probably best remembered today for her role in the 1950 Billy Wilder film *Sunset Boulevard* (fig. 17)—with William Holden and one of her great contemporaries, the actor-director Eric von Stroheim—in which she portrayed a forgotten but proud star of the silent screen. (In that movie she famously said, of the silent era, "We had faces then.") Younger viewers of that movie barely knew who Swanson was, but a quarter of a century earlier she had been one of the most famous women in the world. She went from being, in her teens, a Mack Sennett bathing beauty, to Bobby Vernon's foil in Sennett's Teddy the Dog comedies (for example, *The Nick of Time Baby* [fig. 47]), and then a hugely popular romantic leading lady in marital morality movies for Cecil B. DeMille, reaching perhaps the apex of her career in Raoul Walsh's 1928 film

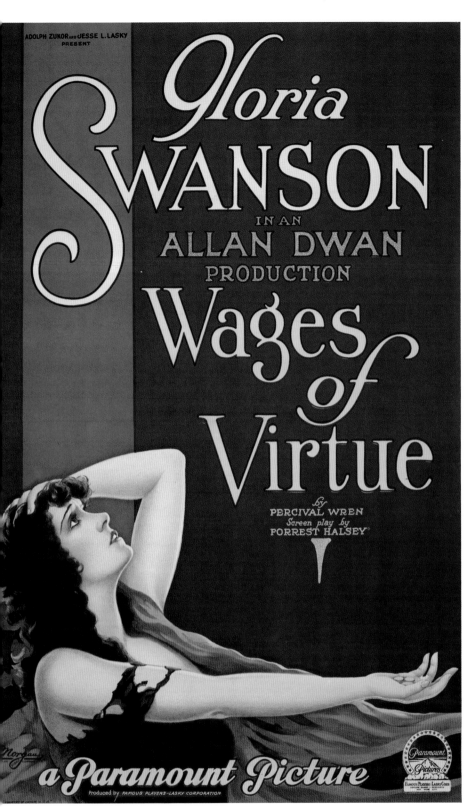

48. *Wages of Virtue*
U.S. (1924)
Paramount
One-sheet
41 × 27 in.
(104.1 × 68.6 cm)

49. Gloria Swanson and
Raoul Walsh in
Sadie Thompson
U.S. (1928)
Gloria Swanson/
United Artists
Still
10 × 8 in.
(25.4 × 20.3 cm)

Sadie Thompson (fig. 49), an adaptation of W. Somerset Maugham's story "Rain." An international celebrity, and famous as a clotheshorse, Swanson was married multiple times and at the end of the silent era embarked on a notorious affair with Joseph P. Kennedy, father of President John F. Kennedy, who was then engaged in film production. She did not succeed in making the transition to sound until belatedly making her spectacular comeback in *Sunset Boulevard* in which she was given another wonderful line, "I'm still big. It's the pictures that got small." To see her in one of her archetypal silent roles, such as *Beyond the Rocks* (fig. 21) or *Wages of Virtue* (fig. 48)—both represented by posters in my collection—is to understand just *how* big she was in her heyday.

'LOVE 'EM AND LEAVE 'EM.
WITH **EVELYN BRENT LAWRENCE GRAY** AND **LOUISE BROOKS**
A FRANK TUTTLE PRODUCTION *A Paramount Picture*

50. *Love 'Em and Leave 'Em*
U.S. (1926)
Famous Players–Lasky/Paramount
Lobby card
11 × 14 in.
(27.9 × 35.6 cm)

Louise Brooks

I have already written about my passion for the exquisite Louise Brooks, who came to movies by way of dancing with the Denishawn group and a stint with the Ziegfeld Follies. She is revered today principally for the three outstanding films that she made in Europe—*Pandora's Box* (fig. 30), *Diary of a Lost Girl* (fig. 32), and *Prix de beauté*. Prior to these successes, she spent three years at Paramount, where she made *It's the Old Army Game*, with W. C. Fields, *Love 'Em and Leave 'Em* (fig. 50), *Beggars of Life* (fig. 51), and *A Girl in Every Port* (fig. 52)—the film that made Pabst decide to cast her as Pandora. At that time, Louise Brooks was perhaps most famous for her archetypal flapper look—with her helmet of bobbed hair—looking almost like a flesh and blood incarnation of one of the Jazz Age girls drawn by John Held. She was also a remarkable actress—utterly natural and unaffected—and a matchless beauty, a fact that cannot be disguised even when, as in *Beggars of Life*, she is passing herself off as a boy. All of her films are worth watching, and her unique glamour and magnetism comes through strongly in stills and lobby cards for movies such as *The American Venus* and *The Canary Murder Case* (fig. 53), which paired her with William Powell.

The one-sheet I have for *The Canary Murder Case* is among my favorites, a dramatic image that shows a sinister black hand reaching for Brooks's shoulder as she—dressed in her character's showgirl costume—flinches from its touch.

BELOW
51. *Beggars of Life*
U.S. (1928)
Famous Players–Lasky/
Paramount
Lobby card
11 × 14 in.
(27.9 × 35.6 cm)

RIGHT
52. *A Girl in Every Port*
U.S. (1928)
Fox
Lobby card
11 × 14 in.
(27.9 × 35.6 cm)

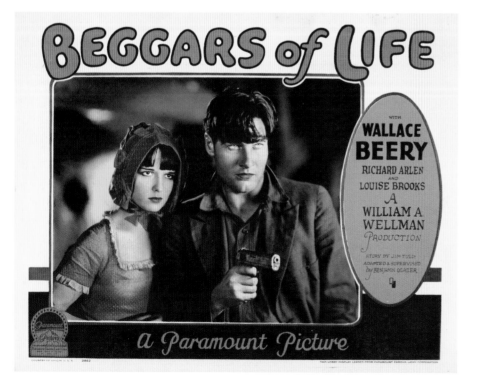

Starstruck

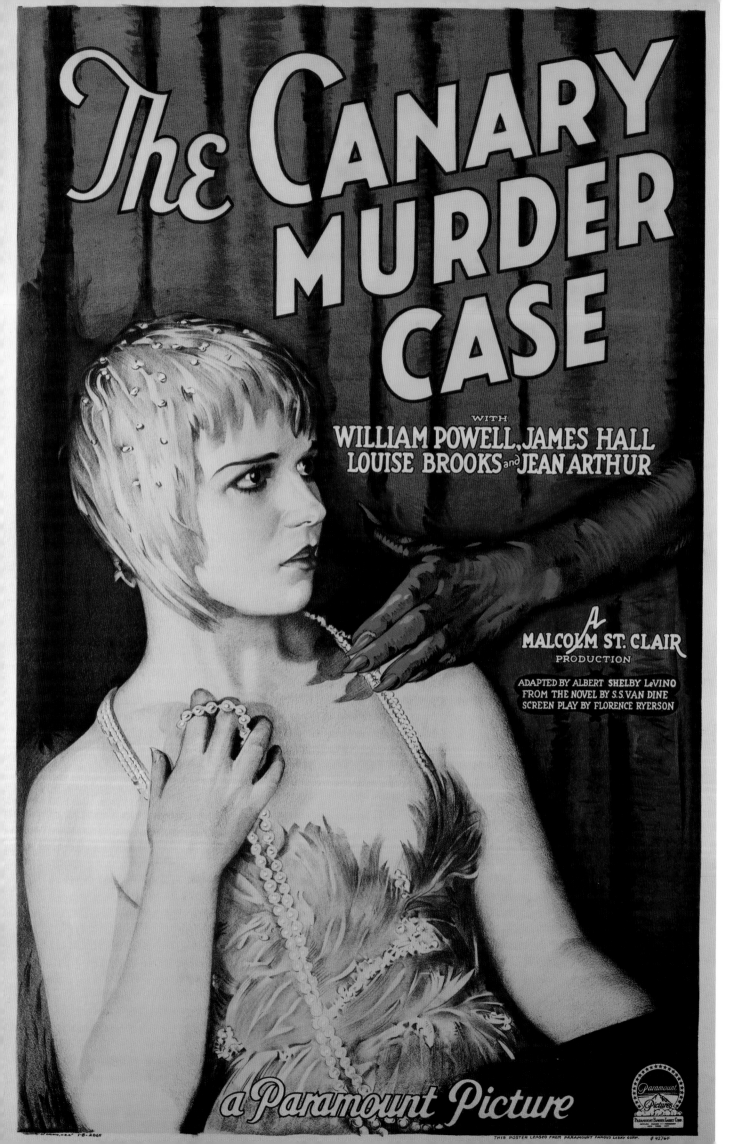

53. *The Canary Murder Case*
U.S. (1929)
Paramount
One-sheet
41 × 27 in.
(104.1 × 68.6 cm)

Starstruck

This was the last important movie she made in America. It was shot as a silent, but B. P. Schulberg, head of production at Paramount, decided to release it as a talkie. Brooks was in Europe for René Clair's *Prix de beauté*, and Schulberg ordered her back to dub her lines. She telegraphed, "Screw you," or words to that effect, and he responded with the already clichéd, "You'll never work in this town again." And she didn't, except for some very minor roles.

As described in the last chapter, I eventually sold the great Austrian poster for *Diary of a Lost Girl* that I had found in California, but Louise Brooks's glittering European career is still represented in my collection by a number of stills and by another poster from *Lost Girl* (fig. 25) in which her naked body is coyly concealed by an oversize diary, worn like a beach towel.

There were of course other great female stars associated with the silent period, such as Norma and Constance Talmadge, Corinne Griffith, Bebe Daniels, and Clara Bow, but for the most part not many people collect them. In addition, there were the many actresses who began their careers in the silent era but then successfully made the transition to sound, a list that would include stars ranging from Marion Davies, Joan Crawford, and Norma Shearer to Mary Astor and Myrna Loy (all of whom will be dealt with more fully in the following chapter). The most famous, of course, was Garbo.

Greta Garbo

Born Greta Lovisa Gustafsson, Greta Garbo had trained at the Royal Dramatic Theater in Stockholm, and in 1924, while still in Sweden, made *The Story of Gösta Berling*—for which I have a remarkable Swedish poster that is almost like a newspaper ad (fig. 56). This film brought her to the attention of MGM's Louis B. Mayer. When she arrived in Hollywood, though, Metro didn't know quite how to promote her and came up with silly ideas such as having her pose in running gear while being barked at through a megaphone by the University of Southern California football coach. She was ordered to lose weight and quickly slimmed down to the wraith who became a global superstar in such silent films as *Flesh and the Devil*, *Love*, and *The Mysterious Lady*, often playing fallen women, though the image she projected was more romantic than sexual. Sadly, very few people today see these early films in which her famously enigmatic persona was formed.

Another of my prized possessions is a one-sheet for the American release of *Streets of Sorrow* (fig. 55)—a very early Garbo film, her second after *Gösta Berling*—which I found, along with a couple of wonderful lobby cards, near the start of my collecting career. It's very dear to me because of the artwork, which has a dark kind of UFA look.

54. *Gösta Berlings saga*
U.S. title:
The Story of Gösta Berling
Sweden (1924)
Poster for U.S. release (1927)
Svensk Filmindustri
Window card
22 × 14 in.
(55.9 × 35.6 cm)

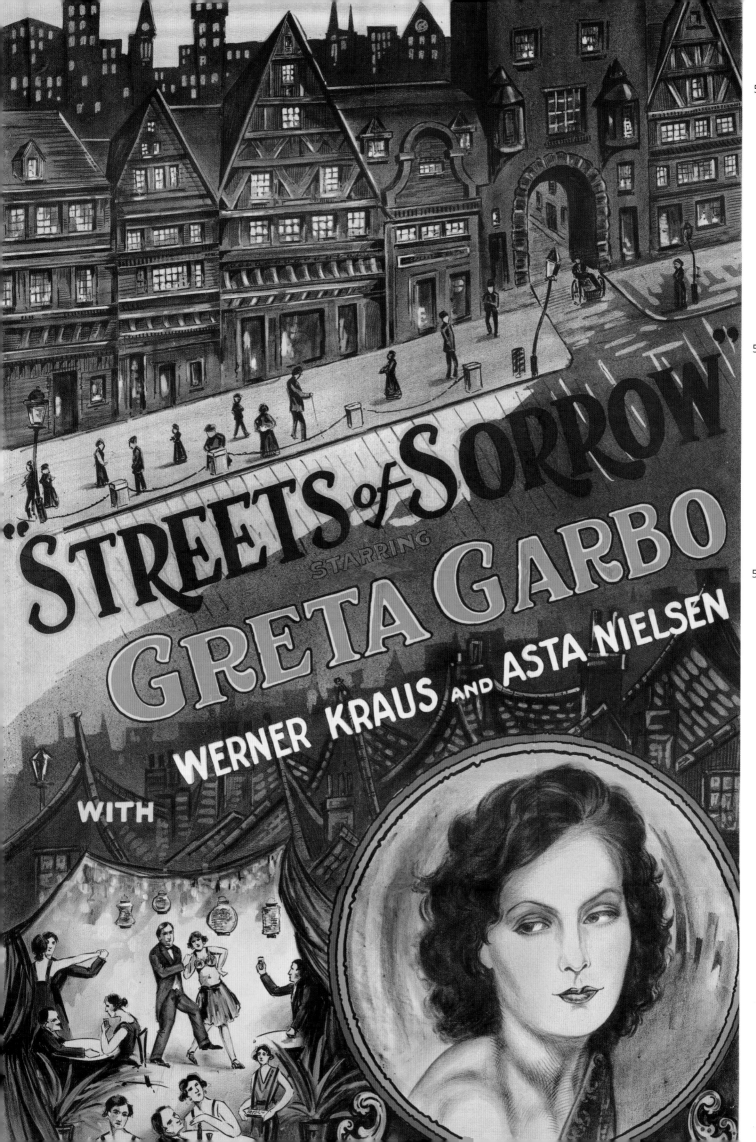

Of course, the silent movies had their share of male heart-throbs such as Douglas Fairbanks Sr., Rudolph Valentino, John Barrymore, and Garbo's lover, John Gilbert, as well as great character actors like Lon Chaney and cowboy heroes like William S. Hart and Tom Mix. Long before Clark Gable earned the title, Doug Fairbanks was the original King of Hollywood—in fact, for audiences in the 1920s, he was Clark Gable and Errol Flynn rolled into one, the archetypal, all-American swashbuckling he-man. In 1920 Fairbanks married Mary Pickford, and for more than a dozen years the pair ruled over the movie colony from their Beverly Hills mansion, Pickfair, the epicenter of Hollywood social life in an era when movie people knew how to party. (There were no lines to memorize in those days, which freed up a lot of time to be spent knocking back bootleg gin at the Sunset Inn or doing the turkey trot at the Cocoanut Grove.)

Douglas Fairbanks

Like Pickford, Fairbanks began his career under the auspices of D. W. Griffith (though Griffith found Fairbanks's flamboyant athleticism alien to his kind of moviemaking). Debuting in 1915, Fairbanks made an immediate impression on the moviegoing public, and was soon one of the biggest box-office draws in the business, a position he held for more than a decade. He is best remembered for swashbuckling, stunt-filled costume dramas such as *The Mark of Zorro*, *The Three Musketeers* (fig. 57), *Robin Hood* (fig. 58), *The Thief of Bagdad* (fig. 284), *The Black Pirate* (fig. 59), and *The Iron Mask*, all made between 1920 and 1927. The exotic subject matter of these films, combined with Fairbanks's irrepressible personality, made for some of the most colorful and dramatic posters of the silent era, featuring the star with sword at the ready and anticipating the opportunity to dice unwary villains, or flying on a magic carpet above minarets and onion-domed palaces.

58. *Robin Hood*
U.S. (1922)
Douglas Fairbanks/
United Artists
One-sheet
41 × 27 in.
(104.1 × 68.6 cm)

Starstruck

59. *The Black Pirate*
U.S. (1926)
Elton/United
Artists
One-sheet
41 × 27 in.
(104.1 × 68.6 cm)

Rudolph Valentino

The name Rudolph Valentino has become synonymous with the Hollywood of the silent years; his real-life romances and the circumstances surrounding his premature death are as enthralling as any of his movies. An immigrant from Italy, he was a taxi dancer in New York, where he became caught up in a society scandal involving a married Chilean heiress, then eventually made his way to Los Angeles, where he had small parts in movies before eventually breaking through to stardom in the 1921 classic *The Four Horsemen of the Apocalypse*.

Valentino, the original Latin lover, was the opposite of Fairbanks, who, despite playing pirates and street Arabs, always remained the all-American boy. Valentino could not challenge Fairbanks's popularity with male audiences, but women went wild for him, making him the cinema's first male sex symbol. His involvement with a number of women, including the costume designer Natacha Rambova and fellow movie star Pola Negri, only stoked the flames, and rumors of homosexuality failed to diminish his erotic appeal. In his short career, he made a number of memorable costume dramas, including *The Sheik*, *Beyond the Rocks* (with Gloria Swanson), *Blood and Sand* (fig. 60), *Monsieur Beaucaire* (fig. 61), and *The Son of the Sheik* (fig. 62), in which Vilma Banky was the lucky girl swept off her feet.

The Son of the Sheik, released in 1926, was Valentino's last great film, and I have a beautiful poster from it, part of a group I purchased that also included an exceptional silent-era Myrna Loy one-sheet from *Renegades* (fig. 115), showing her in a turban back in the days when she, like

ABOVE
60. *Blood and Sand*
    U.S. (1922)
    Paramount
    Lobby card
    11 × 14 in.
    (27.9 × 35.6 cm)

RIGHT
61. *Monsieur Beaucaire*
    U.S. (1924)
    Paramount
    Lobby card
    11 × 14 in.
    (27.9 × 35.6 cm)

OPPOSITE
62. *The Son of the Sheik*
    U.S. (1926)
    Feature/United Artists
    One-sheet
    41 × 27 in.
    (104.1 × 68.6 cm)

John W. Considine, Jr. presents

RUDOLPH VALENTINO

in

"The Son of the Sheik"

a Sequel to "The Sheik"

with VILMA BANKY

from the novel by E. M. HULL = Adapted to the Screen by FRANCES MARION

A GEORGE FITZMAURICE PRODUCTION

- UNITED ARTISTS PICTURE -

JOHN BARRYMORE
in SHERLOCK HOLMES

Directed by ALBERT PARKER

Adapted from WILLIAM GILLETTE'S stage play founded on Sir CONAN DOYLE'S stories

A Goldwyn Picture

Valentino, was playing exotic types. That *Son of the Sheik* poster was expensive, but it was worth it. It shows the Latin Lover holding his luscious costar in his arms, as if carrying her off to his tent, a situation his female fans had no difficulty identifying with. From an artistic point of view, the poster displays a sure sense of design and an exceptionally bold feeling for color.

Then, suddenly and tragically, Valentino's career was over. In the summer of 1926, he collapsed at New York's Ambassador Hotel and was operated on for a perforated ulcer. An apparently good recovery was interrupted by peritonitis, and days later he was dead at the age of thirty-one. The crowds of hysterical women outside the Frank Campbell Funeral Home on Madison Avenue were estimated at 100,000. Inside, Pola Negri created a hysterical scene, claiming that she and Valentino were to have been married. His remains were taken back to California and placed in a crypt at the Hollywood Memorial Park Cemetery, where, ever since, the mysterious "Woman in Black" has, on the anniversary of Valentino's death, famously arrived to mourn him.

John Barrymore

Known as "The Great Profile," John Barrymore was the most famous American stage actor of his day, celebrated for his Hamlet, which he played on Broadway in 1922 before taking it to London where it was received with great acclaim. He had made his film debut almost a decade earlier (when he was considered a light comedian), and throughout the silent era pursued a career in both theater and film. His successes of the period included *Dr. Jekyll and Mr. Hyde*, *Sherlock Holmes* (fig. 63), *Beau Brummel* (fig. 66), and *The Sea Beast* (in which he was a formidable Captain Ahab). His voice made him a natural to make the transition to talkies, and permitted him to fully develop his comedic talents, but his silent movies remain remarkable in their own right, demonstrating that he had the ability to communicate powerfully with gesture, facial expressions, and the sheer magnetism of his screen presence.

Released by Warner Bros. in 1926, Barrymore's *Don Juan* was a film on the very cusp of the talkies—the forerunner of *The Jazz Singer* (fig. 77) in that it was the first movie to use the Vitaphone synchronized sound system, though in this instance it was used only for music and sound effects. The one-sheet I own for that release, showing its star in Renaissance costume, is a rarity I would be loath to part with.

I bought it from Stan Caiden, a lawyer and producer who owned the rights to several old films. He had a house on Roxbury Drive in Beverly Hills—a Spanish house with high ceilings, filled with great posters. The one I always loved most was the one for *Don Juan* (fig. 67). I used to go over to

The Silents, 1912–1929

dinner at the house, and he'd take me to his office in the back, where we spent many evenings trying to make a deal for that poster—but the truth is, he really didn't want to sell it. I know that feeling very well. You have something someone wants, but you just can't give it up. When Stan died, his family put much of his collection up for sale at Christie's, and I ended up buying the poster there.

John Gilbert was less fortunate than Barrymore in making the transition to the talkies, a fact that is often attributed, despite evidence to the contrary, to the fact that his voice did not record well. Apparently his failure may have had more to do with his having knocked out Louis B. Mayer during a fight over his romantic relationship with Greta Garbo, with whom he starred in *Flesh and the Devil*, *Love*, and *A Woman of Affairs*. With his striking good looks, and

OPPOSITE
63. *Sherlock Holmes*
U.S. (1922)
Goldwyn
One-sheet
41 × 27 in. (104.1 × 68.6 cm)

BELOW
64. *Babe Comes Home*
U.S. (1927)
First National
One-sheet
41 × 27 in. (104.1 × 68.6 cm)

his natural acting ability, he remains one of the memorable figures of the silent years.

One of the absolute top posters in my collection is a one-sheet for the film *Babe Comes Home* (fig. 64), a 1927 silent release that starred someone not usually associated with the movie world—the great Babe Ruth, the Sultan of Swat, in his greatest year, when he spearheaded the Yankees with sixty home runs. A rare and irreplaceable item! He appeared in *Speedy* (fig. 75) the following year with Harold Lloyd.

Then there were the silent comedians, without whom the early years of the cinema would have been very different. The academy was Mack Sennett's Keystone Studio, which gave the world the Keystone Cops and the Sennett Bathing Beauties, and from which Charlie Chaplin, Fatty Arbuckle, Ben Turpin, Harry Langdon, Gloria Swanson, and Mabel Normand all graduated. Its biggest rival was the Hal Roach Studio, which produced Harold Lloyd and Laurel and Hardy, while the Talmadge Studio, which became Arbuckle's home base, was where Buster Keaton cut his teeth.

ABOVE LEFT

65. *The Big Parade*
U.S. (1925)
MGM
One-sheet
41 × 27 in.
(104.1 × 68.6 cm)

ABOVE RIGHT

66. *Beau Brummel*
U.S. (1924)
Warner Bros.
One-sheet
41 × 27 in.
(104.1 × 68.6 cm)

OPPOSITE

67. *Don Juan*
U.S. (1926)
Warner Bros.
One-sheet
41 × 27 in.
(104.1 × 68.6 cm)

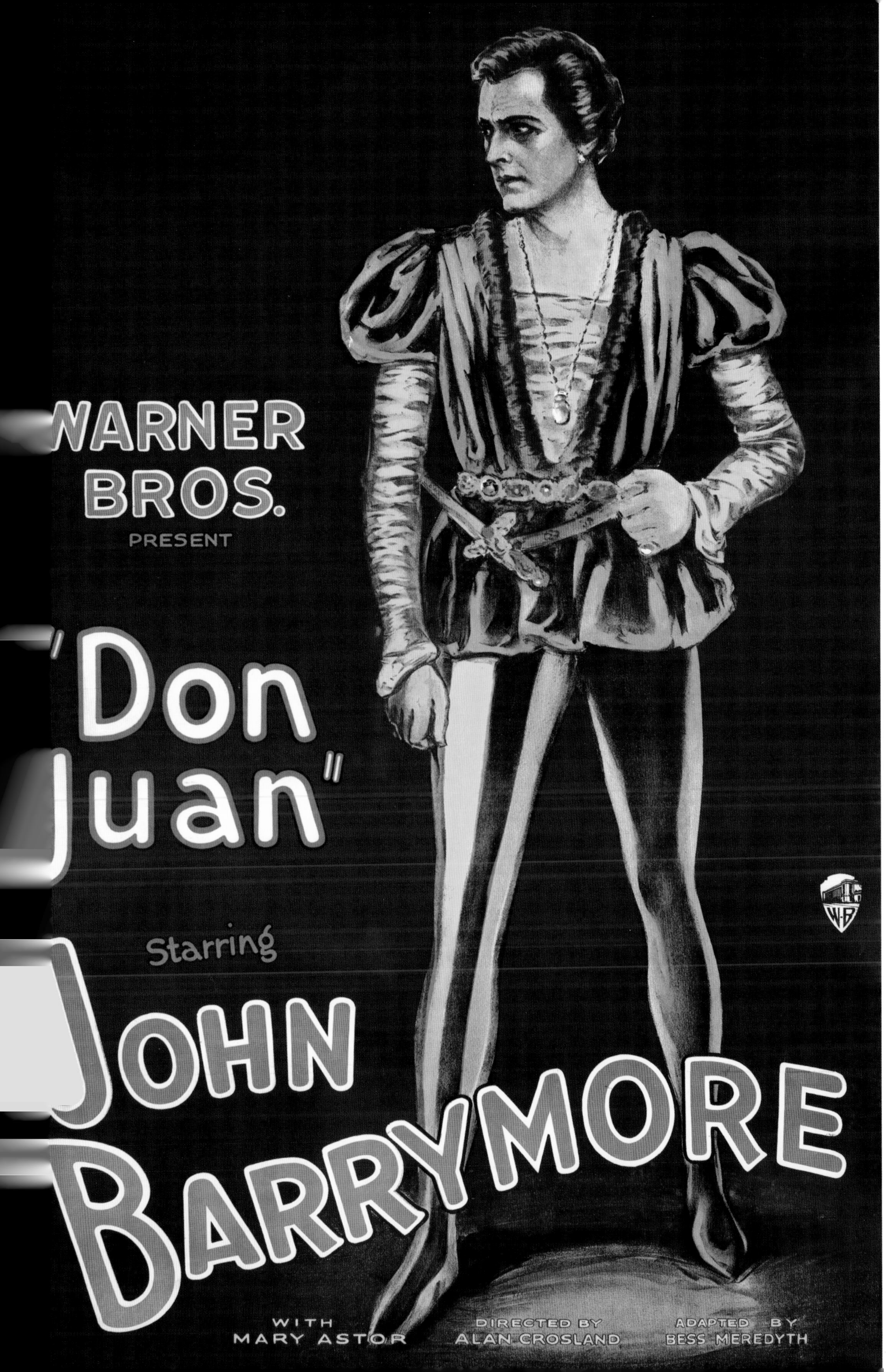
WARNER
BROS.
PRESENT
"Don
Juan"
Starring
JOHN
BARRYMORE
WITH
MARY ASTOR
DIRECTED BY
ALAN CROSLAND
ADAPTED BY
BESS MEREDYTH

Arguably the first great film comedian was the brilliant French star Max Linder, said to have been a huge influence on Chaplin, though in fact he played a character—refined and elegant—that was the exact opposite of Chaplin's tramp. Linder made a few Hollywood movies, but never quite caught on in America and eventually committed suicide. Sadly, he lacks the recognition he deserves, though the evidence of his brilliance and innovative ability is plain to see in his surviving films.

Charles Chaplin

I had the good fortune to be present at Charles Chaplin's triumphant return to America in 1972, when the Film Society of Lincoln Center honored his sixty-five-year career. He had left America in 1952, after being hounded by the FBI and the press for supposed un-American activities, living the rest of his life in Switzerland. Chaplin had begun his career in English music hall shows and first came to America, with the Fred Karno troupe, in 1910, and in 1913 was hired

by Mack Sennett, making his screen debut in 1914. In his second picture for Keystone—*Kid Auto Races at Venice* (in which he took risks that might have ended his career before it had even started)—he adopted the Little Tramp persona that caught the imagination of the entire world, making him perhaps the most famous person alive. It would be presumptuous to summarize Chaplin's extraordinary career, but as everyone knows, he progressed from making hilarious slapstick shorts to directing and starring in full-length features full of sentimentality and pathos as well as brilliant comedic invention. He was such a force in Hollywood that he was able to ignore the talkie revolution, continuing to make what were to all intents and purposes silent movies well into the 1930s (though *City Lights* [1931; fig. 69] and *Modern Times* [1936] did have sound effects, and music written by Chaplin himself).

Chaplin was another star whose private life attracted almost as much attention as his film career, much of this being due to a predilection for very young women. In 1925, while in New York for the premiere of *The Gold Rush* (fig. 68),

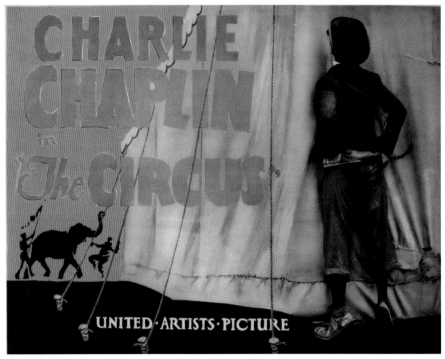

OPPOSITE LEFT

68. *The Gold Rush*
    U.S. (1925)
    Charles Chaplin/
    United Artists
    Window card
    22 × 14 in.
    (55.9 × 35.6 cm)

ABOVE

69. *City Lights*
    U.S. (1931)
    Charles Chaplin/
    United Artists
    Lobby card
    11 × 14 in.
    (27.9 × 35.6 cm)

TOP RIGHT

70. *The Circus*
    U.S. (1928)
    Charles Chaplin/
    United Artists
    Title card
    11 × 14 in.
    (27.9 × 35.6 cm)

BOTTOM RIGHT

71. *Steamboat Bill,
    Jr.*
    U.S. (1928)
    Buster Keaton/
    United Artists
    Title card
    11 × 14 in.
    (27.9 × 35.6 cm)

he began an affair with Louise Brooks, holing up with her for two months in the Ritz Hotel overlooking Central Park. Needless to say, posters for Chaplin movies—especially from the silent years—are very much in demand, and I count myself lucky to own prime examples from *The Gold Rush*, *The Circus* (fig. 70), and *Modern Times*.

Buster Keaton

Like Gloria Swanson and Eric von Stroheim, Buster Keaton was plucked from ill-deserved obscurity to play a role in *Sunset Boulevard* (fig. 17)—only a fleeting one as an expressionless poker player, yet it summed up a rich career that earned him the sobriquet "The Great Stone Face." Keaton learned his trade as part of a family vaudeville act that had seen his abusive father hurling him about the stage when the boy was a mere five years old. The knocks and bruises must have been many, and the need to hide the pain helps explain the rigor with which he was able to maintain a stoic cinematic persona that would have been undermined by the merest hint of a smile. Keaton's acrobatic athleticism was the equal of Fairbanks's, though it was expressed in an entirely different way, and his films are filled with breathtaking stunts, all of which he performed himself (not always true of Fairbanks, even though his publicists claimed otherwise). *Steamboat Bill, Jr.* (fig. 71) was my favorite, until I saw Keaton's greatest movie, *The General,* which was not a hit when first released. Although he did appear in a few talkies, he did not make a successful transition to the new medium, but had a late if improbable moment of triumph in a short movie titled *Film,* written by Samuel Beckett, a great admirer of his work. Like Chaplin, Keaton directed his own films and in 1996 was named the seventh greatest director of all time by *Entertainment Weekly,* placing him well above his comedic rival on the list.

Quite recently, at a gallery in Aspen, I found a marvelous Russian poster for *The General* by the Stenberg brothers, who were important Soviet artists of the period (fig. 72). It consists of a great railroad image and two pictures of Keaton himself. When it comes to Keaton, this is as good as it gets.

Harold Lloyd

My personal favorite among the silent comedians is Harold Lloyd. His screen persona had its origins in a character called Lonesome Luke, which he created when working with Hal Roach. The character evolved into a kind of comedic everyman, a resourceful go-getter who wore glasses and, often, a straw boater, and had a knack for getting into situations that were hilarious, often dangerous, and always beyond his control. This resulted in films that were both funny and thrilling, filled with great chases and daredevil physical feats. In his most famous scene, from the 1923 film *Safety Last!* (fig. 73), he hung from a clock that appeared to

RIGHT
72. *The General*
Soviet title:
Генерал
U.S. (1927)
Poster for Soviet release
Buster Keaton/
Joseph M. Schenck/
United Artists
42.5 × 28.3 in.
(108 × 71.8 cm)

OPPOSITE TOP
73. *Safety Last!*
U.S. (1923)
Hal Roach/Pathé
Title card
11 × 14 in.
(27.9 × 35.6 cm)

OPPOSITE BOTTOM
74. *Hot Water*
U.S. (1924)
Harold Lloyd/Pathé
One-sheet
41 × 27 in.
(104.1 × 68.6 cm)

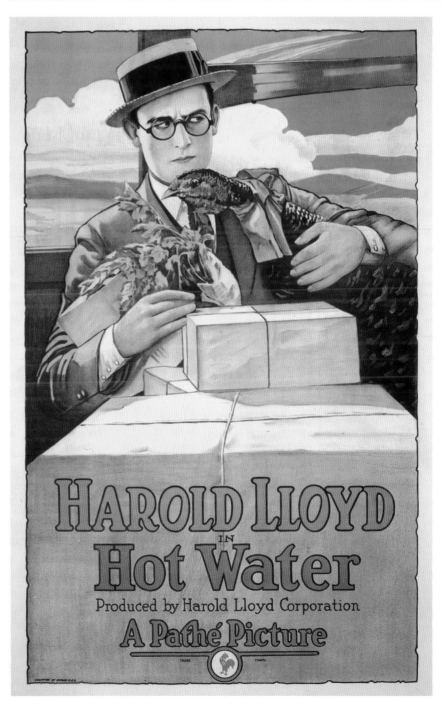

be many stories above a busy city street. Decades later, it was shown that the clock had actually been located not far above ground level at the top of Bunker Hill, a famous Los Angeles landmark overlooking the downtown area. The illusion of dizzying height was created by positioning the camera so that the street at the bottom of the hill, far below, provided the background. When watching the movie, none of this matters, nor does the fact that Lloyd is wearing a prosthetic glove, necessitated by a 1919 accident in which his right hand was mangled by an exploding prop bomb he had taken for a dummy. The injury did not prevent him from continuing to perform amazing stunts.

Unlike most silent comedians, Harold Lloyd had no stage background. He honed his art entirely in movie studios, and I think this gives his films a more modern look and feel than those of Chaplin and Keaton. Lloyd's everyman is very much a twentieth-century character. Chaplin's Little Tramp, by contrast, has roots in an almost Dickensian world— his appeal deriving precisely from the fact that he is an anachronism, out of step with a rapidly changing world and espousing values that are fast disappearing. Moviegoers watching Lloyd, on the other hand, must have felt that he was just like them. Happily we can judge this for ourselves because he carefully kept copyright control of all his films, and his granddaughter, through the Harold Lloyd Trust, has released beautiful prints of his great features and shorts.

Hollywood of the silent era remains more distant, magical, and somehow self-contained than the Hollywood of the 1930s and '40s. Despite scandals, such as the notorious Fatty Arbuckle case, and despite its atmosphere of laissez-faire wildness—unfolding in a world of speakeasies, Charleston contests, gambling ships, and fast cars—an aura of innocence still attaches itself to the period. Even when they misbehaved, movie people seemed somehow innocent, perhaps because they were inventing everything from scratch—a lifestyle as well as an art form and an industry—so that everything was fresh.

Hollywood posters from the silent days reflect that freshness and innocence. They are precious reminders of a glorious moment in the evolution of modern America.

75. *Speedy*
U.S. (1928)
Harold Lloyd/
Paramount
Lobby card
11 × 14 in.
(27.9 × 35.6 cm)

Starstruck

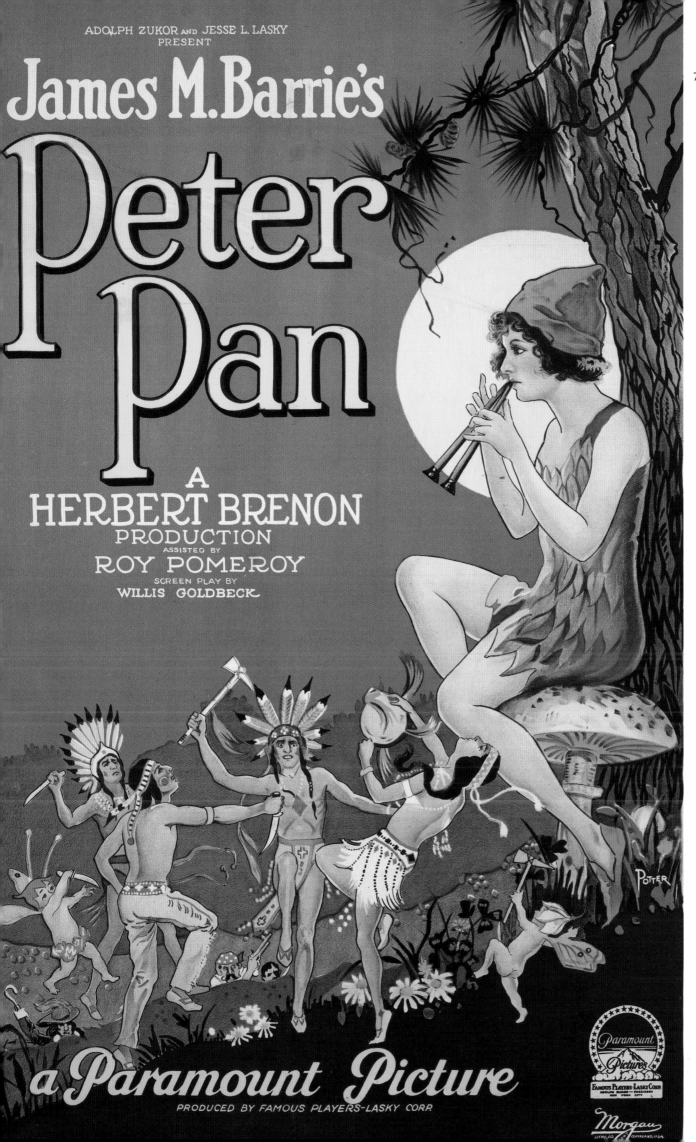

76. *Peter Pan*
U.S. (1924)
Famous
Players–Lasky/
Paramount
One-sheet
41 × 27 in.
(104.1 × 68.6 cm)

4

*The Golden Age
of the Talkies:
The Women, 1927–1941*

PAGES 82–83
White Shoulders
Detail
(See fig. 128 on p. 122)

BELOW
77. *The Jazz Singer*
U.S. (1927)
Warner Bros.
Lobby card
11 × 14 in.
(27.9 × 35.6 cm)

RIGHT
78. *She Done Him Wrong*
U.S. (1933)
Paramount
Lobby card
11 × 14 in.
(27.9 × 35.6 cm)

As everybody knows, it all began with *The Jazz Singer* (fig. 77). When it opened, in October 1927, the Warner Bros. release was an immediate sensation, not so much for Al Jolson's singing, though that didn't hurt, as for the promise contained in one snatch of dialogue—"Wait a minute, wait a minute, you ain't heard nothin' yet." It would be a mistake to think it changed the cinema overnight. No one but Warner Bros. was tooled up for sound, and there were still many kinks to be ironed out of its Vitaphone system. Silent movies continued to appear for a while, but the public's appetite had been aroused, and the industry as a whole—Charlie Chaplin excepted—knew that there was no turning back. By 1929, pretty much all Hollywood production featured synchronized sound, and Europe wasn't far behind.

Not that those early sound movies were technical gems.

Anyone who has seen *Singin' in the Rain* will be familiar with the vicissitudes of the changeover, with microphones hidden in shrubbery and scenes ruined by the leading lady's nasal diction. Many established filmmakers were less than welcoming to the advent of sound, feeling that it took away the poetry and visual flow of silent pictures. Given the primitive nature of the recording systems, fluid movement was virtually impossible for a while. In any case, the die was cast. Some silent stars fell by the wayside, while others—especially those with stage backgrounds—thrived, and Hollywood became a mecca for young hopefuls with bankable voices, and for voice coaches who claimed they could wring dulcet tones from a Bronx accent.

It was amazing, in fact, how quickly Hollywood's behind-the-camera wizards were able to overcome the technical problems involved in shooting with sound. Seen today, many of the early talking pictures are very stagey, but not before

long sound booms were allowing performers to move freely while they delivered their dialogue, and it wasn't long before Busby Berkeley was animating musicals with soaring crane shots.

In many ways, the first dozen years of the sound era—its golden age—breaks down into two distinct phases, the first usually referred to as pre-Code. The Code referred to is the Production Code, better known as the Hays Code after William H. Hays, a former postmaster general who in 1922 had been called upon by the Motion Picture Producers and Distributors of America to clean up Hollywood. The fear was that the federal government might introduce censorship in response to public outcries triggered by movie colony scandals such as the Fatty Arbuckle manslaughter trial, the unsolved murder of director William Desmond Taylor, and a string of drug-related deaths. An early victory for Hays was to persuade the industry to put morality clauses into performers' contracts, permitting termination for perceived misconduct. At first, though, he was far less successful in persuading the studios to avoid "unsavory" subjects such as prostitution and infidelity—staples of the silent era—but in 1927, just as the talkies were born, he drew up a list of things that in his opinion should not appear on movie screens, ranging from those same unsavory topics to suggestive clothing and, in the new era, suggestive language too. This became the basis for the Hays Code, which the studios endorsed but at first paid very little attention to. The Great Depression was on the way, and movie companies wanted to put bodies into their theaters despite the hard times. The audience they targeted was not necessarily looking for moral uplift (though a gesture toward it usually came in the last reel). People who had to watch every dime they spent wanted entertainment pure and simple, and if it involved fallen women, sexy lingerie, and outrageous double entendres, so what? It was a period made to order for someone like Mae West, who said, "Is that a gun in your pocket, or are you just glad to see me?" There wasn't much Will Hays could do about lines like this because he didn't have the clout to enforce his rules.

That all changed in 1934, when another public outcry, spearheaded by the Catholic Church, raised the specter of governmental censorship once more and forced the studios to sign on to strict enforcement of the Hays Code, which from then on was applied with an iron fist by Joseph I. Breen, Hays's Hollywood-based hit man. The Code spelled out the rules in no uncertain terms. If a director was shooting a couple going to bed, he'd better make sure both parties had at least one foot touching the carpet—even if the

79. Carole Lombard
    U.S. (1933)
    Paramount
    Publicity still
    10 × 8 in. (25.4 × 20.3 cm)

LEFT

80. *Gold Diggers of 1933*
U.S. (1933)
Warner Bros.
One-sheet
41 × 27 in.
(104.1 × 68.6 cm)

OPPOSITE

81. *Love Me Tonight*
U.S. (1932)
Paramount
Lobby card
11 × 14 in.
(27.9 × 35.6 cm)

Starstruck

characters were married—or the scene was out. Strictures of this sort remained in force until 1968.

Until 1934, however, things were much looser, so that the first half dozen years of the talkies had a flavor all their own—overtly risqué, though seldom over the top—that can be found not only in the films but also in the cards and posters used to promote them. Mae West—not a great favorite of mine—was perhaps the most obvious beneficiary, but there were plenty of others, Busby Berkeley for one. The kaleidoscopic dance routines in his pre-Code movies like *42nd Street* (fig. 15), *Gold Diggers of 1933* (fig. 80), and *Footlight Parade* (fig. 14) saw the camera track across acres of eroticized flesh, often assuming points of view that were positively voyeuristic. Elaborate numbers like "By a Waterfall" took their cue from Flo Ziegfeld's Broadway revues in terms of ambition, but in spirit they were sometimes closer to burlesque. In Eddie Cantor's 1933 film *Roman Scandals*, Berkeley went so far as to feature "nude" slave girls, their

modesty just barely preserved by thigh-length, Godiva-like blond wigs.

Barbara Stanwyck

An example of an actress whose films clearly break down into pre- and post-Code phases is Barbara Stanwyck. In *Illicit*, from 1931, she's a girl living in sin, and in *Ten Cents a Dance*, released later that year, she's a taxi dancer. In the 1933 film *Baby Face*, among the most notoriously "immoral" of the pre-Code movies, Stanwyck literally sleeps her way to the top, as her overtly seductive charms carry her from a ground-floor office to the penthouse boardroom of an art deco skyscraper, a story conceived by Darryl Zanuck. But detailing plots and roles only hints at the comparative sexual freedom afforded moviemakers prior to the intervention of Joe Breen's scalpel, and much of the eroticism had to do with nuances of dialogue, the way a scene was staged,

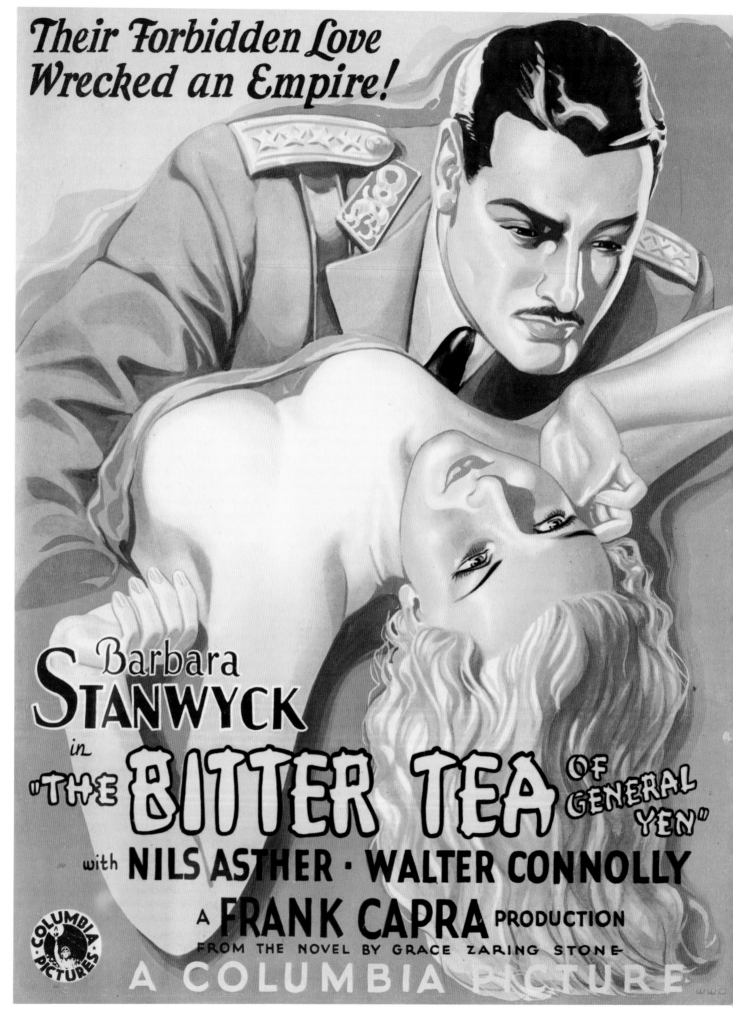

RIGHT

82. *The Bitter Tea
of General Yen*
U.S. (1933)
Columbia
Window card
22 × 14 in.
(55.9 × 35.6 cm)

OPPOSITE

83. *Ladies They
Talk About*
U.S. (1933)
Warner Bros.
One-sheet
41 × 27 in.
(104.1 × 68.6 cm)

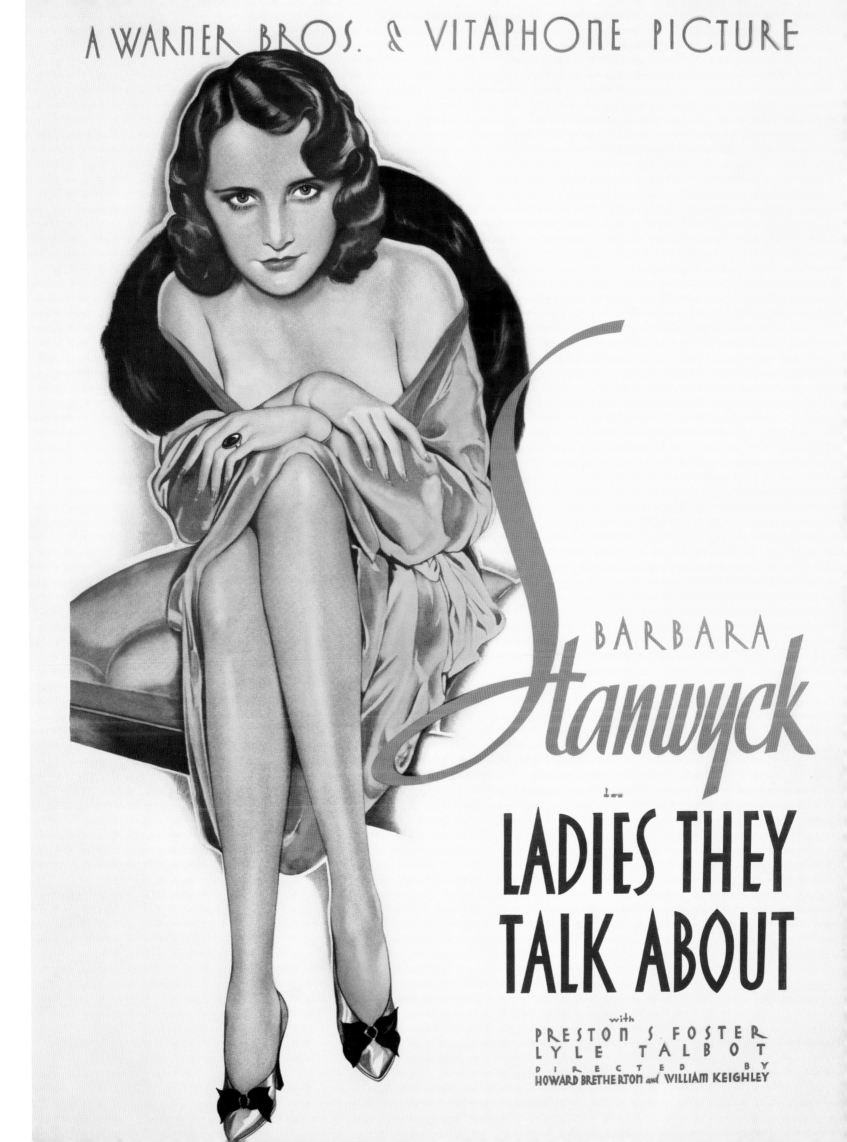

and glimpses of flesh that self-appointed moral arbiters considered offensive. That sexiness often extended to the publicity campaigns. I have a poster for *The Bitter Tea of General Yen*—(fig. 82) an ambitious early Frank Capra film about forbidden love—in which a very blond Stanwyck appears to be almost bare-breasted. Another sexy pre-Code Stanwyck in my collection is a 1933 one-sheet for *Ladies They Talk About* (fig. 83), a much-sought-after poster that took me a long time to find. Luckily for Stanwyck, and for us, her voice alone was enough to allow her to continue to project allure long after the Code came into effect—not to mention her acting skills, which delighted audience in such films as *Golden Boy*, *Double Indemnity* (fig. 232), and *The Lady Eve* (fig. 157).

Stanwyck was just one of a remarkable intake of young and talented actresses whose reputations were established between 1927 and 1933, when sound movies were coming to maturity. The list includes Claudette Colbert, Bette Davis, Irene Dunne, Kay Francis, Jean Harlow, Jeanette MacDonald, Ginger Rogers, Margaret Sullavan, Fay Wray, and the incomparable Katharine Hepburn. Almost all of these stars-in-the-making appeared in films that can be seen as benefiting from the liberality of the pre-Code period. Even Jeanette MacDonald—so proper in her later MGM movies—was positively saucy in her early Paramount outings with Maurice Chevalier. I have a title lobby card from *Love Me Tonight* (fig. 81) in which Chevalier, playing a Parisian tailor, is measuring Princess Jeanette's bust, which is concealed by nothing more than a lacy slip. It's impossible to imagine such a scene when, just a few years later, she was playing opposite Nelson Eddy.

Jean Harlow

An obvious beneficiary of the pre-Code atmosphere was Jean Harlow, who made her name in Howard Hughes's 1930 blockbuster *Hell's Angels*, in which she uttered the then highly provocative line, "Would you be shocked if I changed into something more comfortable?" With her lithe body, her platinum blond hair (which provided the title for one of her early movies [fig. 86]), and her knowing way with innuendo, she became an overnight sex goddess, and remained one until her untimely death, just seven years later, after a troubled life that included multiple marriages, one of which ended with the apparent suicide of her second husband, producer Paul Bern. Her pre-Code movies, in which her performances were often excoriated by the critics, included *The Public Enemy* (with James Cagney; figs. 146 and 151), *Red Dust* (with Clark Gable; fig. 164), *The Beast of the City* (fig. 84), *Dinner at Eight* (fig. 85), and the aptly named *Bombshell*. Even after the Code came into effect, however, her sexuality remained undimmed in films like *Reckless* and *Libeled Lady* (fig. 87). The films she made with Gable, Spencer Tracy, and especially William Powell demonstrated that she was fast maturing as an actress and a comedian.

ABOVE AND DETAIL
OPPOSITE
84. *The Beast of the City*
U.S. (1932)
MGM
Lobby card
11 × 14 in.
(27.9 × 35.6 cm)

LEFT
85. *Dinner at Eight*
U.S. (1933)
MGM
Title card
11 × 14 in.
(27.9 × 35.6 cm)

ABOVE
86. *Platinum Blonde*
U.S. (1931)
Columbia
Title card
11 × 14 in.
(27.9 × 35.6 cm)

OPPOSITE
87. *Libeled Lady*
Belgian title:
Une fine mouche
U.S. (1936)
Poster for Belgian release
MGM
33 × 24 in. (83.8 × 61 cm)

Kay Francis

A favorite of mine, who to my mind did most of her best work in the pre-Code years and just after, was Kay Francis. A stunning tall, dark beauty, her persona was enhanced by a sultry voice inflected with a slight speech impediment—rather like that of Barbara Walters—which led to the nickname "Wavishing Kay Fwancis." One of her first films was the Marx Brothers' *Cocoanuts* (fig. 147), and she then went on to star in another great (though very different) comedy, Ernst Lubitsch's *Trouble in Paradise* (fig. 91), which anticipated the screwball comedy style that would thrive after the introduction of the Code, as humor took the place of overt sexuality (at the same time providing opportunities for more subtle eroticism).

LEFT	ABOVE	OPPOSITE
88. *One Way Passage*	89. *Jewel Robbery*	90. *Confession*
U.S. (1932)	U.S. (1932)	U.S. (1937)
Warner Bros.	Warner Bros.	Warner Bros.
Insert	One-sheet	One-sheet
36 × 14 in.	41 × 27 in.	41 × 27 in.
(91.4 × 35.6 cm)	(104.1 × 68.6 cm)	(104.1 × 68.6 cm)

KAY FRANCIS
Confession

IAN HUNTER • BASIL RATHBONE

JANE BRYAN • DONALD CRISP • MARY MAGUIRE

Directed by Joe May • Original Screen Play by Hans Rameau

Adaptation by Julius J. Epstein and Margaret LeVino

A First National Picture

Presented by

Warner Bros.

ABOVE AND DETAIL
OPPOSITE
91. *Trouble in Paradise*
U.S. (1932)
Paramount
Lobby card
11 × 14 in.
(27.9 × 35.6 cm)

RIGHT
92. *The Mystery*
of the Wax Museum
U.S. (1933)
Warner Bros.
Title card
11 × 14 in.
(27.9 × 35.6 cm)

In that film, Francis benefited enormously from the director's famous "Lubitsch touch." Elsewhere she made a wonderful partner for the stylish and sophisticated William Powell in films such as *Jewel Robbery* (fig. 89) and *One Way Passage* (fig. 88), the latter being a classic among early talkie tearjerkers in which, aboard a trans-Pacific liner, Powell—a charming and debonair condemned man returning to San Quentin for a rendezvous with the electric chair—falls in love with Francis, a beauty languishing from a fatal disease, and she reciprocates in kind. Neither knows the other's secret, and as the idyllic voyage draws to its end, they toast each other and plan a meeting that each knows will never be kept. The film concludes at the planned location of the rendezvous. The same beautiful champagne glasses are on hand, and in the final shot they shatter. They don't make movies like *that* anymore.

Loretta Young

Another dark beauty of the period was Loretta Young, who had played ingénues in the silent period but did not attract too much attention until the sound era, when her screen persona was greatly enhanced by her sultry voice (which has sometimes been attributed to her having taken up smoking at the age of nine). Like many actresses, she had to suffer through her fair share of awful films during the early years of the talkies, but finally came into her own with movies like *Call of the Wild*, in which she played opposite Clark Gable. My own admiration for Loretta Young has always been colored by the fact that she reminds me so much of my mother.

Fay Wray

Fay Wray is, of course, linked forever with the original *King Kong*, from which I have two priceless posters (figs. 267 and 268). Her career had started at the very end of the silent era, when she was selected by Erich von Stroheim to play the female lead in *The Wedding March*. An intelligent actress, she became by chance Hollywood's original "Scream Queen," earning that title through her ability to produce bloodcurdling shrieks in Warner Bros. horror films such as *Dr. X* and *The Mystery of the Wax Museum* (fig. 92). Given this background, it was almost inevitable that Merian C. Cooper would cast her as Ann Darrow in *King Kong*. I had the good fortune to meet her, and have her sign several items, when she spoke after a screening at the Lincoln Center Film Society.

The Golden Age of the Talkies: The Women, 1927–1941

Irene Dunne

Irene Dunne originally made her name in Broadway musicals, and in 1929 she was signed by RKO, who presumably was primarily impressed by her sweet singing voice, which was featured in such movies as *Leathernecking*—her first film—and later even in the Rogers and Astaire feature *Roberta* (fig. 93). Her talents went beyond singing, however, and movies like the 1932 version of the Fannie Hurst story *Back Street* established her as a dramatic leading lady, a reputation that was sealed in 1935 when she starred in *Magnificent Obsession* opposite Robert Taylor. In 1936, she re-created her Broadway role as Magnolia in Jerome Kern's *Show Boat* (fig. 95), demonstrating that her lovely soprano singing voice was still intact. By then, though, she had also developed into a wonderfully gifted comic actress, leading her to star in three of my all-time favorites, a wonderful trio of screwball comedies including *Theodora Goes Wild* (fig. 94), with Melvyn Douglas, *The Awful Truth*, with Cary Grant, and *My Favorite Wife*, with Cary Grant and Randolph Scott, all made between 1936 and 1940. Irene Dunne was one of the most versatile stars of the golden age, and one of the most charming.

ABOVE

93. *Roberta*
U.S. (1935)
RKO
Half-sheet
22 × 28 in.
(55.8 × 71.1 cm)

TOP RIGHT

94. *Theodora Goes Wild*
U.S. (1936)
Columbia
One-sheet
41 × 27 in.
(104.1 × 68.6 cm)

BOTTOM RIGHT

95. *Show Boat*
U.S. (1936)
Universal
Title card
11 × 14 in.
(27.9 × 35.6 cm)

Margaret Sullavan

Another actress with a distinctive voice—husky in this case—was Margaret Sullavan, who began her career on stage in New York with the University Players, a repertory company that was also the proving ground for Henry Fonda (who she later married) and James Stewart. She came to movies in 1933 and was at her best in comedies such as *The Good Fairy* and, opposite her old comrade James Stewart, Ernst Lubitsch's wonderful 1940 version of *The Shop Around the Corner* (fig. 97), one of the great films of the golden age. A volatile personality, she married director William Wyler and super agent Leland Hayward, as well as Fonda, and eventually died of an overdose of barbiturates.

LEFT
96. *Next Time We Love*
U.S. (1936)
Universal
Insert
36 × 14 in.
(91.4 × 35.6 cm)

ABOVE
97. *The Shop Around the Corner*
U.S. (1940)
Loew's/MGM
One-sheet
41 × 27 in.
(104.1 × 68.6 cm)

Claudette Colbert

An instantly recognizable voice was obviously highly desirable in the talkies, especially since radio was being used more and more to promote movies and movie personalities. Claudette Colbert's voice, modulated and melodious, was very different from Sullavan's throaty whisper or Harlow's drawl, but it was just as easy to recognize. Colbert made one silent film but was essentially a product of the sound era, owing her initial stardom not to her voice but rather to taking an on-screen bath in ass's milk while playing Emperor Nero's wife Poppaea, the epitome of decadence, in Cecil B. DeMille's 1932 pre-Code epic *The Sign of the Cross*. Her voice came very much into play, however, in dramas such as *I Cover the Waterfront*, and especially in comedies such as Capra's unforgettable *It Happened One Night*—an Oscar-winning performance alongside Clark Gable—and Preston Sturges's *The Palm Beach Story* (fig. 246).

I have a half-sheet from *It Happened One Night* (fig. 98)—arguably one the most delightful and successful movies of all time—that I think captures Colbert's character in her role as runaway heiress. It catches the slightly askance way she looks at Gable through her overdone eyeliner. She's not yet in love with him—or at least she doesn't know she is—but he's already fallen for her. This is a good example, for me, of how graphics can capture the mood of the film itself, so that when you look at the poster you're instantly carried to a particular moment in the movie.

Another striking poster is a one-sheet for *Midnight* (fig. 99), a memorable 1939 screwball comedy in which Colbert plays a cabaret singer in Paris who becomes involved, against what she sees as her better judgment, with taxi driver Don Ameche. The presence of John Barrymore and Mary Astor—former real-life lovers—adds to the rich-

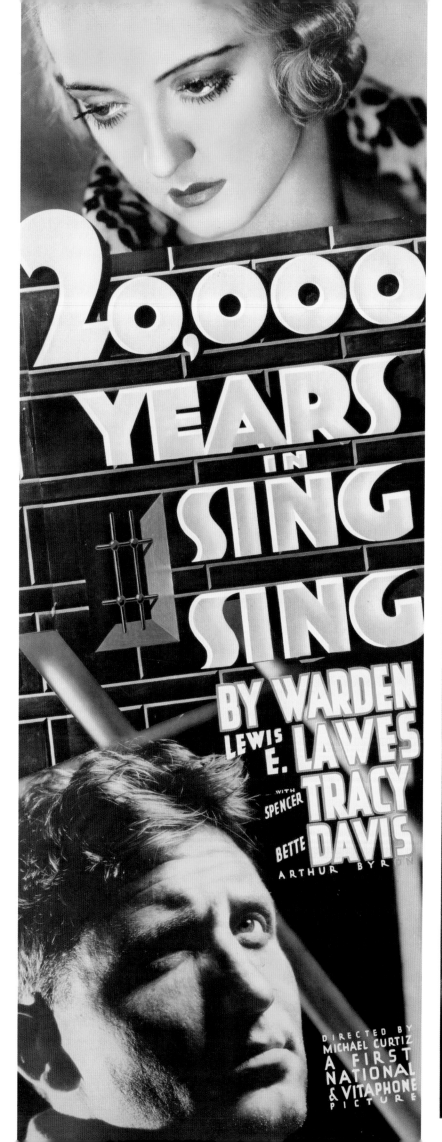

ness of the brew, but the poster focuses on the chemistry between Colbert and Ameche as they kiss against a starry sky.

In the 1970s, I had the good fortune to visit Colbert in her New York apartment, where she entertained me graciously and was generous enough to sign several items from my collection, making them that much more precious to me.

LEFT
100. *20,000 Years in Sing Sing*
U.S. (1932)
Warner Bros.
Insert
36 × 14 in.
(91.4 × 35.6 cm)

BELOW
101. *Of Human Bondage*
U.S. (1934)
RKO
One-sheet
41 × 27 in.
(104.1 × 68.6 cm)

OPPOSITE
102. *Ex-Lady*
U.S. (1933)
Vitaphone/
Warner Bros.
Title card
11 × 14 in.
(27.9 × 35.6 cm)

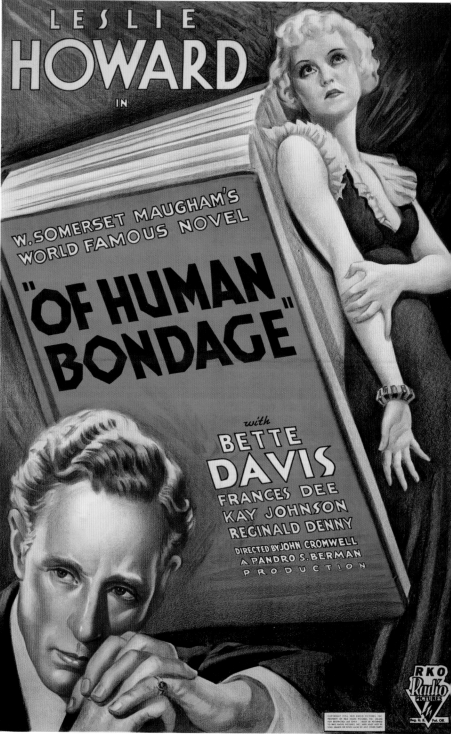

Ginger Rogers

Ginger Rogers made her name in the Gershwin brothers' Broadway musical *Girl Crazy*, which also starred the young Ethel Merman. Her first big movie was *42nd Street*, and she then struck up the partnership with Fred Astaire that she is now remembered for (more of that in the next chapter), but she also had success with dramatic roles in films such as *Stage Door* (fig. 1) and *Kitty Foyle*.

Bette Davis

Much better known as a dramatic actress is Bette Davis. After stage work in New York, she came to Hollywood in 1930 and had an unsuccessful spell at Universal, at which time the studio's boss, "Papa" Carl Laemmle, is reputed to have remarked, "The little brown wren has as much sex appeal as Slim Summerville." In 1932, she bleached her hair and moved to Warner Bros., where she was cast in films that made her clipped accent and haughty manner familiar around the world. Her considerable acting skills were combined with an electric personality that manifested itself on-screen and off. She constantly battled with Jack Warner, demanding better roles and greater respect. She of course continued to work into the 1980s, and in 1962 starred with Joan Crawford in one of her best-known films, *Whatever Happened to Baby Jane?* But it was the pictures that she made in the 1930s and '40s—such as *Ex-Lady* (fig. 102), *Of Human Bondage* (fig. 101), *Bordertown* (fig. 103), *The Petrified Forest* (fig. 155), *Jezebel* (fig. 254), *Dark Victory* (fig. 105), and *The Letter* (fig. 255)—when she was at her peak and her persona was perfected.

The Golden Age of the Talkies: The Women, 1927–1941

LEFT
103. *Bordertown*
    U.S. (1935)
    Warner Bros.
    Midget window card
    14 × 8 in.
    (35.6 × 20.3 cm)

OPPOSITE
104. *Marked Woman*
    U.S. (1937)
    Warner Bros.
    One-sheet
    41 × 27 in.
    (104.1 × 68.6 cm)

Starstruck

FAR LEFT

105. *Dark Victory*
U.S. (1939)
First National/
Warner Bros.
Insert
36 × 14 in.
(91.4 × 35.6 cm)

LEFT

106. Katharine
Hepburn in *A Bill
of Divorcement*
Photographer:
Ted Allan
U.S. (1932)
RKO
Still
14 × 11 in.
(35.6 × 27.9 cm)

Katharine Hepburn

If anyone could be haughtier than Bette Davis, it was the sublime Katharine Hepburn, a screen personality unlike any other. It's fascinating to speculate how it happened that Hepburn, the Connecticut socialite and Bryn Mawr graduate—her father a doctor, her heiress mother a feminist and cofounder of Planned Parenthood—turned first to the stage and then to motion pictures. Certainly her upbringing had encouraged her to be independent, and she was a born iconoclast, but still this was not an obvious career choice for someone of her background.

After a couple of less than world-shattering Broadway outings, she was signed in 1932 by RKO to play opposite the great John Barrymore in *A Bill of Divorcement* (fig. 141). She took Hollywood by storm, and the following year won her first Academy Award, for best performance by an actress, for her role in *Morning Glory* (fig. 108), a "star is born" story in which she played alongside Adolph Menjou and Douglas Fairbanks, Jr. This was quickly followed by her role as Jo in *Little Women*, an enormous hit. There were other early successes, but then she managed to transform herself into box-office poison, thanks to a couple of disappointing movies and the star's perceived arrogance, expressed in ways such as dressing in what Middle America saw as inappropriate male clothing. The cinema, after all, is a medium in which success depends on the approval of a mass audience rather than an elite, and sometimes that wider public rejects the unconventional.

Fame is fickle, however, and things can turn around very quickly, which was certainly the case where Hepburn was concerned. In this instance it was a matter of finding the right vehicle to remind moviegoers of her remarkable

Starstruck

ABOVE
107. Katharine Hepburn
U.S. (1934)
RKO
Publicity still
10 × 8 in.
(25.4 × 20.3 cm)

RIGHT
108. *Morning Glory*
U.S. (1933)
RKO
One-sheet
41 × 27 in.
(104.1 × 68.6 cm)

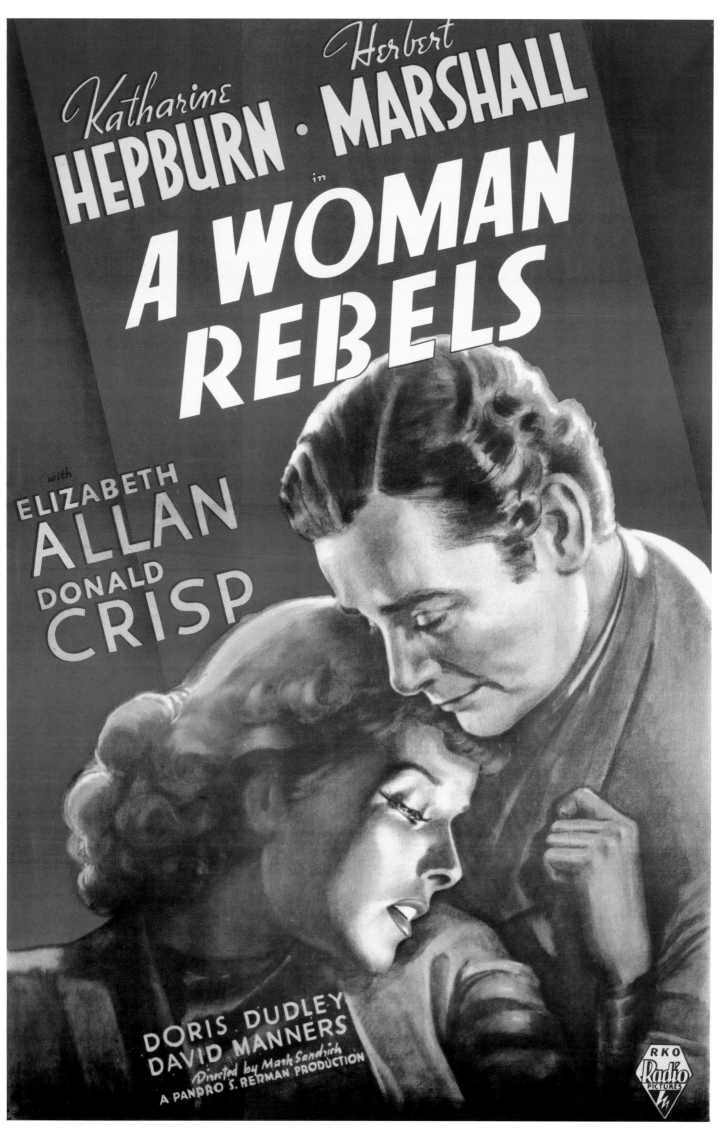

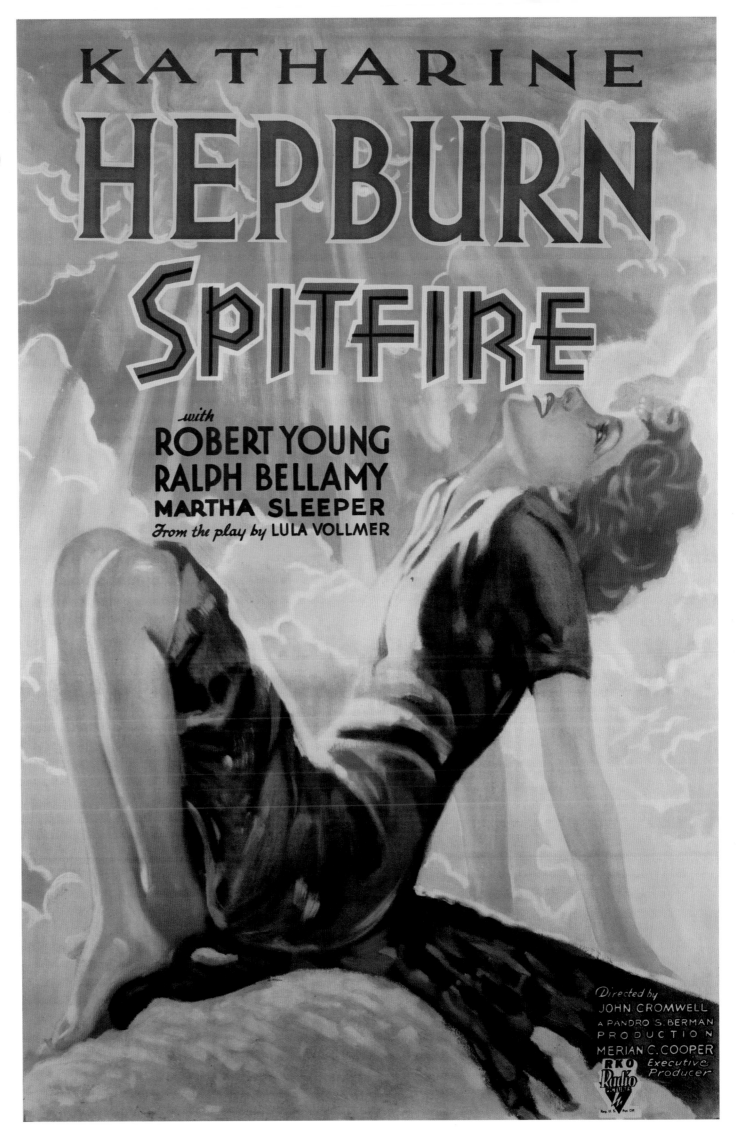

KATHARINE HEPBURN
„ELSKERINDEN"
EN HELT NY HEPBURN · EN HYPERMODERNE KVINDE · I EN HYPERMODERNE FILM
OFFICIN: R KO RADIO PICTURES NEW YORK   ENERET: GLORIA-FILM ⅍, KØBENHAVN
DYVA & JEPPESENS BOGTRYKKERI AKTIESELSKAB

111. *Christopher Strong*
Danish title: *El Skerinden*
U.S. (1933)
Poster for Danish release
RKO
33 × 24 in.
(83.8 × 61 cm)

Starstruck

TOP LEFT

112. *Woman of the Year*
U.S. (1942)
MGM
Title card
11 × 14 in.
(27.9 × 35.6 cm)

BOTTOM LEFT

113. *Bringing Up Baby*
U.S. (1938)
RKO
One-sheet
41 × 27 in.
(104.1 × 68.6 cm)

ABOVE

114. *The Philadelphia Story*
U.S. (1940)
Loew's/MGM
Title card
11 × 14 in.
(27.9 × 35.6 cm)

talents. After appearing to acclaim in the Broadway version of *The Philadelphia Story* (fig. 114)—written for her by Philip Barry—she obtained the film rights to the play and starred along with Cary Grant and James Stewart in the screen version, directed by her great friend George Cukor. It was a triumph and was soon followed by *Woman of the Year* (fig. 112), the first of a series of wonderfully intelligent comedies she made with Spencer Tracy. Hepburn was forgiven. Her great talent was recognized, and she remained a screen icon for the rest of her life.

I make no apologies for my admiration of Katharine Hepburn. The title lobby card for *Stage Door* was one of my first three purchases, and over the years I have accumulated a wealth of Hepburn material—lobby cards, posters, and stills, ranging from earlier films like *Spitfire* (fig. 110) to classics like *Holiday* (figs. 34 and 162)—that is at the core of my collection.

One of the finest Hepburn items I own is a Danish poster for *Christopher Strong* (fig. 111), the second picture she starred in. I don't have many foreign-language posters,

111

but the powerful graphics made it irresistible. The central image is very striking. It shows the star—that young, coltish, slightly odd-looking, angular character that Hollywood had never seen before—dressed in an aviatrix outfit, the lighting slanted to emphasize the bone structure of her face. This is established in subtly modulated monochrome set off by a lovely lime green background. A beauty!

By contrast, my one-sheet for *Bringing Up Baby* (fig. 113) is not particularly rich from a visual viewpoint—it features

ABOVE
115. *Renegades*
     U.S. (1930)
     Fox
     One-sheet
     41 × 27 in.
     (104.1 × 68.6 cm)

ABOVE RIGHT
116. *The Thin Man*
     Belgian title: *L'Introuvable*
     U.S. (1934)
     Poster for Belgian release
     Cosmopolitan/MGM
     33 × 24 in. (83.8 × 61 cm)

RIGHT
117. *Manhattan Melodrama*
     U.S. (1934)
     MGM
     One-sheet
     41 × 27 in.
     (104.1 × 68.6 cm)

OPPOSITE
118. *The Best Years of Our Lives*
     U.S. (1946)
     Goldwyn/RKO
     Lobby card
     11 × 14 in.
     (27.9 × 35.6 cm)

SAMUEL GOLDWYN presents

The Best Years of Our Lives

with MYRNA LOY
FREDRIC MARCH
DANA ANDREWS
TERESA WRIGHT
VIRGINIA MAYO

Released by RKO RADIO PICTURES, Inc.

a kind of combination of artwork and photography that I'm not fond of—but it has meaning for me because the film itself is important. The insert I have from this same movie is stronger than the one-sheet. It shows the battle of the sexes in a scene in which Hepburn has lost her handbag and Cary Grant has managed to accidentally rip her dress in a crowded restaurant. It captures a quintessential moment in the film, and that's yet another reason for collecting a particular image.

Myrna Loy

It was not only newcomers who contributed to the golden age of the talkies. A few stars and some lesser-known actresses successfully made the transition from silent films to fame in the sound era. A good example of the latter would be Myrna Loy. She made her debut in the 1925 film *What Price Beauty?* and for the rest of the silent era

appeared regularly playing vamps, minxes, mantraps, and, occasionally, Asians. Sound was a boon for her because it allowed her to express her sense of humor.

She had a way of hitting it off with her male costars. William Powell—whom she worked with many times, including six films in the Thin Man series (figs. 116 and 175)—loved working with her. Loy said of Powell, "From the first scene we did together on *Manhattan Melodrama*, we felt that particular magic between us. There was this feeling of rhythm, of complete understanding, and an instinct of how each of us could bring out the best in the other."

Myrna Loy was so popular in her day that she was voted Queen of Hollywood—to Clark Gable's king—in the 1936 version of Ed Sullivan's annual poll. Her screen persona reached its apotheosis a decade later when she played the ideal wife in William Wyler's classic *The Best Years of Our Lives* (fig. 118), though it's as Nora Charles in the Thin Man movies that she is probably best remembered today.

The Golden Age of the Talkies: The Women, 1927–1941

Carole Lombard

Another remarkable comedic talent revealed by the talkies was Carole Lombard. Starting at the age of twelve, she worked steadily in silent movies—including some Mack Sennett comedies—first as Jane Peters (her real name) and then as Carol Lombard. (The *e* was added to *Carol* due to a screen-credits error that she decided to let stand.) When the talkies came, her unforced sexiness and her ability to deliver lines with an innate touch of irony saw her elevated to leading lady, though initially she was usually playing second fiddle to an established male star, such as—as in the case of Myrna Loy—the suave William Powell, himself a veteran of the silent era, to whom Lombard was briefly married. Offscreen, she had a reputation as a madcap, throwing some of Hollywood's wildest and most inventive parties, such as when her house was converted into a hospital and guests were asked to come as doctors, nurses, or patients. Not surprisingly, her talent for the outrageous was channeled in her film roles, and she became the queen of screwball comedy in movies such as *Twentieth Century* (fig. 119) and *My Man Godfrey* (fig. 120).

After her divorce from Powell, Lombard dated Gary Cooper and George Raft, among others, and had an affair with crooner Russ Columbo until he was accidentally shot and killed. Then, in 1936, she began a romance with Clark Gable, who had been a casual acquaintance even though they had costarred in *No Man of Her Own* (fig. 283) four years earlier. This relationship eventually led to marriage (at the insistence of Joe Breen of the Hays Office) and Gable and Lombard remained devoted to each other until she was tragically killed in a plane crash in 1942 while traveling back from her home state of Indiana, where she had been participating in War Bond rallies. Because her life was cut short in

119. *Twentieth Century*
U.S. (1934)
Columbia
Lobby card
11 × 14 in.
(27.9 × 35.6 cm)

Starstruck

120. *My Man Godfrey*
U.S. (1936)
Universal
Half-sheet
22 × 28 in.
(55.8 × 71.1 cm)

WHITE WOMAN

WITH
CHARLES LAUGHTON
CAROLE LOMBARD
CHARLES BICKFORD
AND KENT TAYLOR

DIRECTED BY STUART WALKER
FROM A PLAY BY NORMAN REILLY RAINE and FRANK BUTLER
a Paramount Picture

LEFT
121. *White Woman*
U.S. (1933)
Paramount
One-sheet
41 × 27 in.
(104.1 × 68.6 cm)

Starstruck

this way, there's something of a shooting-star quality about her—like Harlow, or James Dean.

If she had lived, I believe Carole Lombard would have turned into a great character actress. Probably she would have continued, like Katharine Hepburn, to be a star into her forties and fifties. She would have matured without losing the wonderful spirit that made her unique and special. She remains one of my greatest favorites, and if I could get hold of all the one-sheets from any single star from the 1930s, I might well pick Lombard, partly because I regard her so highly, and partly because her studio, Paramount, was responsible for producing some of the most beautiful, vivid, and graphically effective posters and lobby cards of the period.

Among the actresses making the transition to the talkies, having already had major careers in the silent era, were Joan Crawford—who went from playing flappers and

The Golden Age of the Talkies: The Women, 1927–1941

TOP

122. *Grand Hotel*
U.S. (1932)
MGM
Title card
11 × 14 in.
(27.9 × 35.6 cm)

BOTTOM

123. *The Women*
U.S. (1939)
MGM
Still
8 × 10 in.
(20.3 × 25.4 cm)

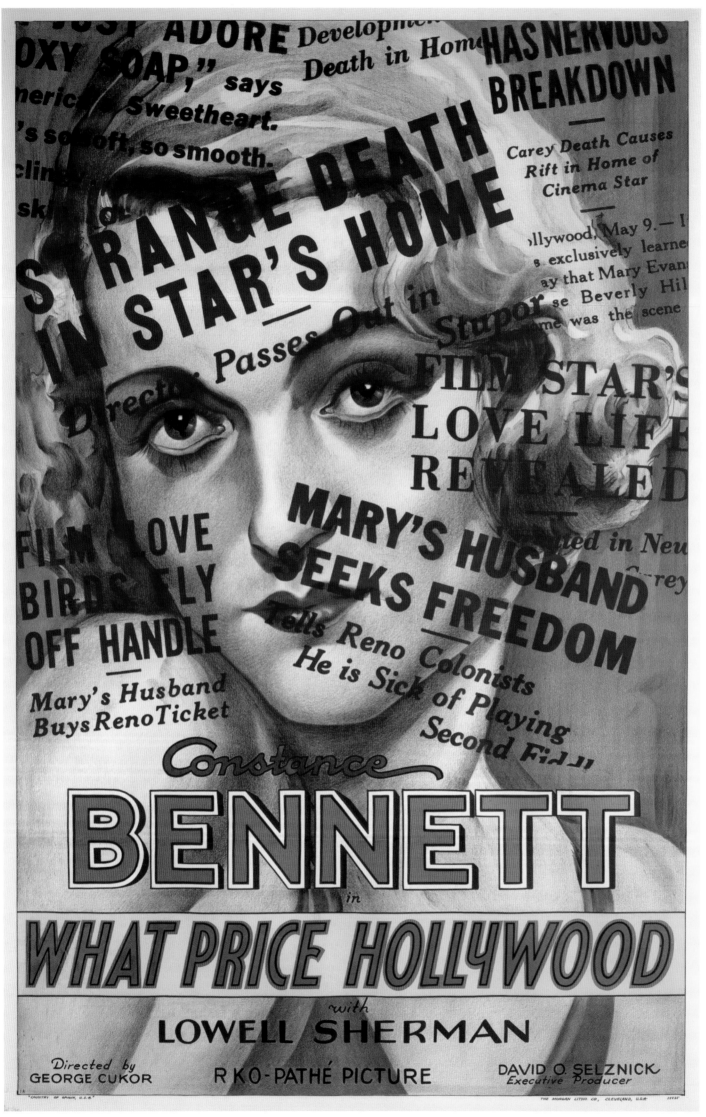

Starstruck

cinematographers—to look good on-screen. In the sound era she made some risqué pre-Code movies, such as *The Divorcee*, *Let Us Be Gay*, and Noel Coward's *Private Lives*, before moving on to "serious" roles like Elizabeth Barrett Browning in *The Barretts of Wimpole Street* and the doomed queen consort of France in *Marie Antoinette*, and then on again to the sophisticated Cukor comedy *The Women* (fig. 123), which gave both Shearer and Crawford the opportunity to be bitchy on camera.

Constance Bennett

More to my taste than any of the previous three actresses is Constance Bennett, one of the most beautiful and elegant actresses of her day, and a prominent, lively figure on the Hollywood social scene. Born into a leading New York theater family, she married at sixteen to escape her father's influence, and then, after that union was promptly annulled, signed with Goldwyn, had a brief but promising career in silent pictures, got married a second time, to the playboy Henri de la Falaise, the marquis de la Falaise de la Coudraye—an ex of Gloria Swanson's—and retired from films once more, but returned to become a star of the talkies. In the pre-Code era, she played her share of fallen women, but her most memorable role of that period was in *What Price Hollywood?* (fig. 124), one of the best films about Hollywood ever made. A direct precursor to *A Star Is Born*, *What Price Hollywood?* is the story of a Brown Derby waitress who gets her big break but finds that life in the limelight comes at a price. The poster for this movie is one of the most sought after by collectors, partly due to its rarity but especially because it really says something about the film. Bennett's beautiful face is overlaid with headlines that trumpet the tragic story of her relationship with the alcoholic director who wanted to control her career but couldn't keep pace with her burgeoning fame. It's a poster that begs the question, "What price are *you* willing to pay for fame?"

Janet Gaynor

The first version of *A Star Is Born*, released five years after *What Price Hollywood?*, starred Janet Gaynor. As a teenager, Gaynor had been cast in two-reelers at Hal Roach Studios and Universal. Starting in 1926 Fox began to feature her in more ambitious silent films, culminating in the 1927 classic *Sunrise* (figs. 126 and 229) and the very first Oscar for best actress, awarded for her role in *7th Heaven* (fig. 125). Gaynor made the transition to talkies comfortably, the soft texture of her voice contributing to the illusion of a childlike woman that was her specialty. Besides *A Star Is Born*, she made successful talkies such as *The Farmer Takes a Wife* and *The Young in Heart* before retiring in 1939 and marrying MGM costume designer Gilbert Adrian.

showgirls in the 1920s to roles in films like *Grand Hotel* (fig. 122) and *Letty Lynton* in the 1930s—and William Randolph Hearst's mistress Marion Davies. There are many who view the latter as a sublime comedian, but I can't help from seeing her, perhaps unfairly, through the prism of the ridiculously untalented Susan Alexander character in *Citizen Kane*, said by some to be based on Davies (as the Kane character was at least partially based on Hearst).

Norma Shearer

Another silent star who would thrive in the golden age of the talkies was Norma Shearer. Described by Crawford, her rival at MGM, as "cross-eyed and knock-kneed," she nonetheless was able to pass herself off to the public as an elegant and sophisticated beauty, perhaps thanks to the fact that she married head of production Irving Thalberg, who made sure that she was provided with all the help the studio could provide—including great

The Golden Age of the Talkies: The Women, 1927–1941

126. *Sunrise: A Song
of Two Humans*
U.S. (1927)
Fox
Title card
11 x 14 in.
(27.9 x 35.6 cm)

ABOVE

127. *Lady from Nowhere*
U.S. (1936)
Columbia
One-sheet
41 × 27 in.
(104.1 × 68.6 cm)

RIGHT

128. *White Shoulders*
U.S. (1931)
RKO
One-sheet
41 × 27 in.
(104.1 × 68.6 cm)

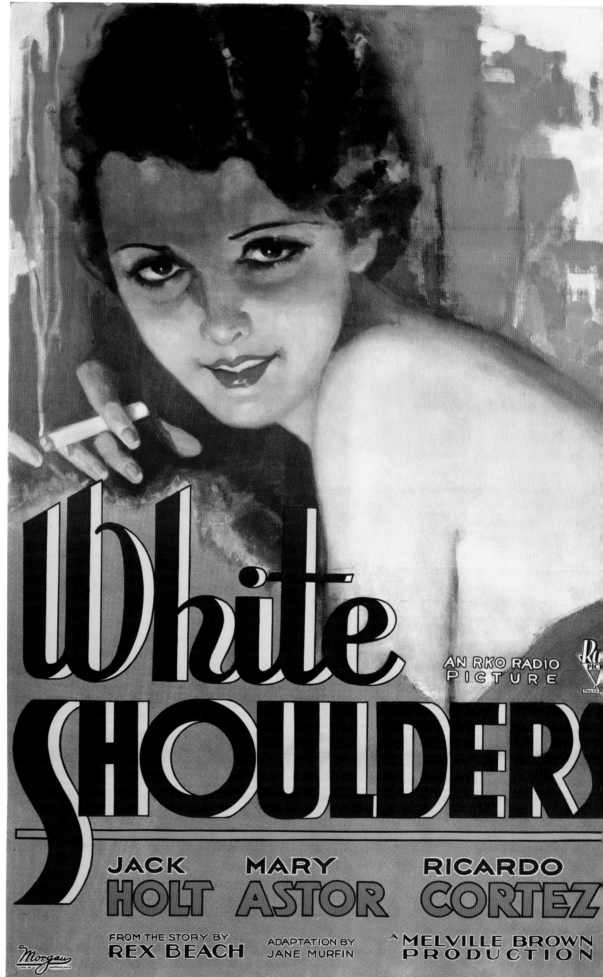

Mary Astor

One of the most fascinating careers to span both silent and sound eras was that of Mary Astor. A great beauty in her early years, she had a famous affair with John Barrymore, whom she costarred with in both *Beau Brummel* (1924; fig. 66) and *Don Juan* (1926; fig. 67). (A decade later, the purple press had a field day with her diary, which detailed an even more notorious affair with the playwright George S. Kaufman.) Astor prepared herself for the transition to the talkies by appearing in a number of theatrical productions. After the changeover—her face still beautiful but now a tad weary and sometimes wounded—she became a marvelous blend of leading lady and character actress whose ability to help carry a movie always justified costar billing. She was a marvelous foil for Clark Gable and Harlow in the 1932 picture *Red Dust*, and she was magnificent in William Wyler's 1936 masterpiece *Dodsworth* (fig. 222), though today she is perhaps even better known for her unforgettable role as the dangerous but pitiful Brigid O'Shaughnessy opposite Bogart in 1941's *The Maltese Falcon* (fig. 193).

An archetypal pre-Code poster is the one-sheet that portrays a seductive Mary Astor in the 1931 film *White Shoulders* (fig. 128), in which she plays a rich man's bride seduced by a gigolo. I had seen this poster in the collection of someone who refused to part with it, then encountered it again at a show at a New York hotel at the stand of the Sally Brothers, dealers who had been on the scene for a long time. This time it was for sale, and the price was right—high but appropriate. I also have a poster for a 1936 B movie, *Lady from Nowhere* (fig. 127), which once again features a bare-shouldered Mary Astor, though by now the Code was in full force and the poster is significantly more understated in its sexuality.

Greta Garbo

In 1930 the MGM publicity department announced the release of *Anna Christie* (fig. 133) with the exclamatory statement "Garbo Talks!" That alone was enough to put people into theaters. Garbo had ended the silent era as an enormous star, but Louis B. Mayer, Irving Thalberg, and the rest of the Metro hierarchy were understandably nervous about whether she could make the transition to sound, the unknown factor being whether the public would accept her Swedish accent. (The last film MGM released without dialogue was Garbo's 1929 picture *Kiss*.) As it turned out, Garbo's lilting, rather melancholy Scandinavian contralto perfectly matched the persona she had created for herself and ensured another decade of stardom that included such films as *Queen Christina* (fig. 130), *Grand Hotel*, *Anna Karenina* (fig. 131), *Camille*, and *Ninotchka* (fig. 132). As I mentioned in the last chapter, *Ninotchka* is my favorite among Garbo's sound films, the reason being that she lightened up

The Golden Age of the Talkies: The Women, 1927–1941

TOP

129. Greta Garbo
U.S. (1931)
MGM
Publicity still
10 × 8 in.
(25.4 × 20.3 cm)

BOTTOM

130. *Queen Christina*
U.S. (1933)
MGM
Title card
11 × 14 in.
(27.9 × 35.6 cm)

and demonstrated that she had a real feel for sophisticated comedy—that it was not incompatible with her screen personality—and the same can be said to an extent of *Two-Faced Woman*, her final film, released in 1941, though that movie made the mistake of trying to take her down off her pedestal. It's too bad she didn't have more outings that utilized her comedic gifts, but unfortunately her carefully nurtured image stood in the way.

BELOW
131. *Anna Karenina*
U.S. (1935)
MGM
Title card
11 × 14 in.
(27.9 × 35.6 cm)

RIGHT
132. *Ninotchka*
U.S. (1939)
MGM
Lobby card
11 × 14 in.
(27.9 × 35.6 cm)

ABOVE

133. *Anna Christie*
U.S. (1930)
MGM
Lobby card
11 × 14 in.
(27.9 × 35.6 cm)

RIGHT

134. *Blonde Venus*
U.S. (1932)
Paramount
Insert
36 × 14 in.
(91.4 × 35.6 cm)

Marlene Dietrich

It's conventional, and probably appropriate, to link Garbo's name with that of Marlene Dietrich, the other preeminent European-raised Hollywood star of the 1930s. She had had a career in silent movies in Germany and Austria starting in 1924, while also appearing onstage in plays, musical shows, and as a cabaret performer. She lost out to Louise Brooks for the starring role in Pabst's *Pandora's Box* (fig. 30), but shortly after landed the lead in one of the key movies of the early sound era, UFA's 1930 melodrama *The Blue Angel*, directed by Josef von Sternberg, which proved to be the great turning point in Dietrich's career. The film was an international hit and led to Dietrich being offered a contract from Paramount, where von Sternberg directed her in a string of movie hits including *Morocco, Dishonored, Shanghai Express*—which was *Grand Hotel* on wheels—*Blonde Venus* (figs. 134 and 161), *The Scarlet Empress* (fig. 139), and *The Devil Is a Woman* (fig. 138).

The Golden Age of the Talkies: The Women, 1927–1941

ABOVE
135. *Der blaue Engel*
U.S. title: *The Blue Angel*
Germany (1930)
Poster for U.S. release
UFA/Paramount
Title card
11 × 14 in.
(27.9 × 35.6 cm)

OPPOSITE
136. *Morocco*
U.S. (1930)
Paramount
One-sheet
41 × 27 in.
(104.1 × 68.6 cm)

Starstruck

MOROCCO

The unforgettable story of LOVE-of a -fiery-all consuming LOVE!

WITH

GARY COOPER
MARLENE DIETRICH
ADOLPHE MENJOU

137. *Shanghai Express*
U.S. (1932)
Paramount
Half-sheet
22 × 28 in.
(55.8 × 71.1 cm)

These Dietrich/von Sternberg movies deal with decadence, desire, hope, and hopelessness. They still seem beautifully modern and are loaded with visual poetry. Despite their exotic settings, they were in fact all shot entirely on Paramount's Hollywood lot, making them masterpieces of artifice. They provided poster designers with spectacular opportunities, ranging from the rich color used in one version of the *Morocco* one-sheet (fig. 136) to the stark black and white of a half-sheet for *Shanghai Express*

(fig. 137) that I think of as being almost Cubist. Two of my most important cards are from *The Blue Angel* (figs. 135 and 237). By the 1940s Dietrich had lost the quality of haunted beauty that I always found so affecting, and for me she became less interesting.

The silent movies had played a significant role in the rise of women toward equality in the first quarter of the twentieth century. Hollywood studios were far too conservative to support something as radical as the suffragettes, but they understood the importance of female stars to their industry and provided roles—often written by women such Frances Marion—that gave actresses opportunities to express their talent and sexuality. A few women, most notably Lois Weber, were given the opportunity to direct. Certainly American women were not unaware of the implications of

138. *The Devil Is a Woman*
U.S. (1935)
Paramount
Lobby card
11 × 14 in.
(27.9 × 35.6 cm)

the success—both as a celebrity and a businesswoman—of Mary Pickford, which coincided with women winning the right to vote.

The early talkies continued this trend, which was boosted by the fiercely independent spirits of stars like Bette Davis and Katharine Hepburn, and by the fact that the movies had now given women a voice, which could be sassy or seductive, winsome or witty. They could hold their own in the give-and-take of the battle of the sexes, though the studios' underlying conservatism—not to mention the interventions of Joseph Breen's interpretations of the Hays Code—generally dictated that the male worldview had to prevail in the final reel.

In those early years of sound, everyone went to the movies—this was the ultimate in family entertainment—but audiences were still weighted toward women, and so it was important for producers to provide male stars who could hold their own with sharp-tongued rebels like Davis and Hepburn, or who could strike up partnerships based on edgy or knowing chemistry, like those between Spencer Tracy and Hepburn, or William Powell with first Kay Francis, then Myrna Loy.

Marlene DIETRICH

"The Scarlet Empress"
directed by
JOSEF von STERNBERG
A Paramount Picture

Starstruck

ADOLPH ZUKOR PRESENTS

MARLENE DIETRICH and GARY COOPER

in 'Desire'

A Paramount Picture

JOHN HALLIDAY · WILLIAM FRAWLEY · ERNEST COSSART · AKIM TAMIROFF · ALAN MOWBRAY · Directed by Frank Borzage
From a comedy by Hans Szekely and R. A. Stemola

It's fair to say that the women stars are my primary passion, but—like those audiences of the Depression years—I know and appreciate a great male star when I see one. In particular I am drawn to those male stars who brought out the best in my favorite actresses, and I have collected their posters with enthusiasm.

OPPOSITE
139. *The Scarlet Empress*
U.S. (1934)
Paramount
Lobby card
11 x 14 in.
(27.9 x 35.6 cm)

ABOVE
140. *Desire*
U.S. (1936)
Paramount
Lobby card
11 x 14 in.
(27.9 x 35.6 cm)

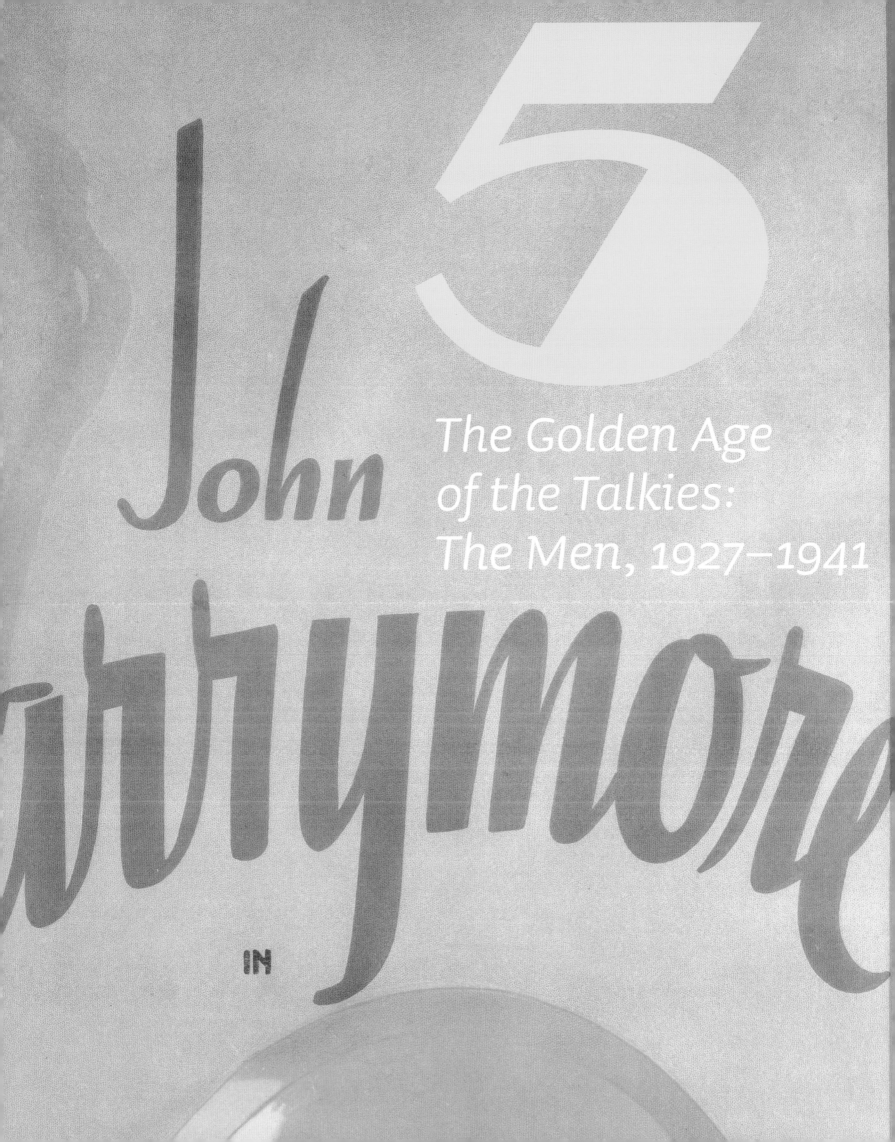

John

Barrymore

IN 5

The Golden Age
of the Talkies:
The Men, 1927–1941

PAGES 132–33
Twentieth Century
Detail
(See fig. 142 on p. 136)

RIGHT AND
DETAIL OPPOSITE
141. *A Bill of
Divorcement*
U.S. (1932)
RKO
One-sheet
41 × 27 in.
(104.1 × 68.6 cm)

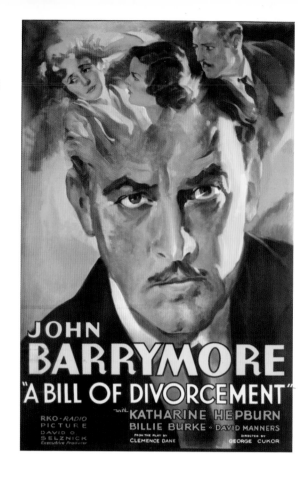

Major male stars that made the transition from silent movies to sound were relatively few. Chaplin was one of them, of course, though his contribution to the golden age of the talkies was almost nonexistent, since he kept the spirit of the silent screen alive with his own unique form of artificial respiration.

John Barrymore had long been known as "The Great Profile," but along with the profile went a great speaking voice so that he was a natural for sound movies. He had passed his prime as a romantic lead by then, but there were other kinds of roles that allowed him to demonstrate his gifts, ranging from scenery-chewing parts such as the title role in *Svengali* to genuine dramatic roles such as Baron Felix von Geigern—opposite Garbo—in *Grand Hotel* and as a Jewish attorney in *Counsellor-at-Law*. Best of all, though, he demonstrated his comedic gifts—well known to Broadway audiences—most notably with Carole Lombard in *Twentieth Century* (figs. 119 and 142). Sadly, his addiction to alcohol reduced him to a parody of himself in his later films, and he died in 1942, though not, it's said, without firing off a closing line worthy of one of his own movies. "Die? I should say not, dear fellow. No Barrymore would allow such a conventional thing to happen to him." Convention did catch up with him, but was defiantly ignored by a group of friends, led by director Raoul Walsh, who "kidnapped" Barrymore's body from the funeral home where it was laid out and brought it to Errol Flynn's house, where it was propped up in a chair, a fright for Flynn when he arrived home from a late-night drinking session.

Racketeer, cowboy, cop, playboy, clown, song-and-dance man, gambler, sophisticate, war hero, drifter, con man, champion of the people, and even the occasional bumbling academic (think of Gary Cooper in *Ball of Fire* or Cary Grant in *Bringing Up Baby* [figs. 113 and 242]), the male hero came in many guises during the golden age of the talkies.

As with their female counterparts, however, the roles that male stars found themselves in changed significantly when the Hays Code came into full effect in 1934. The difference between the two eras can be illustrated succinctly by looking at the early career of James Cagney. When he made *The Public Enemy* (figs. 146 and 151) in 1931, audiences were watching newsreels that featured stories about bread lines and bank closures. The mood was solidly antiestablishment. In theory, Cagney's ambitious mobster should have been a heel and a villain. He not only squashed a grapefruit into Mae Marsh's pretty face in the film's most famous scene, but also cynically bullied and murdered his way to success. Despite all this, audiences rooted for Cagney's gangster because they understood the forces that had driven him to a life of mayhem, and had no problem identifying with him. (Cagney's inherent joie de vivre and charm had something to do with that too, of course.) Even in the pre-Code era, crime could not pay, so the movie ends with Cagney's brutal death, but people still left the theater rooting for him. The character had shown that he didn't take crap from anyone. He was moxie personified.

But audiences identified with him just as easily when, not long after, he gave up playing charismatic bad guys and became a solid upholder of the law in 1935's *"G" Men*. Cagney was still embodying a version of the same

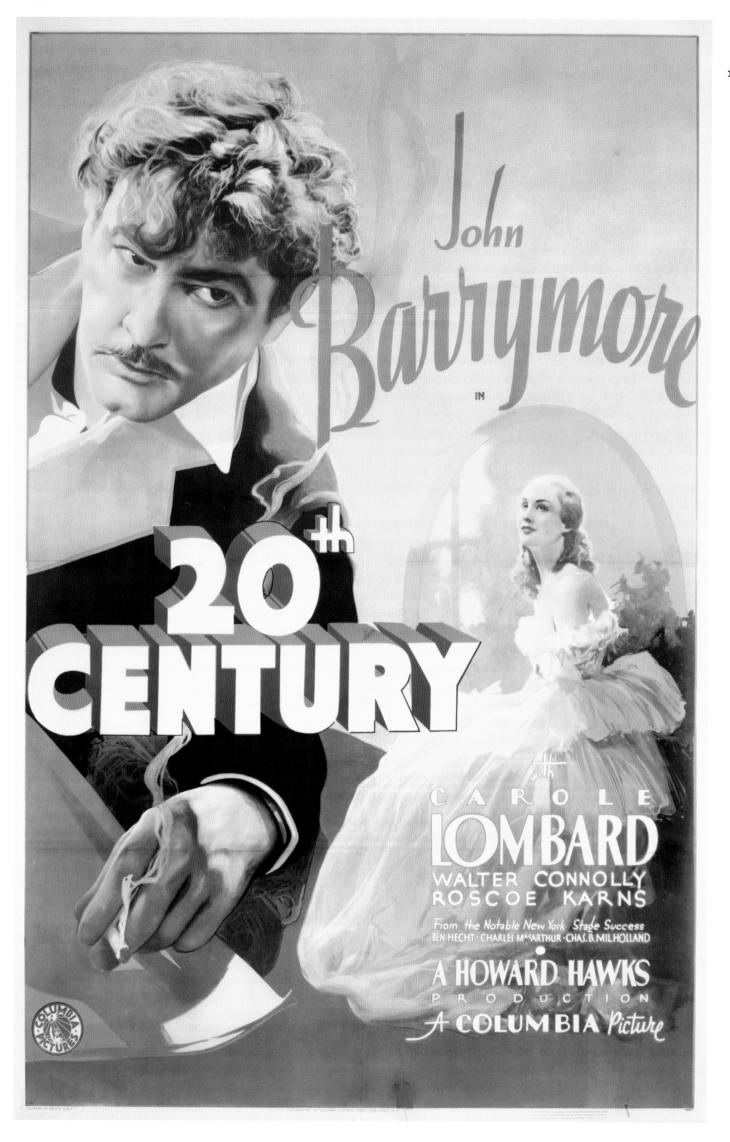

142. *Twentieth Century*
U.S. (1934)
Columbia
One-sheet
41 × 27 in.
(104.1 × 68.6 cm)

Starstruck

character, of course—a hard-nosed tough guy with a no-nonsense style and a sure sense of when to flash that irresistible toothy grin. What had changed was the mood of the times and the studio's acquiescence to the demands of Will Hays and his powerful backers. Mobsters were still a box-office draw, but now the "crime does not pay" theme was the whole point of the movie, not just a token gesture tagged onto the final reel.

Similarly, Edward G. Robinson, star of *Little Caesar* (fig. 144)—said to be based on the career of Al Capone—

went from playing criminals to playing good guys, often representatives of law enforcement.

It's not surprising that the anarchic spirit of the Marx Brothers enjoyed many of its greatest triumphs during the pre-Code era. *The Cocoanuts* (fig. 147), *Animal Crackers* (fig. 148), *Monkey Business* (fig. 150), *Horse Feathers*, and *Duck Soup* (figs. 36, 149, and 185) all appeared before the enforcement of the Code. As already remarked, Busby Berkeley musicals benefited from pre-Code conditions where eroticism was concerned, but they were also marked

143. *Rasputin and the Empress*
U.S. (1932)
MGM
One-sheet
41 × 27 in.
(104.1 × 68.6 cm)

137

by the us-against-them attitude so typical of the early Depression, embodied in male heroes played by Dick Powell and especially, once again, James Cagney.

In a sense, though, male stars were less affected by the Code than their female equivalents. The situations they found themselves in on-screen might be less risqué, but in general the way they expressed their masculinity didn't depend on revealing glimpses of flesh, though Clark Gable's bare chest in the pre-Code classic *It Happened One Night* (fig. 98) did cause hearts to flutter. When it comes to the posters of the era, those that feature a male star are far less likely to have been impacted by the Code than those that feature a woman. There's no such thing, after all, as a revealing suit and tie.

As with actresses, actors of the early sound era break down into those who had enjoyed careers in the silent era, and those that became known in the wake of *The Jazz Singer* (fig. 77). Since I've mentioned James Cagney already, I'll start with him as an example of the latter.

144. *Little Caesar*
U.S. (1931)
First National/
Warner Bros.
Lobby card
11 × 14 in.
(27.9 × 35.6 cm)

Starstruck

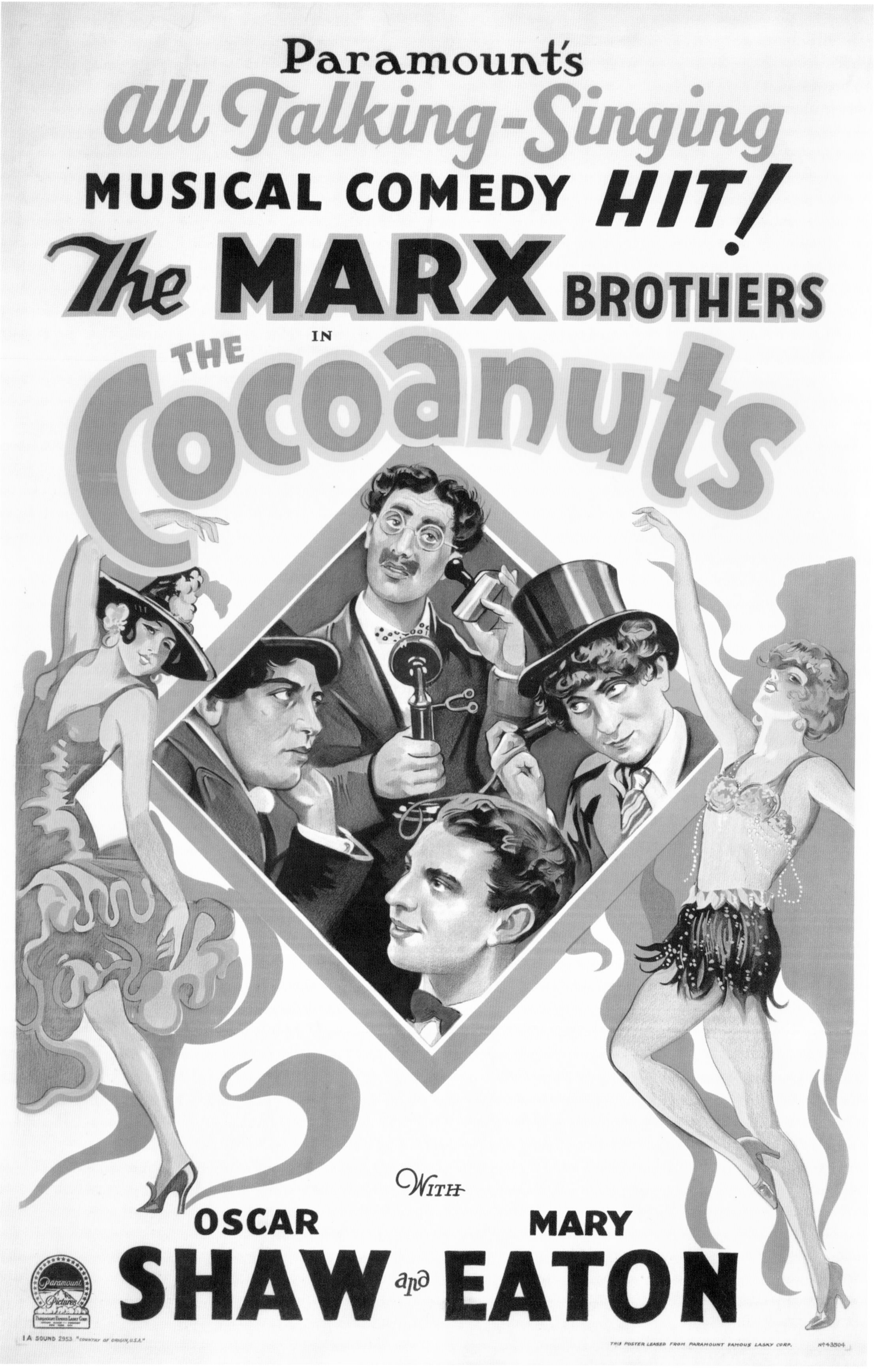

147. *The Cocoanuts*
U.S. (1929)
Paramount
One-sheet
41 × 27 in.
(104.1 × 68.6 cm)

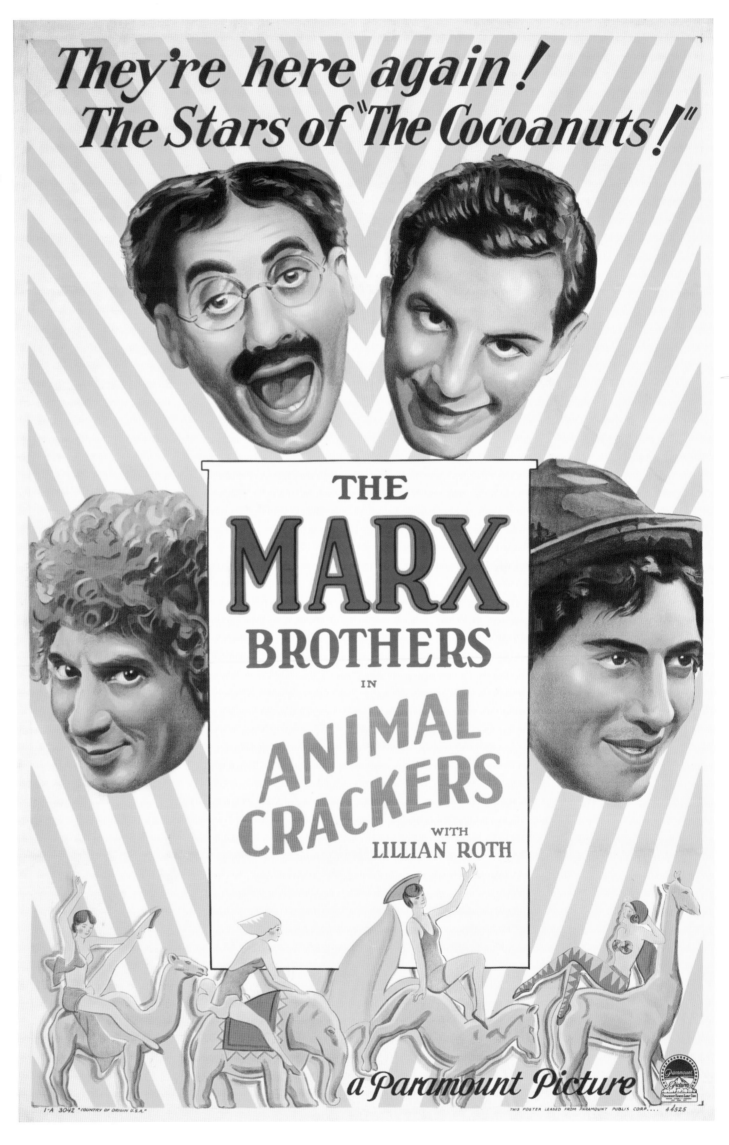

148. *Animal Crackers*
U.S. (1930)
Paramount
One-sheet
41 × 27 in.
(104.1 × 68.6 cm)

Starstruck

James Cagney

Cagney began his career in 1919, almost by accident, as a chorus girl in a stage production called *Every Sailor*. (Yes, that's right—a chorus girl. *Every Sailor* was a play about World War I servicemen who put on a show in which the female parts have to be played by men in drag.) For the next dozen years he earned his living in the theater, appearing in everything from Broadway plays to vaudeville, honing both his acting skills and his remarkable song-and-dance talent. By the time he came to Hollywood in 1930—touted to Warner Bros. by none other than Al Jolson—he was already thirty-one years old. Jolson had bought the screen rights to a play called *Penny Arcade* that Cagney had starred in on Broadway opposite Joan Blondell, and the pair of them reprised their roles for the screen, Cagney playing a prototype version of what was to become his classic tough

guy character, driven to crime by circumstance and social injustice. Then came the real McCoy—*The Public Enemy*—and it etched his persona into the American collective psyche forever.

I have in my collection a lobby card that catches the film's defining moment—rendered into color—where Cagney gives Mae Marsh the grapefruit treatment. The expression on his face says it all, and the impact of the image is amplified by a vignetted portrait in the upper right-hand corner. My Cagney collection is weighted toward early pre-Code movies—posters that capture the raw energy of the Warner Bros. pictures of that period. *Blonde Crazy* released in 1931, paired Cagney with Joan Blondell once again, and was the film in which he says, "That dirty, double-crossing rat!" The poster (fig. 152) is rather beautiful, a pastel-colored image of the stars in a simple deco setting. Also influenced by art deco is the window card I own from *42nd Street* (fig. 15), showing chorus girls stepping out through the footlights' stylized beams. Equally striking is a large door panel for the same movie in which Cagney—life-size in white tie and tails—is silhouetted against a red-and-white background, an image that beautifully captures the character of the Broadway director he plays in the film.

The title lobby card I have from *The Mayor of Hell* (fig. 154), a 1933 reform school story, sums up Warner Bros. aesthetics of the early sound era in its no-nonsense directness. A contrasty portrait of Cagney, in red and white, is set against a simple geometric black-and-white background. That's all there is, except the red-and-black block lettering spelling out the title and credits. The poster is deliberately cheap-looking, almost like a print ad in the back section of a comic book. This is extremely effective because it's not promoting some big-budget costume extravaganza, but rather a hard-hitting contemporary story rooted in the realities of the Great Depression.

Cagney would go on to have a long and glittering career, with features such as *Angels with Dirty Faces*, *The Roaring Twenties* (fig. 153), *White Heat*, and, most unforgettably, *Yankee Doodle Dandy* (fig. 10)—the film that did so much to introduce me to the excitement of Hollywood—but it was in these rough and ready, but always solidly crafted, early Warner Bros. talkies that he became the star we will always remember. It was at that time too that he proved his remarkable versatility. He was always James Cagney, but how many performers could switch from creating archetypal gangsters to carrying two of Hollywood's greatest musicals?

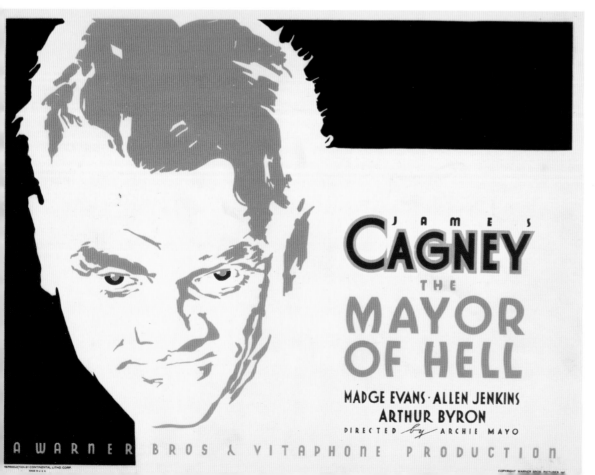

TOP

152. *Blonde Crazy*
U.S. (1931)
Warner Bros.
Lobby card
11 × 14 in.
(27.9 × 35.6 cm)

ABOVE

153. *The Roaring Twenties*
U.S. (1939)
Warner Bros.
Lobby card
11 × 14 in.
(27.9 × 35.6 cm)

LEFT

154. *The Mayor of Hell*
U.S. (1933)
Warner Bros.
Title card
11 × 14 in.
(27.9 × 35.6 cm)

Humphrey Bogart

The musical was a genre that Humphrey Bogart, another resident Warner Bros. tough guy, never attempted. Bogart grew up in a well-to-do household on New York's Upper West Side. His father was a surgeon; his mother—like Katharine Hepburn's—was a suffragette. She was also a very successful commercial artist who sometimes used Humphrey as a model, notably for Gerber's baby food ads. At the end of World War I Bogart had a spell in the navy, then drifted into various professions, culminating in an undistinguished theatrical career in which he was often cast as a feckless socialite in white flannels and a striped blazer, roles that his background had prepared him for but that hardly suited his temperament. Bogart was the same age as Cagney, and came to Hollywood at the same time, but where Cagney clicked immediately, Bogart failed to find his enduring persona till the mid-1930s. That came with *The Petrified Forest* (fig. 155), for which he had created the role of the tough hoodlum "Duke" Mantee in the 1935 Broadway production. The following year—at the insistence of Leslie Howard, who owned the movie rights, and who costarred along with Bette Davis—Bogart re-created the role on-screen. It won him great reviews and a string of gangster roles in B movies, as well as some good supporting roles in films like *Dark Victory* (fig. 105). It wasn't until the early 1940s, though—thanks to *High Sierra* (fig. 31), *The Maltese Falcon* (fig. 193), and, especially, his signature role in *Casablanca* (figs. 191, 273, and 274)—that he finally became a star of the first magnitude. Many of the highlights of his career—from *The Big Sleep* (fig. 198) to *Sabrina* (fig. 212) and *The African Queen* (fig. 202)—belong to future chapters, but Bogart remained very much a product of that first age of the talkies.

Henry Fonda

Most of the male stars who grew up with the talkies had long careers. This was certainly true of Henry Fonda, who spent almost half a century in front of the movie cameras. Before that, he'd put in his time in front of the footlights, graduating from the University Players, the summer stock company that was also the proving ground for James Stewart (who became Fonda's lifelong friend) and Margaret Sullavan (to whom Fonda was briefly married). He commenced his screen career in 1935 with *The Farmer Takes a Wife* in a role he'd created on Broadway. Critical successes in films like *You Only Live Once* and *Jezebel* (fig. 254) led to his defining role in *The Grapes of Wrath* (fig. 156).

No matter what the role, though, the characters Henry Fonda played always seemed to take the world pretty seriously. He was well suited to portraying idealists, whether

BELOW
155. *The Petrified Forest*
U.S. (1936)
Warner Bros.
Lobby card
11 × 14 in.
(27.9 × 35.6 cm)

RIGHT
156. *The Grapes of Wrath*
U.S. (1940)
20th Century-Fox
Insert
36 × 14 in.
(91.4 × 35.6 cm)

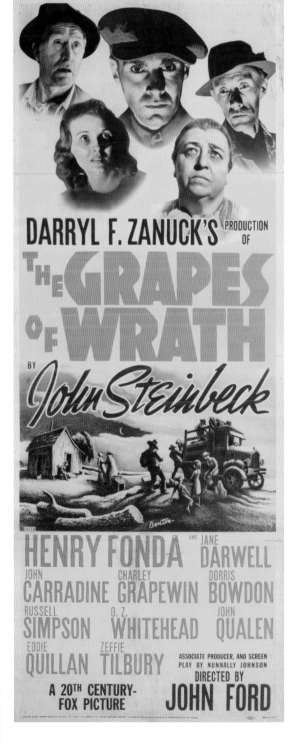

157. *The Lady Eve*
U.S. (1941)
Paramount
One-sheet
41 × 27 in.
(104.1 × 68.6 cm)

in contemporary settings or in westerns. Surprisingly, he also thrived in screwball comedies. In that context his seriousness and sincerity provided the other players with something wonderful to play off, and he teamed up especially well with ex-wife Sullavan in *The Moon's Our Home*. His greatest comedy role, however, was in Preston Sturges's 1941 masterpiece *The Lady Eve*, in which Barbara Stanwyck's confidence artist with a heart of gold provided the perfect foil for Fonda's wet-behind-the-ears rich kid, Charles Pike, heir to the Pike Ale fortune. I have a one-sheet (fig. 157) and a lobby card (part of a full set) from that film that share the same imagery—very typical of the period—in which Stanwyck in a short black dress lavishes her attentions on a confused Fonda, who is half hidden by a gigantic apple with a bite out of it. A smirking serpent in a top hat serves as a further reminder of mankind's expulsion from the Garden of Eden.

James Stewart

Fonda's University Players cohort and lifelong pal James Stewart followed him out to Hollywood. Stewart was signed by MGM, but surprisingly—given the range of roles he would eventually play—the studio had difficulties casting him. This was partly due to his natural shyness, and it was University Players alumna Margaret Sullavan who coached him, helping him deal with his diffidence and encouraging him to make use of his drawling speech mannerisms rather than suppress them. She persuaded the studio to cast him as her leading man in the 1936 comedy *Next Time We Love* (fig. 96), and he was on his way. Later Stewart and Sullavan were brilliantly reunited in *The Shop Around the Corner* (figs. 97 and 231).

A fruitful partnership between Stewart and director Frank Capra resulted in films such as *You Can't Take It with You* (fig. 240) and *Mr. Smith Goes to Washington* (fig. 158), and in 1940 Stewart starred with Katharine Hepburn and Cary Grant in the classic comedy *The Philadelphia Story* (fig. 114). In 1941, months before Pearl Harbor, he enlisted in the U.S. Army, the first Hollywood star to don uniform in response to the threat of war. He had held a pilot's license for several years, so it was natural that he should serve in the U.S. Army Air Corps, first as an instructor but then as a combat pilot, leading missions deep into occupied Europe, ending the war as a full colonel. Later he was promoted to brigadier general in the USAF Reserve.

After the war he resumed his career where he had left off with Capra's *It's a Wonderful Life* (fig. 241) before forging a new partnership with Alfred Hitchcock, for whom he starred in *Rope* (1948), *Rear Window* (1954), *The Man Who Knew Too Much* (1956; fig. 248), and *Vertigo* (1958). There were other hits too, including a couple of great westerns, *Winchester '73* and *The Man Who Shot Liberty Valence*, and

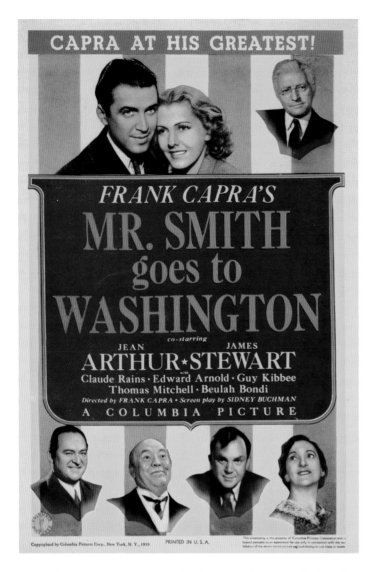

the Otto Preminger courtroom drama *Anatomy of a Murder*. It's impossible to do justice to Stewart's remarkable career without stepping out of a specific period, though the Stewart items in my collection are primarily from the golden age of the talkies. A measure of his achievement is the fact that, according to the American Film Institute, he starred in more movies, out of the hundred voted the greatest, than any other performer, male or female.

Cary Grant

Born in Bristol, England, Cary Grant spent his first twenty-eight years as Archie Leach, before he signed a contract with Paramount and they assigned him the name by which he became world famous. (It's said that he chose it from the options offered because it shared the initials of the names of two established stars, Clark Gable and Gary Cooper). He had run away from home at thirteen to work with the Bob Pender troupe of jugglers and acrobats, and the physical skills he acquired at that time would stand him in good stead even when he was playing the most sophisticated roles: no one could handle a pratfall with greater aplomb than Cary Grant. The Pender troupe brought him to America, and he stayed on, keeping body and soul together by taking a variety of jobs ranging from Coney Island barker to vaudeville straight man.

He graduated to light comedies, first in provincial theaters, then on Broadway, which brought him to the attention of Paramount. He became a beneficiary of the pre-Code era by being cast alongside Marlene Dietrich in *Blonde Venus* (figs. 134 and 161), in which he was a playboy, and—at the star's insistence—opposite Mae West in two 1933 outings, *I'm No Angel* and *She Done Him Wrong* (fig. 78). Paramount did not fully appreciate what they had, however, and he starred in movies ranging from the indifferent to the ridiculous (such as the B-picture melodrama *Wings in the Dark* in which he was cast as an aviator who, having almost perfected a blind flying device, is himself blinded). In 1935, however, Grant was loaned to RKO to play opposite Katharine Hepburn in George Cukor's wonderfully bizarre *Sylvia Scarlett*. Throughout much of the movie, Hepburn passes herself off as a boy. Grant, meanwhile, took advantage of the opportunity to showcase his comedic talent in the role of a roguish Cockney—essentially playing a part he

160. *His Girl Friday*
U.S. (1940)
Columbia
One-sheet
41 × 27 in.
(104.1 × 68.6 cm)

Starstruck

LEFT
161. *Blonde Venus*
U.S. (1932)
Paramount
Lobby card
11 × 14 in.
(27.9 × 35.6 cm)

ABOVE
162. *Holiday*
U.S. (1938)
Columbia
Lobby card
11 × 14 in.
(27.9 × 35.6 cm)

knew all too well from his early show-business experiences. The movie's gender ambiguities, played for all they were worth, contributed considerably to Hepburn's temporary fall from favor, but the film earned Grant a new level of recognition.

Until then he had been a little callow, with a hint of baby fat in his face and a career that lacked direction. Now he was cast in a string of outstanding screwball comedies that began in 1937 with *Topper* and included *The Awful Truth* (fig. 7), *Bringing Up Baby*, *Holiday*, *His Girl Friday* (figs. 160 and 243), *My Favorite Wife*, *The Philadelphia Story*, *The Talk of the Town*, and *Arsenic and Old Lace*—all released between 1937 and 1944.

In these films Grant perfected his persona as the impossibly handsome and debonair leading man—sometimes a touch feckless, sometimes a trifle arrogant, occasionally verging on the pompous, but always brave and oozing charm. His accent—an improbable hybrid of London's East End and New York's Upper East Side—was a marvelous tool that he exploited to the fullest. His sense of timing was immaculate, and he had learned a great deal from his days as a vaudeville straight man: he knew how to keep a straight face and how to set up his fellow performers for a gag as slickly as George Burns. And what made his characters so irresistible was his ability to undermine his carefully

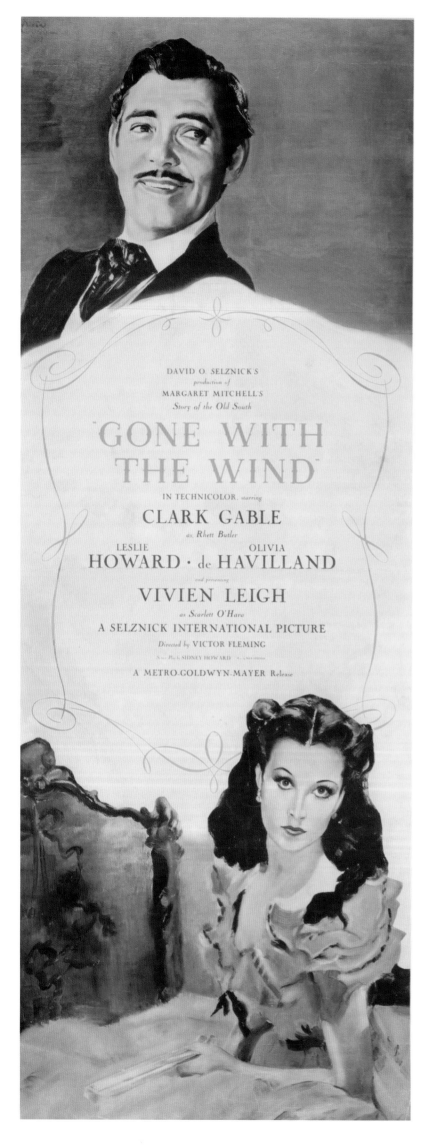

crafted persona at just the right moment, so that hint of arrogance or pomposity would be punctured before it got out of hand, making his characters vulnerable and human.

Like Bogart, Fonda, and Stewart, Cary Grant's career would continue well into the postwar era, with enormous hits such as *To Catch a Thief* (fig. 210), *Charade*, and the iconic Hitchcock thriller *North by Northwest* (fig. 253). Later Grant movies are represented in my collection, but once again my taste is reflected with a predilection for the early comedies.

Clark Gable

Today, stars of the 1930s like Cagney, Bogart, Fonda, Stewart, and Grant remain as highly regarded as ever, at least by fans of old movies. Back then, Clark Gable was known as the King of Hollywood—the star of stars so far as the men were concerned—but to many fans his crown has lost some of its luster. It may be that today it's harder to identify with the wholesome, uncomplicated he-man parts he so often played. It's not difficult to imagine Humphrey Bogart or Cary Grant thriving in Hollywood today, whereas Gable, I suspect, would be a fish out of water. His lasting fame is guaranteed, of course, by his role as Rhett Butler in *Gone with the Wind* (figs. 163, 271, and 272)—a part he reportedly had no interest in playing. By then he had been under contract to MGM for almost a decade. (Prior to that he had been an extra in several silent movies, but otherwise his career had been on the stage.) He started playing supporting roles, but MGM publicity boss Howard Strickling—who became a close friend—systematically built up Gable's he-man image, and the studio began to pair him with established female stars like Garbo, Norma Shearer, and Joan Crawford (with whom he had a torrid affair). His on-screen romance with Jean Harlow in the 1932 picture *Red Dust* (fig. 164) was hot even by pre-Code standards—she braless, he nuzzling her cheek with his six o'clock stubble (though the poster in my collection presents him as clean-cut and clean-shaven).

That movie established Gable as a top box-office star, and not surprisingly he and Harlow made six films together, including the racetrack movie *Saratoga*, during the shooting of which Harlow died. Although comedy was not his primary talent, Gable could more than hold his own given the right role, and a great one came along in 1934 when he was cast—supposedly as punishment by MGM—as down-on-his-luck newspaper reporter Peter Warne in Frank Capra's

163. *Gone with the Wind*
U.S. (1939)
Selznick/MGM
Insert
36 × 14 in.
(91.4 × 35.6 cm)

It Happened One Night, which, as already mentioned, was a huge hit for both Gable and Claudette Colbert (both won Oscars, as did the movie). This was another film to benefit from pre-Code standards, slipping in just before Joe Breen was set loose with his scissors. A few months later, scenes such as Colbert flashing her leg to hitch a ride, not to mention intimations of intimacy in an auto court, would almost certainly have been snipped out of the release print.

For the next several years, there was no one bigger in Hollywood as one hit followed another: *Manhattan Melodrama* (fig.117), *The Call of the Wild*, *Mutiny on the Bounty*, *San Francisco*, *Too Hot to Handle*, *Idiot's Delight* (in which Gable sings "Puttin' on the Ritz"), *Strange Cargo*, *Boom Town*, and *Honky Tonk*. Not to mention *Gone with the Wind*. In these movies he was cast with leading ladies ranging from Myrna Loy to Lana Turner. In real life, he fell in love with Carole Lombard, their all-too-brief marriage ending with her tragic death. Shortly after, Gable followed James Stewart into the U.S. Army Air Corps, where he was trained as an aerial gunner, then assigned to head a film unit, though he managed to fly a number of combat missions

from a bomber base in the United Kingdom. After the war, he resumed his acting career, which continued until his death in 1960, shortly after completion of *The Misfits* (fig. 219) with Marilyn Monroe. Like the other actors already mentioned in this chapter, however, he was very much a product of the golden age of the talkies, and to fully appreciate his gifts, it's necessary to immerse oneself in that period.

Like Gable, Spencer Tracy came to Hollywood in 1930. Initially he signed with Fox, but his career didn't really take off until he moved to MGM in the mid-1930s, and even then Gable was given the most desirable roles until he won consecutive Academy Awards, in 1937 and 1938, first for Victor Fleming's *Captains Courageous* and then for his role as Father Flanagan in *Boys Town*. It was, however, his partnership with Katharine Hepburn, starting in 1942 with *Woman of the Year* (fig. 112), that best defined his reputation, though he too must be counted among the entry class that attained stardom during the golden age of the talkies.

164. *Red Dust*
U.S. (1932)
MGM
Title card
11 × 14 in.
(27.9 × 35.6 cm)

165. *Dodge City*
U.S. (1939)
Warner Bros.
Midget window card
14 × 8 in.
(35.6 × 20.3 cm)

Errol Flynn

Spencer Tracy is often described as an actor's actor. A very different kind of star was Errol Flynn, a swashbuckler worthy of comparison with Douglas Fairbanks. With a sardonic personality that was all his own, Flynn had a predatory gleam in his eye when women were around (though his priapism was tempered by elaborately perfect manners— nobody could bow quite like Flynn), and the ability to deliver absurd lines with humor and conviction.

Flynn was born in Australia in 1909 and spent some time in New Guinea before making his way, in his early twenties, to England, where his acting career began. A Warner Bros. executive spotted him in a now-lost British film, and he was promptly signed to a contract and shipped to America, where he instantly made his mark as the star of the 1935 film *Captain Blood*, his handsome features and superb athleticism making him the ideal hero for exotic costume dramas, in which he was often paired with Olivia de Havilland, and memorably with Bette Davis in *The Private Lives of Elizabeth and Essex*.

The kind of films that Flynn was cast in—movies such as *The Adventures of Robin Hood* (fig. 20), *The Sea Hawk*, *The Charge of the Light Brigade*, *The Adventures of Don Juan*, *Dodge City* (figs. 11 and 165), and *Dawn Patrol*—were ideal subjects for poster artists. As had been the case with Fairbanks, Flynn was often shown sword in hand against a background packed with dramatic action, a classic example being the one-sheet for his breakthrough picture *Captain Blood* (fig. 166).

It would have been interesting had Flynn been cast in a few screwball comedies, because there's plenty of evidence that he possessed a self-deprecating sense of humor and an innate attraction to wildness that—along with his out-front sex appeal—might have brought the best out of Carole Lombard or even Katharine Hepburn.

Fred Astaire

If Flynn was among the most overtly erotic of male movie stars, Fred Astaire may well have been the least, yet he possessed an ability that none of his contemporaries could match. He could spin a web of romance that was, and still is, completely captivating. It was not his way with playing a scene, of course, though he had a knack with wry comedic dialogue, but how he staged and performed—with Ginger Rogers and then other partners—dance number after dance number, each seemingly more magical than the last and for the most part satisfyingly embedded into the movie as a whole. It's famously been said of Rogers and Astaire that she gave him sex appeal and he gave her class. There's probably some truth to that, though it only partially explains the extraordinary chemistry that existed between

166. *Captain Blood*
U.S. (1935)
Warner Bros.
One-sheet
41 × 27 in.
(104.1 × 68.6 cm)

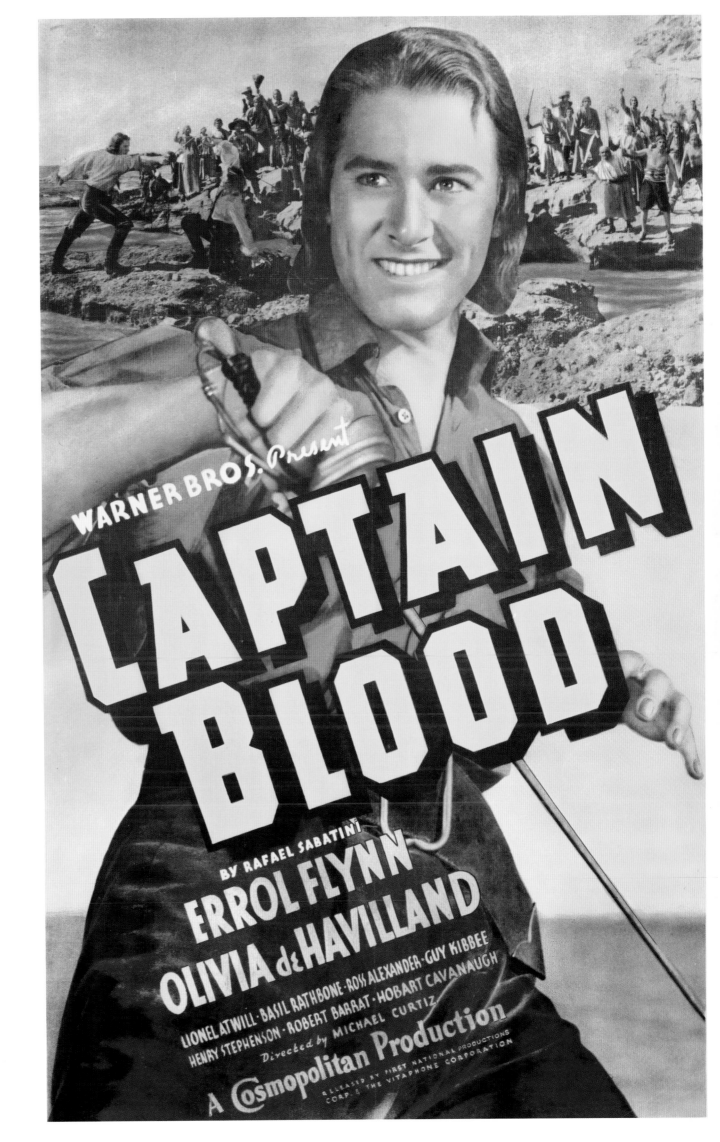

them on-screen (a chemistry that reputedly ceased to exist when the cameras were not rolling).

Astaire and his sister Adele had been a dance team since childhood, and during the 1920s and the early 1930s they were major stage stars both on Broadway and in London's West End. In 1932, the partnership came to an end when Adele married Lord Charles Cavendish. Earlier, the pair of them had failed a screen test at Paramount, and now Astaire was tested by RKO, where a legendary (and possibly apocryphal) memo is reported to have read, "Can't sing. Can't act. Balding. Can dance a little." David Selznick, who had commissioned it, agreed that the test was dreadful but remained convinced that Astaire had a charm that movie audiences would respond to. When Astaire was cast as Rogers's partner in *Flying Down to Rio* (fig. 167), Selznick

was proven correct, and Astaire and Rogers went on to star in a string of hits, including *The Gay Divorcee, Roberta* (fig. 93), *Top Hat* (fig. 169), *Follow the Fleet, Swing Time* (fig. 171), *Shall We Dance* (fig. 172), and *The Barkleys of Broadway*. In all these movies, and others that he made at RKO and other studios, principally MGM, Astaire planned and controlled all the dance sequences, essentially reinventing the concept of cinematic dance, insisting that his full figure and his partner's be kept on camera through the entire routine—with as few edits as possible—so that the audience would experience the dance as if they were seeing it in person. This was the opposite of Busby Berkeley's technique of using swooping camera angles, fast cuts, and shots of isolated body parts.

Not surprisingly, posters for the Astaire/Rogers movies

mostly try to capitalize on the grace of the pair dancing, a difficult feat to pull off, though there are some striking efforts that often incorporate jazzy '30s lettering, as in my examples from *Swing Time* and *Shall We Dance*. A rather bizarre exception is the midget window card for *The Gay Divorcee* (fig. 170). This too features deco-ish lettering, but combines it with caricatures of the two stars—Ginger pop-eyed, and Astaire slightly ghoulish with an enormous forehead.

The Golden Age of the Talkies: The Men, 1927–1941

OPPOSITE
167. *Flying Down to Rio*
U.S. (1933)
RKO
Title card
11 × 14 in.
(27.9 × 35.6 cm)

ABOVE
168. *The Gay Divorcee*
U.S. (1934)
RKO
Title card
11 × 14 in.
(27.9 × 35.6 cm)

FRED ASTAIRE
GINGER ROGERS
in
"TOP HAT"
Lyrics and Music by
IRVING BERLIN
RKO·RADIO PICTURE

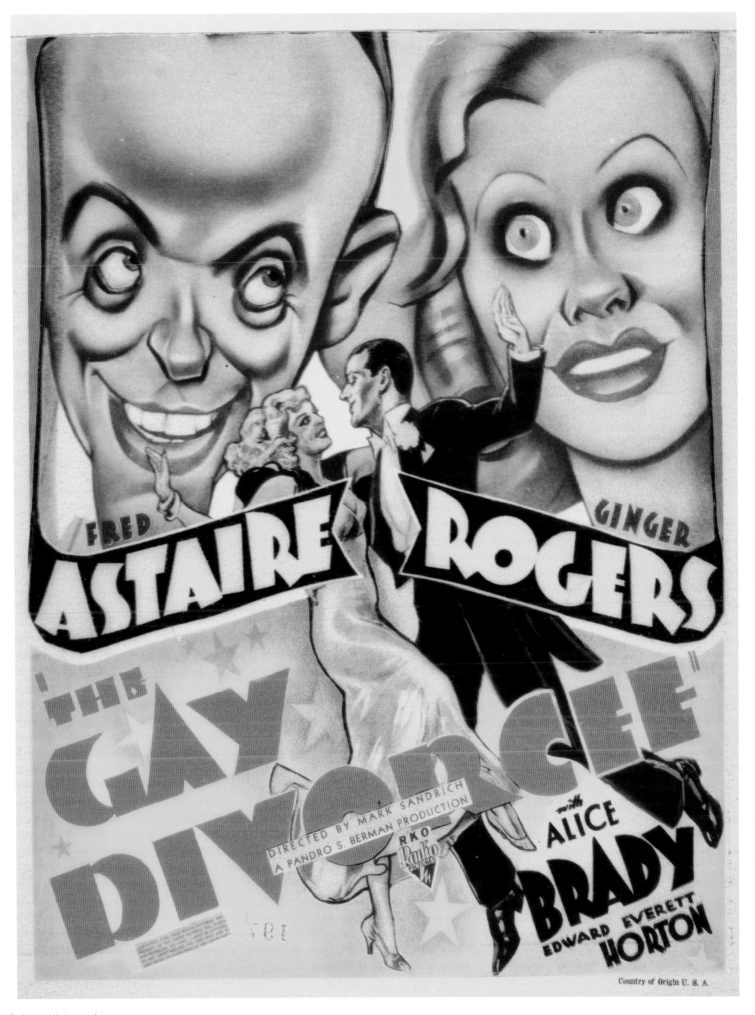

The Golden Age of the Talkies: The Men, 1927–1941

William Powell

After a successful stage career, William Powell—another of my special favorites—made his screen debut in Barrymore's 1922 version of *Sherlock Holmes* (fig. 63). During the silent era, he was often cast as a sneering villain, but with the advent of sound a whole new Powell emerged— urbane and sophisticated—starting in 1929 with *The Canary Murder Case* (fig. 53), in which he played S. S. Van Dine's detective Philo Vance opposite Louise Brooks. This started out as a silent film, but recorded dialogue was added when it became apparent that the public was demanding talkies. Brooks's refusal to return from Europe to dub her part effectively ended her Hollywood career.

Powell, meanwhile, went from strength to strength, displaying his ability to play smart and witty roles in partnership with actresses like Kay Francis and Carole Lombard, to whom he was briefly married. (Later he was involved in a serious romance with Jean Harlow—his costar in the 1935 movie *Reckless*—and their affair lasted until her sudden death.) In 1934 he made *The Thin Man* (figs. 116 and 175), based on Dashiell Hammett's novel of the same name, playing urbane society detective Nick Charles, who seems to subsist on cocktails and caviar and throws off witticisms as dry as a martini. In this film, and five more in the series, he was wonderfully partnered with Myrna Loy, with whom, as noted in the previous chapter, he enjoyed an on-screen chemistry that puts them among the greatest and most winning of Hollywood romantic comedy teams. They made fourteen films together, most of them—and especially the Thin Man series—still compulsively watchable.

The popularity of the Thin Man films, however, should not be allowed to detract from other Powell outstanding efforts such as *My Man Godfrey* (figs. 120 and 176), with Lombard, and *Libeled Lady* (fig. 87), with Loy, Harlow, and Spencer Tracy, among the films well represented in my collection. It was Powell more than anyone else who anticipated the persona that Cary Grant—a dozen years his junior—took on in the late 1930s.

173. *Street of Chance*
U.S. (1930)
Paramount
Insert
36 × 14 in.
(91.4 × 35.6 cm)

with
MARGARET LINDSAY · ARTHUR BYRON
RUTH DONNELLY GORDON WESTCOTT
DIRECTED BY MICHAEL CURTIZ
A WARNER BROS. & VITAPHONE
PRODUCTION

WILLIAM

Powell

in

PRIVATE
DETECTIVE 62

Starstruck

OPPOSITE

174. *Private Detective 62*
U.S. (1933)
Warner Bros.
One-sheet
41 × 27 in.
(104.1 × 68.6 cm)

ABOVE

175. *The Thin Man*
U.S. (1934)
Cosmopolitan/MGM
Lobby card
11 × 14 in.
(27.9 × 35.6 cm)

The Golden Age of the Talkies: The Men, 1927–1941

176. *My Man Godfrey*
U.S. (1936)
Universal
One-sheet
41 × 27 in.
(104.1 × 68.6 cm)

Gary Cooper

I've had the pleasure of knowing Gary Cooper's beautiful daughter, Maria Cooper Janis, for many years. Her father was, of course, one of the biggest stars of the talkies, drop-dead handsome, with an understated, gentlemanly screen presence that owed a good deal to his Montana ranch upbringing, though both his parents were English by birth, and Cooper for several years attended school in England. He did not become a major force in Hollywood until the sound era, but he had had minor parts in silent movies from 1925 onward, coming to the attention of the public—and the Paramount brass—thanks to a small but pivotal role in William Wellman's 1927 World War I epic *Wings*. His first sound picture, *The Virginian* (1929; fig. 2), made him a star, and he became one of the busiest actors in Hollywood, playing the lead in movies that included *Morocco* (figs. 136 and 177), *A Farewell to Arms*, *The Lives of a Bengal Lancer*, *Mr. Deeds Goes to Town*, *The General Died at Dawn* (fig. 179), *The Plainsman*, *The Cowboy and the Lady*, *Beau Geste* (fig. 178), *Sergeant York*, *The Pride of the Yankees*, and *For Whom the Bell Tolls*—all these (and a couple of dozen more) between 1930 and 1943.

Along the way he proved that he could play roles that ranged from cowboys who let actions speak louder than words to the pedantic foil for burlesque queen Barbara

The Golden Age of the Talkies: The Men, 1927–1941

Stanwyck—aka "Sugarpuss" O'Shea—in Howard Hawks's hilarious *Ball of Fire*, written by Billy Wilder and Charles Brackett. In *Mr. Deeds* he was so natural that he inspired Carl Sandburg to remark, "He is one of the most beloved illiterates this country has ever known." "Coop"—as he was universally known—went on to win Academy Awards for his roles in *Sergeant York* (1941) and *High Noon* (1952).

Most of the male and female stars of the early talkies were adept at playing comedy of one sort or another, but then there were the pure comedians who thrived in the sound era, especially W. C. Fields and the Marx Brothers, with an honorable mention going to Laurel and Hardy, though their comedy was less sophisticated and their films more modest

in their ambitions. Stan and Ollie first worked together in the early 1920s and became a successful team starting in 1926, easily making the transition to talkies, their humor actually accentuated by their somewhat stilted way of delivering lines. I have a handsome Al Hirschfeld caricature poster (fig. 180) for their first full-length talkie, *Pardon Us* (1931), and another for one of their most famous films, *Sons of the Desert* (1933; fig. 181).

179. *The General Died at Dawn*
U.S. (1936)
Paramount
Lobby card
11 x 14 in.
(27.9 x 35.6 cm)

ABOVE

180. *Pardon Us*
U.S. (1931)
Hal Roach/MGM
Title card
11 × 14 in.
(27.9 × 35.6 cm)

RIGHT

181. *Sons of the Desert*
U.S. (1933)
Hal Roach/MGM
Lobby card
11 × 14 in.
(27.9 × 35.6 cm)

W. C. Fields

W. C. Fields was over fifty by the time he became a full-
fledged Hollywood star. Before that, though, he had been
a huge draw in vaudeville and in Broadway reviews, most
notably various editions of the Ziegfeld Follies. Many of
his comedy routines were very visual—he was an accomplished juggler and comic mime—and he did make some
silent movies, though relatively few, in part because he was
so busy and successful on stage. When sound came along,
it added a new dimension to his decidedly misanthropic
screen persona because Fields had a wonderful and expres-
sive voice, even though he seemed to mumble half the time,
and to be talking to himself as much as to anyone else. This
was aided by the fact that he wrote his own material and

The Golden Age of the Talkies: The Men, 1927–1941

came up with wonderful lines for himself—"Anyone who hates children and animals can't be all bad," or "A woman drove me to drink, and I didn't even have the decency to thank her." Then there were the inimitable exclamations such as "Godfrey Daniel!" and expressions of affection such as "my little chickadee." With his well-larded but surprisingly graceful body, his bulbous nose, and his way of flinching neurotically whenever his universe showed signs of becoming bent out of shape—which was most of the time—"Bill" Fields was one of a kind.

Fields's screen appearances range from the broad physical humor of *If I Had a Million* (fig. 182), in which he and the formidable Alison Skipworth take revenge on "road hogs"—a term that rolls beautifully off Fields's eloquent tongue—to the far more structured and subtle comedy of *The Bank Dick*. My favorite Fields movie is the 1934 film *It's a Gift*, in which the star plays Harold Bissonette, a provincial grocer beleaguered by his family and other assorted pests, pets, incompetents, and small children (including his nemesis Baby LeRoy). I have a handsome insert for this picture, and a lobby card that captures the famous scene in which Mr. Muckle, a blind customer, stumbles around the store spreading mayhem (figs. 19 and 183).

ABOVE
182. *If I Had a Million*
U.S. (1932)
Paramount
Lobby card
11 × 14 in.
(27.9 × 35.6 cm)

LEFT
183. *It's a Gift*
U.S. (1934)
Paramount
Lobby card
11 × 14 in.
(27.9 × 35.6 cm)

OPPOSITE
184. *A Night at the Opera*
U.S. (1935)
MGM
Lobby card
11 × 14 in.
(27.9 × 35.6 cm)

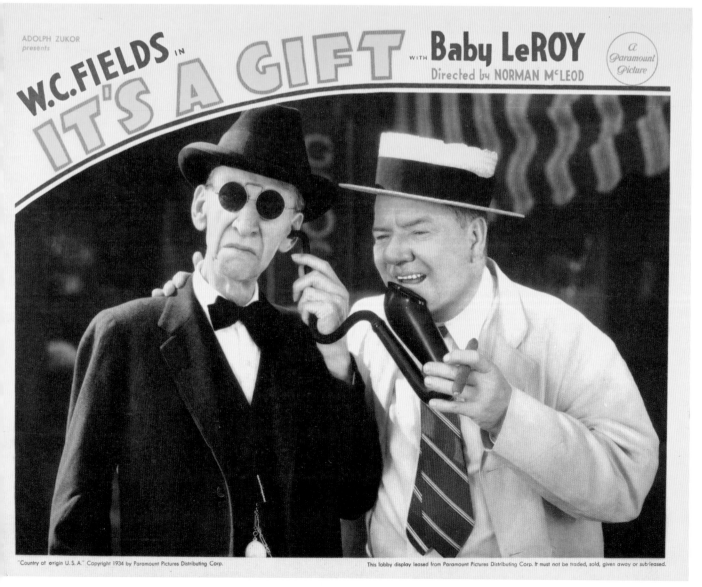

Starstruck

The Marx Brothers

As memorable as Fields was at his best, for me the greatest comedy of the early sound years was produced by the Marx Brothers. The sons of Jewish immigrant parents—Simon Marrix (who became Sam Marx) and the formidable Minnie Schoenberg—Chico, Harpo, Groucho, Gummo, and Zeppo grew up in the tough Yorkville section of Manhattan, just a few blocks from where my family settled when we moved from New Rochelle. Minnie's boys grew up the hard way, taking all kinds of menial jobs to help the family out. They were encouraged to study music, however, which led to gigs in bars and taverns, and eventually to Broadway. At first the Marx Brothers team leavened their musical presentations with comedy, but it was when they put the comedy first that they became really successful, and in the 1920s they were major stage stars, audiences flocking to see shows that featured their unique cocktail of satire, wisecracks, slapstick, and musical interludes, shaken well with a splash of vaudeville vermouth and served with a surrealistic twist.

The brothers hit their peak as a live act just as the talkies arrived, and were quickly signed by Paramount, making their earliest films at the studio's New York lot, in Astoria, just across the East River from the mean streets where they

had grown up. *The Cocoanuts* (1929) and *Animal Crackers* (1930) were adapted from Marx Brothers stage hits written by George S. Kaufman and Morrie Ryskind. They made three more features for Paramount—*Monkey Business*, *Horse Feathers*, and *Duck Soup*—before switching to MGM, where they made half a dozen films, including *A Night at the Opera* (1935; figs. 184 and 186) and *A Day at the Races* (1937; fig. 187).

Like W. C. Fields, the Marx Brothers offered plenty of visual gags—think of the stateroom scene in *A Night at the Opera* or the avalanche of purloined silverware falling from Harpo's tattered coat in *Animal Crackers*—but it was sound that gave them the means to mock the establishment and to deflate pretension. They were more anarchistic than selective when it came to choosing their targets. Favorites were the interchangeable characters—Mrs. Rittenhouse, Emily Upjohn, Mrs. Gloria Teesdale—superbly embodied by Margaret Dumont (though Groucho insisted she didn't understand many of the jokes made at her expense).

Groucho got the best lines. ("I never forget a face, but in your case I'll be glad to make an exception.") Chico played the gambler who allegedly thought up the crazy schemes that got them into trouble. Harpo, voiceless and seemingly

LEFT
185. *Duck Soup*
U.S. (1933)
Paramount
Midget window
card
14 × 8 in.
(35.6 × 20.3 cm)

OPPOSITE TOP
186. *A Night at the
Opera*
U.S. (1935)
MGM
Title card
11 × 14 in.
(27.9 × 35.6 cm)

OPPOSITE
BOTTOM
187. *A Day
at the Races*
U.S. (1937)
MGM
Title card
11 × 14 in.
(27.9 × 35.6 cm)

a simpleton, was the most complex. All emotions came easily to him. He was a wild child, whether chasing women or practicing petty larceny. If he took a liking to you, he was apt to give you his leg to hold. All three displayed advanced symptoms of lechery, and each in his own way personified the belief that authority is inevitably accompanied by corruption and abuse. In the eight years between *The Cocoanuts* and *A Day at the Races*, the Marx Brothers provided a string of classic comedies fueled by satire that was motivated in equal parts by amusement and contempt.

Happily, the Marx Brothers were very well served by poster designers. MGM is not my favorite studio when it comes to posters, but the designs they came up with for *A Night at the Opera* and *A Day at the Races* are superb examples of pop culture, blending caricatures by Al Hirschfeld, bold lettering, and bright colors to capture the spirit of freshness, wild invention, and freedom that permeates these movies.

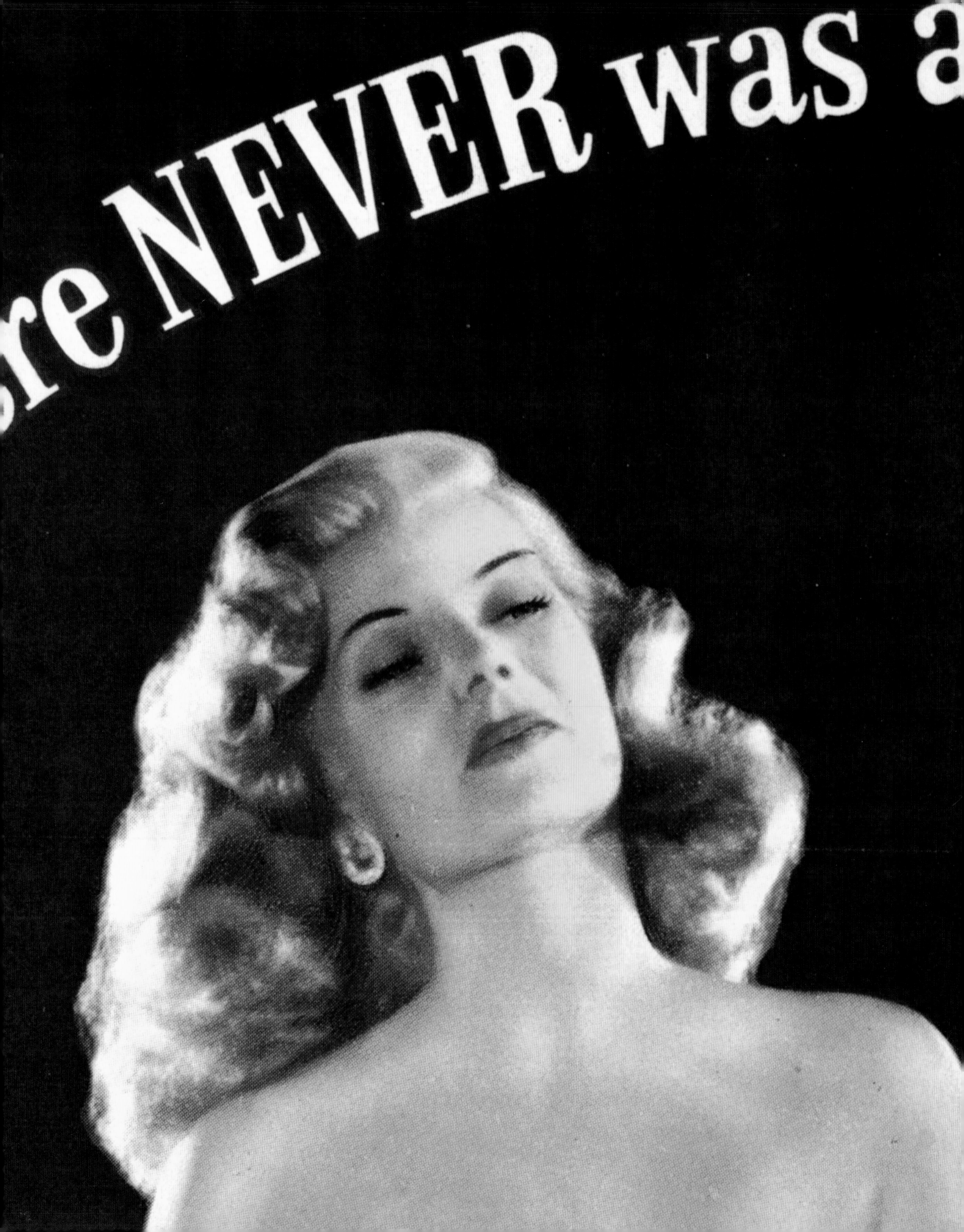
re NEVER was a

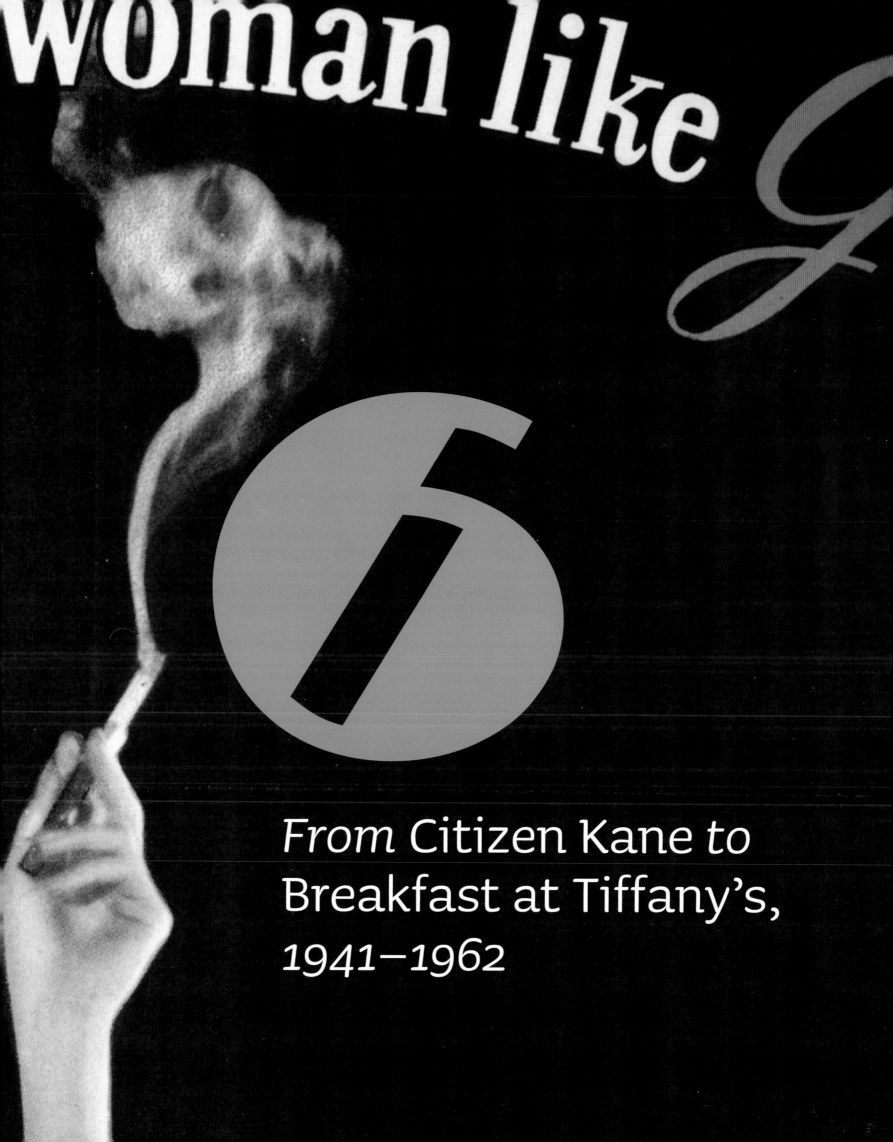

woman like *G*

6

From Citizen Kane *to* Breakfast at Tiffany's, 1941–1962

PAGES 170–71
Gilda
Detail
(See fig. 205 on p. 186)

When Japanese planes bombed Pearl Harbor in December of 1941, an era came to a close both in America as a whole and in Hollywood, though Hollywood had been ahead of most of America in making movies that directly or indirectly dealt with the war that was already raging in Europe, and in reflecting the view that sooner or later the United States would be drawn into what the studios painted as a simple confrontation between good and evil. When the bombs began to fall, America lost some of the innocence that had survived the deprivations of the Great Depression. This is not to say that the average American became cynical, but he was aroused to the fact that there were dangerous forces in the world—forces it had been possible to overlook until then, partly because of the distraction of hard times at home—that could no longer be ignored. Isolationism was over, but ironically its demise forced filmmakers to look inward and take a new and more psychologically oriented look at some of the fault lines that lay beneath the fabric of American society.

Anyone searching for presages of this change need look no further than May 1, 1941—seven months and a few days before Pearl Harbor—when a bombshell of a movie, made by a twenty-six-year-old prodigy, had its premiere. That director was Orson Welles; the film was *Citizen Kane* (figs. 189, 190, and 282), and it changed filmmaking forever, just as the Japanese attack on Hawaii would alter the course of history. Welles's theme—a great man and his flaws—had been tackled before, of course, but never with the kind of insight, sharpened by an awareness of modernism, that the young director brought to it. The technical brilliance of the film—typified by Gregg Toland's innovative cinematography—was used to probe the psychology of the characters and to peer beneath the self-regarding surfaces of American society.

As everyone interested in the cinema knows, *Citizen Kane* was the focus of violent controversy and shrill criticism. It certainly didn't do much to change the way that Louis B. Mayer or Jack Warner thought about making films, and on the surface Hollywood went about its business the same as ever. Other features released that year included *Here Comes Mr. Jordan*, *How Green Was My Valley*, *The Little Foxes*, and *Meet John Doe*, and the following years saw the release of mainstream—and often wonderful—films such as *Mrs. Miniver*, *Random Harvest*, *Woman of the Year* (fig. 112), *Pride of the Yankees*, and *Yankee Doodle Dandy* (fig. 10), not to mention two Andy Hardy movies, and Walt Disney's *Bambi*.

November 26, 1942—Thanksgiving Day—saw the New York premiere of a film that was superficially mainstream Hollywood fare but that in retrospect can be seen as being as iconic, and in its own way almost as revolutionary, as *Citizen Kane*. This was Michael Curtiz's *Casablanca* (figs. 191, 273, and 274), a film that was routine from a cinematic point of view, but that shook up Hollywood because in it Humphrey Bogart embodied the archetype of a new kind of American hero—or antihero—with a decidedly jaded view of life, who ends up doing the right thing as much out of his feelings for a lost love as from a somewhat tenuous sense of patriotism. Bogart had played similar parts before, most notably the previous year in John Huston's *The Maltese Falcon* (fig. 193), another terrific movie, but it was

188. *My Darling
    Clementine*
    U.S. (1946)
    20th Century-Fox
    Three-sheet
    81 × 41 in.
    (205.7 × 104.1 cm)

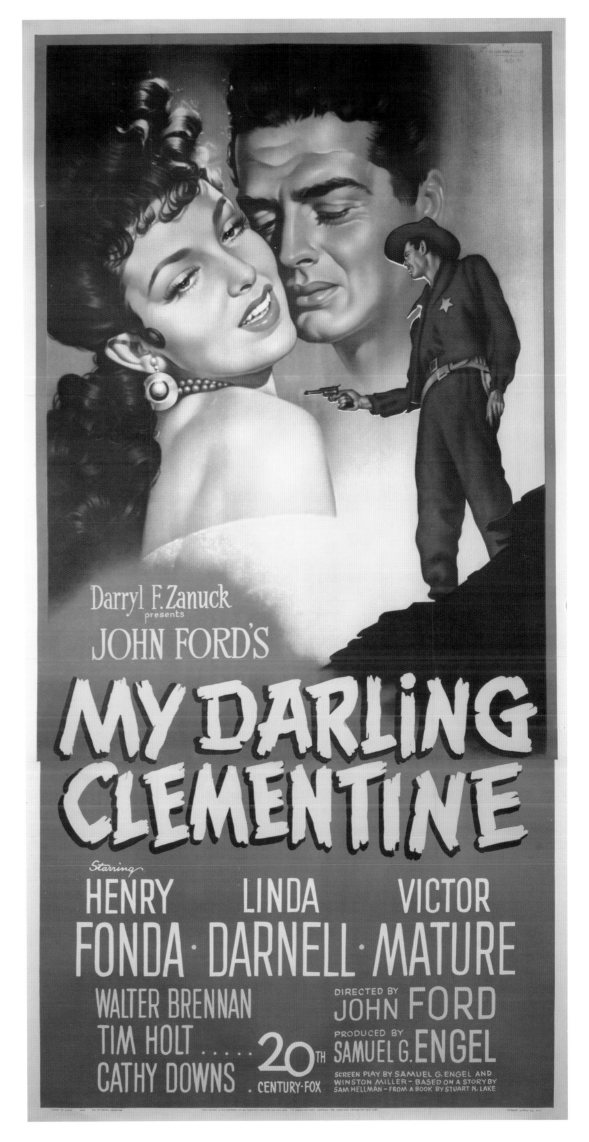

189. *Citizen Kane*
    U.S. (1941)
    Mercury/RKO
    Half-sheet
    22 × 28 in.
    (55.8 × 71.1 cm)

174

190. *Citizen Kane*
U.S. (1941)
Mercury/RKO
Lobby card
11 × 14 in.
(27.9 × 35.6 cm)

From Citizen Kane *to* Breakfast at Tiffany's, *1941–1962*

in *Casablanca* that he perfected the antihero persona. He would play it again in films like *To Have and Have Not* (1944; figs. 197 and 201) and *The Big Sleep* (1946; fig. 198). Both were directed by Howard Hawks, and the latter is now considered a pivotal example of the film noir genre, a staple of the 1940s and '50s.

191. *Casablanca*
      U.S. (1942)
      Warner Bros.
      Title card
      11 × 14 in.
      (27.9 × 35.6 cm)

Film Noir

Film noir had its roots in the Warner Bros. crime movies of the 1930s, but took on a whole new aspect with the arrival in the early '40s of films like *The Maltese Falcon*, *The Glass Key* (1942), starring Brian Donlevy, Alan Ladd, and Veronica Lake, and *Murder, My Sweet* (1944), starring Dick Powell and Claire Trevor. Although it did not belong to the genre, the psychological influence of *Citizen Kane* on these films cannot be discounted. Ultimately, though, the genesis of film noir was primarily the crime stories published in pulp magazines like *Black Mask*, and especially the hard-boiled fiction of Dashiell Hammett, Raymond Chandler, and James M. Cain. Both *The Maltese Falcon* and *The Glass Key* originated with Hammett, while *Murder, My Sweet* and *The Big Sleep* were based on novels by Chandler, who helped adapt Billy Wilder's *Double Indemnity* (1944) from Cain's story.

Another Cain story was the basis for *The Postman Always Rings Twice* (fig. 195), a proto-noir starring Lana Turner and

John Garfield. Garfield, born Jacob Julius Garfinkle, was the son of Jewish immigrants who grew up in New York and became one of the most interesting actors of his generation, in some ways anticipating Marlon Brando and the Method school. Along with *Postman* he had pivotal roles in films such as *Gentleman's Agreement* and *Body and Soul*, but his movie career was cut short when he was blacklisted for refusing to name Communist Party members when called before the House Un-American Activities Committee.

All of the movies mentioned in this chapter so far were major studio productions with major stars. *Double Indemnity*, for example, paired Fred MacMurray with the durable Barbara Stanwyck and the equally durable Edward G. Robinson. Bogart's costars of the period included Mary Astor, Ingrid Bergman, his wife, Lauren Bacall, and—in *High Sierra* (fig. 31) and, another proto-noir film, *They Drive By Night* (fig. 194)—Ida Lupino, a British-born actress who had been around since the early 1930s in minor parts and B movies. In her pioneering roles opposite Bogart she emerged as a full-blown star of the hard-boiled genre who would go on to appear in classic noirs such as Jean Negulesco's 1948 *Road House* (in which she memorably sang the Harold Arlen– Johnny Mercer song "One for My Baby [and One More for the Road]") and Nicholas Ray's *On Dangerous Ground* (1952). She even got to direct an example of the genre, the 1953 picture *The Hitch-Hiker*.

I became hooked on Ida Lupino partly because I found so many terrific posters featuring her at Bob Colman's Hollywood Poster Exchange on Santa Monica Boulevard. My enthusiasm for her was further aroused by the dramatic

ABOVE

192. Ida Lupino
U.S. (1940)
Warner Bros.
Publicity still
10 × 8 in.
(25.4 × 20.3 cm)

LEFT

193. *The Maltese Falcon*
U.S. (1941)
Warner Bros.
Title card
11 × 14 in.
(27.9 × 35.6 cm)

LEFT

194. *They Drive By Night*
U.S. (1940)
Warner Bros.
Half-sheet
22 × 28 in.
(55.8 × 71.1 cm)

BELOW

195. *The Postman
Always Rings Twice*
U.S. (1946)
MGM
Lobby card
11 × 14 in.
(27.9 × 35.6 cm)

scene at the trial in *They Drive By Night* when her character cracks up on the stand and screams, "The doors made me do it." Half crazed, she's blaming her murder of her husband on the doors of a garage slamming open and shut. It's a Lady Macbeth moment that climaxes the movie, and I've loved it from the first time I encountered it. Later I saw her in *The Sea Wolf* and some early 1940s films that made me think she was just so terrific and smart—and then I discovered her earlier films, and poster and lobby cards from when she was really young. An unusual type, reminiscent of Katharine Hepburn physically, Lupino had come to Hollywood when she was seventeen, and the town really went to work on her, glamorizing her, making her sexy. I have a poster (fig. 196) for a 1934 film called *Ready for Love* that really gets to me because she's so young and beautiful. I also love the colors in this poster—the green of the dress she's wearing—and the strange thing is that I've never managed to see this film, only this one-sheet and some stills. This is an example of a poster that other collectors

From Citizen Kane *to* Breakfast at Tiffany's, *1941–1962*

ABOVE LEFT

196. *Ready for Love*
U.S. (1934)
Paramount
One-sheet
41 × 27 in.
(104.1 × 68.6 cm)

TOP

197. *To Have and Have Not*
U.S. (1944)
Warner Bros.
Lobby card
11 × 14 in.
(27.9 × 35.6 cm)

ABOVE

198. *The Big Sleep*
U.S. (1946)
Warner Bros.
Lobby card
11 × 14 in.
(27.9 × 35.6 cm)

ALAN LADD
VERONICA LAKE
WILLIAM BENDIX

in THE BLUE DAHLIA

a GEORGE MARSHALL production
with HOWARD da SILVA · DORIS DOWLING · TOM POWERS · FRANK FAYLEN
Produced by JOHN HOUSEMAN · Directed by GEORGE MARSHALL · Written by RAYMOND CHANDLER · A Paramount Picture

might not find that interesting, because it's a film she made in the 1940s and it's the '50s that people remember her for, but to me it's precious because I love the image of her it presents.

Lauren Bacall emerged in the early years of film noir. The daughter of Jewish immigrants, she was born in the Bronx and had modeled while studying acting, until her photograph on the cover of *Harper's Bazaar* led Howard Hawks to sign her for *To Have and Have Not*. (Apparently he fell in love with her, but Bogart got the girl in real life as well as on-screen.) Her husky voice—the result of careful coaching—and her knowing way with repartee added a sexy dimension to her stylish good looks, creating a screen image that was much imitated. Among her later film roles opposite Bogart were *Dark Passage*, *The Big Sleep*, and John Huston's 1948 thriller *Key Largo*.

Also born in New York—though in Brooklyn—was Veronica Lake, who had memorable noirish roles in *The*

Glass Key and the 1946 film *The Blue Dahlia* (fig. 199), an original for the screen by Raymond Chandler, with Alan Ladd as a World War II bomber pilot suspected of murdering his wife. (The film was produced by John Houseman, a key figure in the development of *Citizen Kane*, though he and Welles fell out before the movie went before the cameras.) Veronica Lake had one of the briefest careers of any Hollywood star. Audiences took a shine to her in the 1941 film *I Wanted Wings*, and she was quickly embraced as much for her peekaboo hairstyle as for her acting ability. That same year she had a choice role opposite Joel McCrea in *Sullivan's Travels* (figs. 200 and 247), Preston Sturges's road film with a difference. For half a dozen years, Lake was at the top of the heap, but her box-office appeal waned, and *The Blue Dahlia* was the last decent movie she appeared in. Her downfall was precipitous. She became an alcoholic—at one point tending bar for a living—and died of hepatitis at the age of fifty-three.

JOEL McCREA

VERONICA LAKE

in

SULLIVAN'S TRAVELS

A PARAMOUNT PICTURE

with
ROBERT WARWICK
WILLIAM DEMAREST
MARGARET HAYES
PORTER HALL
FRANKLIN PANGBORN
ERIC BLORE
Written and
Directed by PRESTON STURGES

Country of Origin U. S. A.

The big studio film noir productions of the early and mid-1940s anticipated, without fully exploiting, the mannerist style that came to characterize later examples of film noir, especially the B movies turned out by major studios and the efforts of smaller outfits like Republic and Monogram. The noir idiom lent itself especially well to low-budget production, since it didn't require too many elaborate sets—well-chosen location shots added to the sense of grittiness—and atmosphere could be created with fog machines and dramatic lighting, making these movies descendants of both the stylization of comic strips and—more unexpectedly, perhaps—the German Expressionist cinema tradition of the 1920s.

The German connection becomes less surprising when one considers the involvement in film noir of refugees from the Nazis, like director Robert Siodmak and former UFA cinematographer Franz Planer, who worked together on a classic of the genre, *Criss Cross* (1949), starring a young Burt Lancaster and Yvonne de Carlo. Planer's lighting and high-contrast photography are pure UFA. Ultimately, though, film noir was explicitly American, set in unfinished cities like Los Angeles—as is the case with *Criss Cross*—or parched towns alongside desert highways, the plot often propelled by a voice-over that borrowed its knowing and jaded tone from Raymond Chandler's Philip Marlowe and from Bogart's Rick Blaine.

201. *To Have and
Have Not*
U.S. (1944)
Warner Bros.
Lobby card
11 x 14 in.
(27.9 x 35.6 cm)

War Movies

Another major genre of the 1940s and '50s was the war movie, which took off even before America became engaged in the war, with films like *Confessions of a Nazi Spy*, which starred Edward G. Robinson, and *Sergeant York*, starring Gary Cooper, as well as a rash of comedies about conscription featuring everyone from Bob Hope to the Three Stooges. After Pearl Harbor, Hollywood was converted into a propaganda factory turning out films designed to maintain the morale of America and its allies. There's nothing quite like an unmitigated villain to guarantee the success of even a mediocre script, and so writers under contract built stories around evil Nazi spies and ruthless Japanese warriors. Opposed to these villains would be a brave unit of American soldiers/sailors/airmen made up of a smorgasbord of stereotypes. There was likely to be a former playboy who under fire proves to be one of the lads, a laconic New Englander, a cowboy, a farmhand, and invariably—or so it seemed—a kid from Brooklyn. There were also films based on actual war stories, such as *Thirty Seconds Over Tokyo*, starring Spencer Tracy and Van Johnson, and movies that extolled the virtues of allies, of which the most notable was William Wyler's *Mrs. Miniver*, starring Greer Garson and Walter Pidgeon.

The importance of movies to wartime morale-building can be illustrated by the case of the Aero Theater in Santa Monica. The theater was built in 1939 by the Douglas Aircraft Company, which at that time was gearing up to produce planes for the military. The Aero was for the exclusive use of the thousands of workers employed at the manufacturer's huge plant just a couple of miles away. Like the assembly lines, it operated twenty-four hours a day, seven days a week, so that employees could catch a movie no matter what shift they were working. The Aero has survived and is now one of the homes of the American Cinematheque.

202. *The African Queen*
United Kingdom/U.S. (1951)
Horizon/United Artists
Still
10 × 8 in. (25.4 × 20.3 cm)

RITA HAYWORTH
GENE KELLY
Cover Girl
in TECHNICOLOR
A COLUMBIA PICTURE

Lovely Rita Hayworth at her entrancing best!

203. *Cover Girl*
U.S. (1944)
Columbia
Lobby card
11 × 14 in.
(27.9 × 35.6 cm)

Escapist Fare

Many of the movies shown at the Aero in those years, and in theaters all over the country, were pure escapist fare, as important to the country's morale as films extolling the bravery of America's forces in the face of Axis aggression. This was the era of lightweight Betty Grable musicals like *Coney Island*, and *Springtime in the Rockies*, and the early Road series of movies featuring Bing Crosby, Bob Hope, and Dorothy Lamour. Crosby also starred in Paramount's 1942 version of *Holiday Inn*, with Fred Astaire. The war years were well supplied with musicals, including classics such as *Yankee Doodle Dandy* and Vincent Minelli's *Meet Me in St. Louis*, a feast of nostalgic Americana with Judy Garland and Margaret O'Brien in top form. Another musical heavy on nostalgia was *Tin Pan Alley*, starring Alice Faye and John Payne. Samuel Goldwyn, meanwhile, had lured Danny Kaye

away from Broadway, and starting in 1944 he was featured in comedy musicals beginning with *Up in Arms*.

A major star who emerged in the early 1940s was Rita Hayworth. Born Margarita Carmen Cansino, she was the daughter of a Spanish dancer, Eduardo Cansino, and joined the family onstage when she was just eight years old. Her exceptional good looks and dancing ability won her some small film parts in the 1930s, and she began to draw attention following her first sizable role in Howard Hawks's 1939 movie *Only Angels Have Wings*, alongside Cary Grant and Jean Arthur. The 1941 Warner Bros. picture *The Strawberry*

Fred Astaire and Rita Hayworth—dancing and singing together!

FRED ★ RITA
ASTAIRE ★ HAYWORTH
in
"YOU WERE
NEVER LOVELIER"
A COLUMBIA PICTURE

204. *You Were Never
Lovelier*
U.S. (1942)
Columbia
Lobby card
11 × 14 in.
(27.9 × 35.6 cm)

Blonde, in which she was James Cagney's love interest, made Hayworth a star, and she quickly followed it up with *You'll Never Get Rich*, partnered with Fred Astaire in spectacular dance numbers. Her career peaked in 1946 with Charles Vidor's classic melodrama *Gilda* (fig. 205). Her 1943 marriage to Orson Welles did not work out, and her films of the late 1940s—including Welles's 1948 *The Lady from Shanghai* (fig. 257)—did not perform well at the box office. She married Prince Ali Khan, but the union was dissolved in 1951 and she returned to making movies, though she never again achieved the level of stardom she had enjoyed in the 1940s.

The postwar era saw the return to the screen of stars who had served in the military like James Stewart and Clark Gable, and Hollywood did its best to return to normal despite serious distractions such as the court-ordered divestiture of theaters—which meant that the big studios no longer controlled the outlets for their films—politically motivated congressional investigations of the movie industry, and the advent of television. As a result, Hollywood went in several different directions at the same time. Film noir was now at its height, its longevity guaranteed by the fact that most films in this category required relatively low budgets, but also because it touched some raw nerves. A related phenomenon was a move toward a kind of gritty realism, typified by films like Jules Dassin's *Naked City*

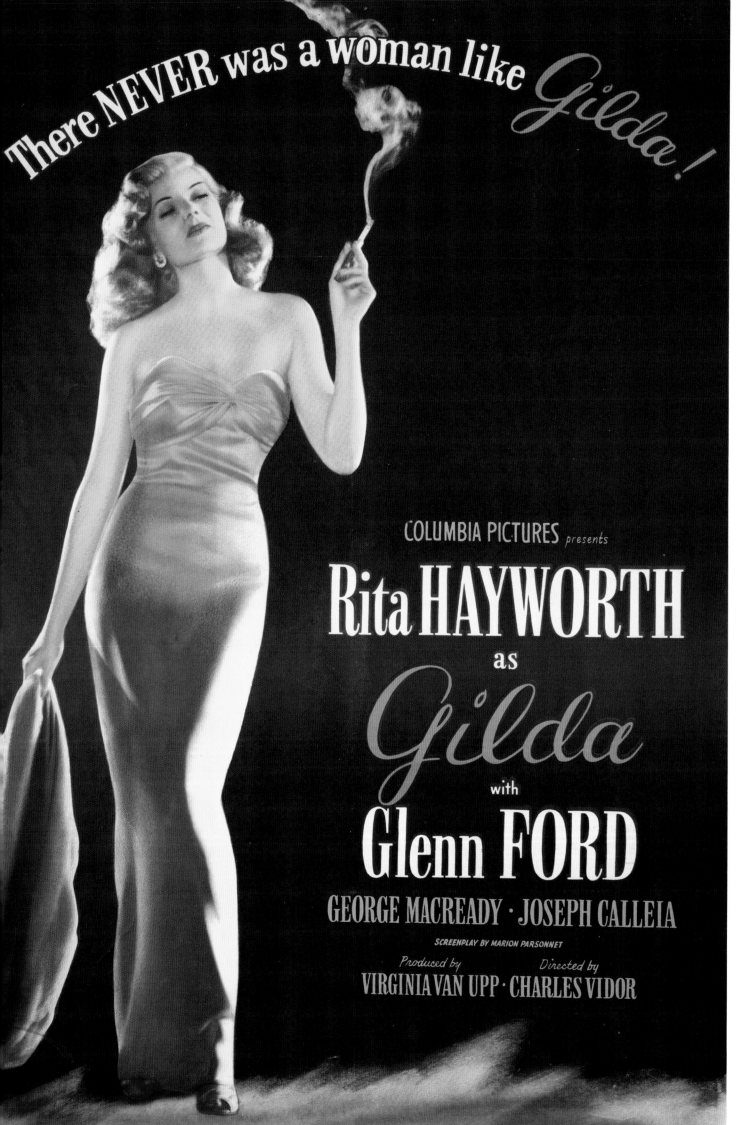

There NEVER was a woman like *Gilda*!

COLUMBIA PICTURES presents

Rita **HAYWORTH**

as

Gilda

with

Glenn **FORD**

GEORGE MACREADY · JOSEPH CALLEIA

SCREENPLAY BY MARION PARSONNET

Produced by
VIRGINIA VAN UPP

Directed by
CHARLES VIDOR

Starrstruck

(1948), shot on the streets of New York rather than the back lot, and John Huston's caper movie *The Asphalt Jungle* (1950; figs. 206 and 216), which also made effective use of location footage. At the other extreme was a move toward blockbusters, partially inspired by the prewar success of films like *Gone with the Wind* (figs. 163, 271, and 272), but primarily a response to the competition offered by television. "You can stay at home and watch in black and white on a nine-inch screen," the argument went, "or you can head for your local theater and enjoy a *real* spectacle in full color on the big screen."

This move toward blockbusters really took off with the advent of CinemaScope and other widescreen formats. The first CinemaScope movie to be released was 20th Century-Fox's 1953 biblical epic *The Robe*, starring Richard Burton, Jean Simmons, and Victor Mature. A string of epics climaxed a decade later with the same studio's disastrous version of *Cleopatra*, starring Elizabeth Taylor and Richard Burton, but by then widescreen formats were being used for every imaginable kind of movie, from Alfred Hitchcock thrillers like *North by Northwest* to animated features such as Disney's *Lady and the Tramp*.

Older stars like Humphrey Bogart, Cary Grant, James Stewart, Henry Fonda, Clark Gable, Fred Astaire, Spencer Tracy, James Cagney, Bette Davis, and Katharine Hepburn continued to thrive. In 1951, for example, Bogart and Hepburn enjoyed great success in John Huston's *The African Queen* (fig. 202). Hepburn also continued her partnership with Spencer Tracy, while both Cary Grant and James Stewart displayed their talents in suspense films by Hitchcock, and Fred Astaire danced his way through lavish MGM musicals with much younger partners, including Jane Powell, Vera-Ellen, Cyd Charisse, and Leslie Caron. Gable worked steadily until his death following completion of *The Misfits* (fig. 219). Fonda chose to work on Broadway for several years, then returned to the screen to star with Cagney, William Powell, and newcomer Jack Lemmon in *Mister Roberts* (during the filming of which he and director John Ford had a famous fight). As for Bette Davis, she kicked off the decade with one her greatest successes, *All About Eve*.

Brando, Dean, and Elvis

The 1950s also saw the emergence of a new generation of stars. Among the men, these ranged from a Shakespearean actor like Richard Burton to a Method actor like Marlon Brando and even a rock star, Elvis Presley. (The 1950s also saw the birth of the rock-and-roll movie, in the form of producer Sam Katzman's *Rock Around the Clock*, which featured Bill Haley and DJ Alan Freed.)

There has probably never been a more influential actor than Brando. The ultimate exponent of Konstantin Stanislavski's system as taught by Stella Adler at her Studio of

From Citizen Kane *to* Breakfast at Tiffany's, *1941–1962*

STARRING
ELIZABETH TAYLOR · ROCK HUDSON · JAMES DEAN   *PRESENTED BY WARNER BROS. IN WarnerColo*

2

56 \ 497

ABOVE
207. *Giant*
U.S. (1956)
Giant/Warner Bros.
Lobby card
11 × 14 in.
(27.9 × 35.6 cm)

OPPOSITE
208. Marlon Brando in
The Wild One
U.S. (1953)
Stanley Kramer/Columbia
Still
10 × 8 in. (25.4 × 20.3 cm)

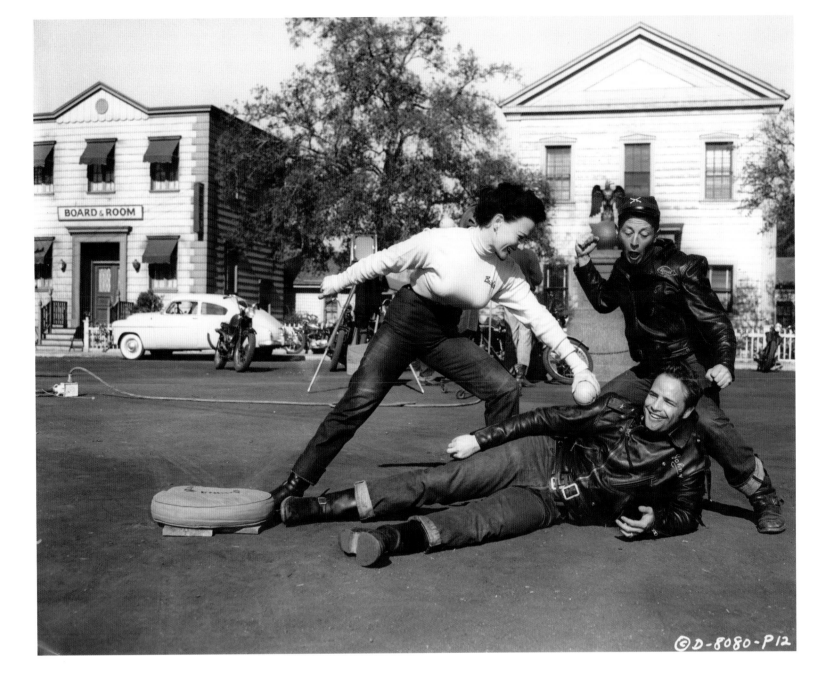

©D-8080-P12

Acting in New York, Brando made his name onstage in Elia Kazan's production of *A Streetcar Named Desire* and in 1951 played his Stanley Kowalski character in the screen version of Tennessee Williams's play. I have a great still from *The Wild One* (fig. 208), a film that could not more aptly describe Brando's persona (he rides his own personal Triumph motorcycle in the movie). These roles were the first in a series of groundbreaking roles that would continue from *The Godfather* and beyond.

Another star who owed a great deal to Elia Kazan was James Dean. It was Kazan who cast the young actor as Cal Trask in his 1955 adaptation of John Steinbeck's *East of Eden*, remarking, "I wanted a Brando for the role." Dean wasn't formally a follower of the Stanislavski system, but he had Method acting in his bones. He understood how to fully enter a character. Reportedly a number of his scenes in *East of Eden* are entirely improvised. He followed this film up with his pitch-perfect performance in *Rebel Without a Cause* and his Academy Award–nominated role in *Giant* (fig. 207),

and then he was gone, though in death he became more famous than ever.

Even more of a teenage icon than Dean was Elvis. He was already a huge recording star when he tested for the role in *The Rainmaker* that subsequently went to Burt Lancaster. Instead Elvis made his big screen debut in 1956 in the movie *Love Me Tender*, and he continued to star in films—some musical, some primarily dramatic—for the next fourteen years at a steady rate of two releases a year.

Grace Kelly

The major women stars who came up in the 1950s were more in the mold of traditional movie stars, though each in her own way was completely unique. Grace Kelly was the daughter of a self-made Philadelphia millionaire—a three-time Olympic gold medalist in rowing events—and the head of the physical education department at the University of Pennsylvania. She went to the right schools

"dial M for Murder" ARNER BROS. PRESENT ALFRED HITCHCOCK'S STARRING RAY MILLAND · GRACE KELLY · ROBERT CUMMINGS

6

LEFT
209. *Dial M for Murder*
U.S. (1954)
Warner Bros.
Lobby card
11 × 14 in.
(27.9 × 35.6 cm)

BELOW
210. Cary Grant and
Grace Kelly in
To Catch a Thief
U.S. (1955)
Paramount
Still
10 × 8 in.
(25.4 × 20.3 cm)

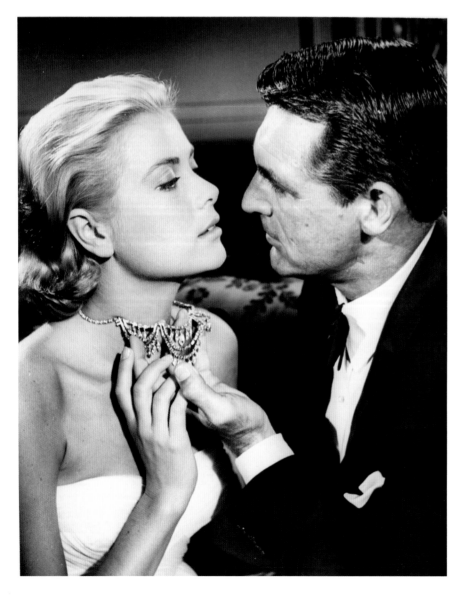

and acquired the social polish that would be so much a part of her on-screen persona. In the late 1940s, she studied acting in New York, did some modeling, and began to win parts in television dramas, then still shot live. She had her first film role in 1951, and the following year won the lead opposite Gary Cooper in *High Noon*. She acted in only eleven films altogether, but they make up an impressive list that includes *Mogambo* (1953) with Clark Gable, *Dial M for Murder* (1954; fig. 209) with Ray Milland, *Rear Window* (1954) with James Stewart, *The Country Girl* (1954) with Bing Crosby and William Holden, *Green Fire* (1954) with Stewart Granger, *The Bridges at Toko-Ri* (1954) with William Holden and Fredric March, *To Catch a Thief* (1955) with Cary Grant, *The Swan* (1956) with Alec Guinness, and finally—perhaps her most memorable role—*High Society* with Bing Crosby and Frank Sinatra. Then, abruptly, after only five years in Hollywood, she forsook her distinguished coterie of leading men to become the bride of Prince Rainier of Monaco.

Audrey Hepburn
Equally beautiful and equally graceful was the irresistible Audrey Hepburn, who was born in Brussels to an English father and an aristocratic Dutch mother. (Coincidentally, Hepburn was distantly related to Prince Rainier.) After

Starstruck

LEFT
211. *The Lavender Hill Mob*
United Kingdom (1951)
Poster for U.S. release
Ealing/Universal
Lobby card
11 × 14 in (27.9 × 35.6 cm)

her parents divorced when she was young, Hepburn was brought up largely in Holland, where she spent the war years under harrowing conditions. After the war she went to London, modeling to help support herself and studying dance with Marie Rambert. She began her acting career on the London stage and had small parts in a handful of British films, including the classic 1951 Ealing comedy *The Lavender Hill Mob* (fig. 211), starring Alec Guinness. That same year, Hepburn was brought to America to play the lead in the Broadway production of Gigi. Her first American picture was William Wyler's *Roman Holiday*, in which she played a moonlighting princess who falls for handsome American reporter Gregory Peck and learns a few lessons about the real world. Her performance in this film revealed an actress of charm, wit, and winning vulnerability and was rewarded with the 1954 Academy Award for best performance by a lead actress.

This marked the beginning of an illustrious career. Next came Billy Wilder's *Sabrina* (fig. 212) opposite Humphrey Bogart and William Holden, the first film in which Hepburn was costumed by the Paris couturier Hubert de Givenchy, inaugurating a partnership that was to become as important to her career as any of her leading men. Givenchy's stylings played a big part in the 1957 musical *Funny Face*, with her leading man Fred Astaire, almost twice Hepburn's

ABOVE
212. *Sabrina*
U.S. (1954)
Paramount
Lobby card
11 × 14 in.
(27.9 × 35.6 cm)

ABOVE

213. *Charade*
U.S. (1963)
Universal-Donen/
Universal
Insert
36 × 14 in.
(91.4 × 35.6 cm)

RIGHT

214. *Breakfast at Tiffany's*
U.S. (1961)
Jurow-Shepherd/
Paramount
Lobby card
11 × 14 in.
(27.9 × 35.6 cm)

Starstruck

ED BY OWARDS · MARTIN JUROW AND RICHARD SHEPHERD · GEORGE AXELROD · SCREENPLAY BY GEORGE AXELROD · BASED ON THE NOVEL BY TRUMAN CAPOTE MUSIC — HENRY MANCINI **T**ECHNICOLOR®
A PARAMOUNT RELEASE

From Citizen Kane to Breakfast at Tiffany's, 1941–1962

age. (He had starred in the original Broadway production of *Funny Face* in 1927). In *Funny Face*, in which she played a would-be intellectual transformed into a reluctant fashion icon, Hepburn's dance training was used to good effect, and she also sang.

Hepburn had success with more serious roles such as *War and Peace* (1956), *The Nun's Story* (1959), and the John Huston western *The Unforgiven* (1960). In 1961 she returned to the world of Givenchy in one of her most enchanting roles as Holly Golightly in the film adaptation of Truman Capote's *Breakfast at Tiffany's* (fig. 214). Two years later she starred opposite Cary Grant in *Charade* (fig. 213), and the following year had one of her defining roles as Eliza Doolittle in *My Fair Lady*.

Audrey Hepburn made relatively few films, but the impression she left in movies like *Sabrina* and *Breakfast at Tiffany's* was indelible. She was the ultimate in stylish sophistication but could bring a childlike innocence to the

screen. She defined the word *gamine*, yet at the same time she could convincingly convey an impression of having seen it all—perhaps because she *had* seen it all during the nightmare years of World War II, witnessing, among other horrors, an uncle and a cousin shot to death for their work with the Resistance. Despite making the transition from wartime Arnhem to the soundstages of Hollywood, Hepburn never forgot those harrowing experiences and devoted much of her adult life to helping the children of the world through relief work for UNICEF.

BELOW
215. *Love Happy*
U.S. (1949)
Artists Alliance/
United Artists
Lobby card
11 × 14 in.
(27.9 × 35.6 cm)

OPPOSITE
216. *The Asphalt Jungle*
U.S. (1950)
MGM
Lobby card
11 × 14 in.
(27.9 × 35.6 cm)

Marilyn Monroe

Marilyn Monroe—born Norma Jean Mortensen but baptized Norma Jean Baker—was a very different kind of star, with a very different kind of past, though one that was harrowing enough to leave deep scars. Her mother was mentally disturbed, and she never knew her father. The future star was brought up largely in Los Angeles–area foster homes and public institutions but, encouraged by a friend of her mother's, imagined she would become a movie star. After a brief early marriage—entered as an alternative to remaining a ward of state—and a job in a munitions factory, she became a successful model. This led, in 1946, to her being signed to a six-month contract by 20th Century-Fox, but nothing much happened, and she returned to modeling, posing at that time for the notorious nude photographs later used as calendar art.

Adopting the name Marilyn Monroe, she finally attracted some attention in the film world with a small role in the Marx Brothers' 1949 picture *Love Happy* (fig. 215). This in turn led to a part as a gangster's moll in John Huston's *The Asphalt Jungle*, which was followed up with a short but memorable appearance in *All About Eve*. Now Fox was interested again, and she signed a seven-year contract.

In 1952 the nude calendar appeared, and the brouhaha that ensued threatened to cut short her career before it had really begun. In the end, however, the calendar helped ensure Monroe's celebrity and set her up to become a major sex symbol. A *Life* cover story later that year emphasized the traumatic nature of her upbringing, which earned her sympathy with audiences. The following year she was featured on the inaugural cover of *Playboy*. By then she had

217. Cary Grant and
Marilyn Monroe in
Monkey Business
U.S. (1952)
20th Century-Fox
Still
10 × 8 in.
(25.4 × 20.3 cm)

begun dating Joe DiMaggio, and the whole country knew about it. She had not yet made any of her iconic films, but she was a star just as she had dreamed she would be.

The first of those iconic films was *Niagara* (1953), noted for the long take in which Monroe, seen from the rear, walks toward the falls. Famously, Constance Bennett is reported to have remarked of this scene, "There's a broad with her future behind her." Next came *Gentlemen Prefer Blondes* (1953), in which Monroe was paired with veteran sex symbol Jane Russell and gave her breathy, Helen Kane–like rendition of "Diamonds Are a Girl's Best Friend." After that she starred in the similarly themed *How to Marry a Millionaire*, with Betty Grable and Lauren Bacall, then went on to make *River of No Return*, an Otto Preminger western with Robert Mitchum.

Her on-screen presence was so extrovert, and even exhibitionistic, that it was a shock for producers and crews to discover that she was chronically camera shy—to the

extent that many mornings she had difficulty making it onto the set. In these earlier movies, costars like Russell and Robert Mitchum did their best to help her out—Russell would calm her down and escort her to the set—but things got much worse. Toward the end of 1953, she was scheduled to begin work opposite Frank Sinatra in *The Girl in Pink Tights* but repeatedly failed to show up and was promptly suspended by the studio. A few weeks later she married DiMaggio, then returned to Fox to make *There's No Business Like Show Business*, a forgettable musical, and then the 1955 romantic comedy *The Seven Year Itch* (fig. 218), which proved to be one of her most memorable roles. A quarrel over the famous scene in which Monroe's skirt is blown above her waist is said to have infuriated DiMaggio, eventually leading to their divorce.

Monroe left Fox, spent time in New York studying at the Actors Studio, and renewed an acquaintanceship with playwright Arthur Miller, whom she later married. Back in front of

218. *The Seven Year Itch*
U.S. (1955)
20th Century-Fox
Title card
11 × 14 in.
(27.9 × 35.6 cm)

the cameras, she delivered her most dramatic performance in Josh Logan's 1956 film *Bus Stop*, taking the critics by surprise. Then things started to go downhill again. She clashed with Laurence Olivier during filming of *The Prince and the Showgirl* (1957), and with Billy Wilder during the making of *Some Like It Hot* (1959; fig. 220), though ukulele-playing vocalist "Sugar Kane" proved to be one of the defining roles of her career.

Monroe had one more great performance to offer, in the 1961 John Huston film *The Misfits*, costarring Clark Gable (who she'd once fantasized was her father) and Montgomery Clift. Despite the fact that she had become hopelessly dependent on alcohol, and sometimes did not show up on set, she received critical accolades for the movie, as did her two costars. Gable, who died just days after shooting was finished but had seen rushes, pronounced his own performance the best of his career. Monroe never completed another film. On August 5, 1962, she was found dead in her Brentwood home, an apparent suicide.

219. Clark Gable and
Marilyn Monroe in
The Misfits
Photographer:
Cornell Capa
U.S. (1961)
Seven Arts/United
Artists
Still
10 × 8 in.
(25.4 × 20.3 cm)

OPPOSITE
220. *Some Like It Hot*
U.S. (1959)
Ashton/Mirisch/
United Artists
Lobby card
11 × 14 in.
(27.9 × 35.6 cm)

Starstruck

MARILYN MONROE *and her bosom companions* TONY CURTIS JACK LEMMON

in a BILLY WILDER Production "SOME LIKE IT HOT"

CO STARRING GEORGE RAFT · PAT O'BRIEN · JOE E. BROWN · SCREEN PLAY BY BILLY WILDER and I.A.L. DIAMOND · DIRECTED BY BILLY WILDER An Ashton Picture · A Mirisch Company Presentation UNITED ARTISTS RELEASED THRU The music from "Some Like It Hot" (and Marilyn sings!) is available on United Artists Records at all record shops.

By the time Marilyn Monroe—ultimate sex symbol—died, the Hays Code was on its last legs. *Some Like It Hot* is an example of a film—Alfred Hitchcock's *Psycho* is another—that was released without a Production Code certificate. Because of its gender-bending humor, it was condemned by the Catholic League of Decency, which pretty much guaranteed that it would be refused a certificate. United Artists decided to go ahead and distribute it anyway, a move that would have been unthinkable even a few years earlier.

Leading the way in his opposition to the strictures of the Code was Otto Preminger, whose 1953 film *The Moon Is Blue* was the first significant American production to be released without a certificate. (Its crimes against the Code included the use of the words "pregnant" and "virgin.") Two years later, Preminger's *The Man with the Golden Arm* was also released without the blessing of the Motion Picture Association of America, this time because it dealt frankly with the taboo subject of drug addiction. The facade was crumbling, but it would be 1968 before the Code was definitively

abandoned and replaced by the ratings system we are familiar with today.

Partly because of the demise of the Code, the 1960s signaled the arrival of a new era in filmmaking, free of the notion that absolute moral values should be imposed from above by self-appointed arbiters of the public good. The end of censorship did away with many absurdities, but it didn't necessarily guarantee better movies. For all its faults, the Code had forced writers and directors to use their imaginations. If you couldn't use the word "virgin," then you had to find some subtle way of signaling that a character was indeed a virgin. Making films in Hollywood during the years of the Production Code had been a little bit like writing novels in the Soviet Union during the same period. You had to find ways to express yourself while dancing around the obstacles placed in your way. The great filmmakers of the era knew how to do that. The greatest of them were as important to Hollywood—and to me, as a collector of poster art—as any star.

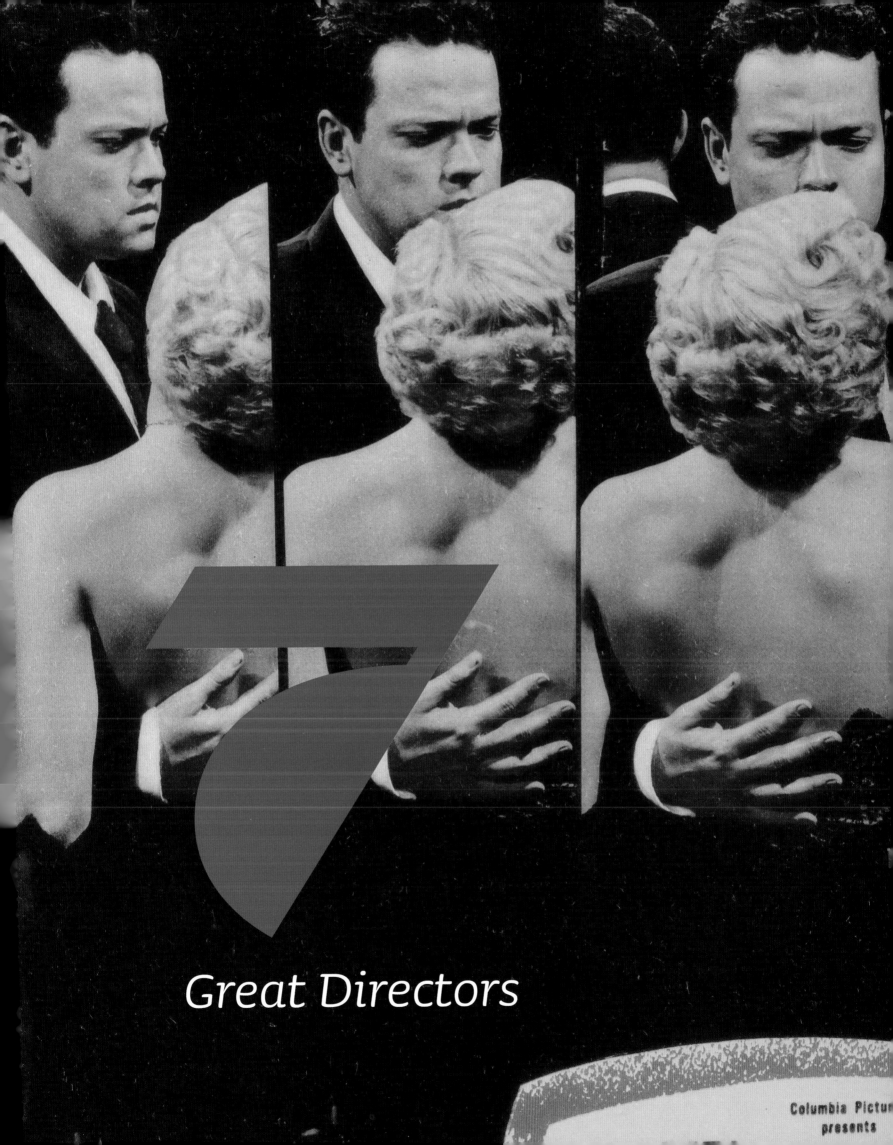

Great Directors

Columbia Pictu...
presents

PAGES 200–1
The Lady from Shanghai
Detail
(See fig. 256 on
p. 231)

RIGHT
221. *The Birth of a Nation*
U.S. (1915)
Griffith/Epoch
Lobby card
11 × 14 in.
(27.9 × 35.6 cm)

OPPOSITE
222. *Dodsworth*
U.S. (1936)
Goldwyn/United
Artists
One-sheet
41 × 27 in.
(104.1 × 68.6 cm)

I suppose it's the stars that all of us are attracted to initially. They're the ones up there on-screen putting their talent on the line, daring us not to adore them. But if you take the cinema at all seriously, sooner or later you begin to think about the talent on the other side of the camera— the writers, cinematographers, set designers, costumiers, makeup artists, film editors, and especially the directors. In the 1950s, writing in the French magazine *Cahiers du cinéma*, the fledgling director François Truffaut famously wrote, "There are no good or bad movies, only good or bad directors." It was an idea that was at the heart of the "auteur theory" espoused by the young filmmakers and critics associated with *Cahiers*, people like Jean-Luc Godard, Eric Rohmer, Claude Chabrol, and Truffaut himself, heroes of my film-school days. This theory proposes that great directors have signature styles—approaches to making movies as distinctive as the style of a great poet, a great novelist, or a great painter. Looking back at the history of Hollywood, it's possible to argue that certain studios at certain times—Warner Bros. and Paramount in the 1930s, for example—had distinctive styles that sometimes trumped the styles of individual directors, or that some stars like Fred Astaire or the Marx Brothers were the true auteurs of their movies. Nonetheless there's no denying that the directors that the *Cahiers* writers singled out—men like Alfred Hitchcock, Howard Hawks, John Huston, and John Ford, as well as great European directors like Jean Renoir— possessed "autograph" styles as distinctive as handwriting. It's a phenomenon almost as old as the cinema itself.

D. W. Griffith

The prototypical example of the great director has to be D. W. Griffith, who not only forged the language of the American film and defined the scale of Hollywood's ambition but also launched the careers of some of the earliest superstars, including Mary Pickford and the Gish sisters. If he differs from later auteurs, it's because he was working at a time when the movies were evolving so rapidly—largely in response to *his* powers of invention—that he never developed a signature style as clear-cut as that of, say, Howard Hawks. From his Biograph period to his days at United Artists, Griffith was constantly refining the syntax of the medium, and that is perhaps his greatest contribution, though in his best films he also displayed a remarkable mastery of narrative.

Griffith made many films, and it's been calculated that, adjusted for inflation, his 1915 blockbuster *The Birth of a Nation* (fig. 221) was probably the greatest box-office hit of all time. Still, Griffith collectible material remains rare. Earlier in this book I told the story of how I rushed to New Jersey to see what I hoped would be a pristine poster from the initial release of *The Birth of a Nation*, only to be sadly disappointed. I have other fine Griffith items, however, including lobby cards for his classic films *Broken Blossoms* (1919; fig. 224) and *Orphans of the Storm* (1921; fig. 223), the first featuring Lillian Gish with Richard Barthelmess, the other showing Lillian with her sister Dorothy in the setting of a formal garden. Both are tinted with color, as were the movies themselves in prints intended for major theaters.

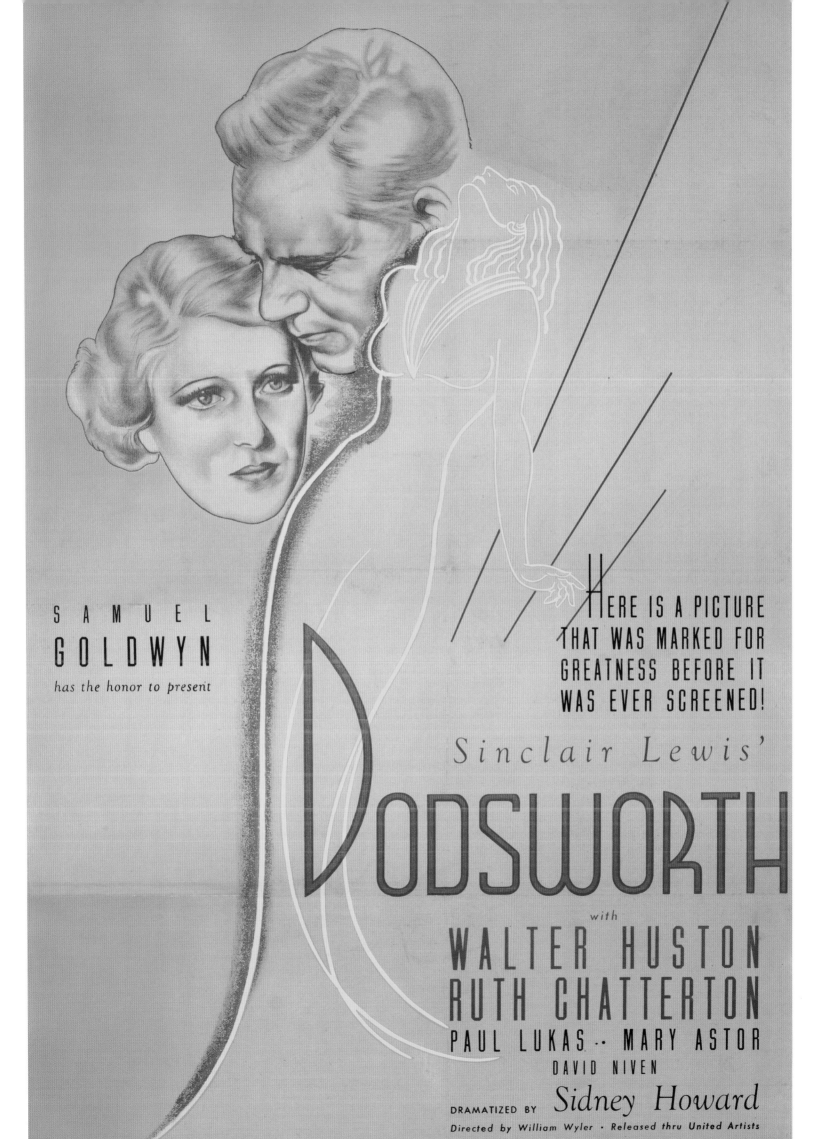

SAMUEL GOLDWYN

has the honor to present

HERE IS A PICTURE THAT WAS MARKED FOR GREATNESS BEFORE IT WAS EVER SCREENED!

Sinclair Lewis'

DODSWORTH

with

WALTER HUSTON
RUTH CHATTERTON

PAUL LUKAS ·· MARY ASTOR

DAVID NIVEN

DRAMATIZED BY *Sidney Howard*

Directed by William Wyler · Released thru United Artists

D.W. GRIFFITH
Presents
'Orphans of the Storm'

LEFT	ABOVE
223. *Orphans of the Storm*	224. *Broken Blossoms*
U.S. (1921)	U.S. (1919)
Griffith/United Artists	Griffith/United Artists
Lobby card	Title card
11 × 14 in.	11 × 14 in.
(27.9 × 35.6 cm)	(27.9 × 35.6 cm)

Erich von Stroheim

One of the first true auteurs, in the sense in which the word was used by the *Cahiers du cinéma* crowd, was Griffith's protégé Erich von Stroheim. Born in 1885, Stroheim claimed to be descended from Austro-Hungarian nobility, a part he played to perfection for the benefit of the Hollywood press corps, though it now seems probable that he was born in Vienna to a Jewish family of modest means. Leaving Europe behind as a young man, he had the opportunity to reinvent himself and, arriving in Hollywood just in time for the outbreak of World War I, contrived to hire himself out to movie studios as an expert on all things Germanic. This led to bit parts in films such as *In Old Heidelberg*, and Griffith used him in *Intolerance* as both an actor and an assistant. With America's entry into the war came larger roles, usually as a loathsome, stereotyped, militaristic Hun, and he attained a degree of fame as "the man you love to hate."

While acting, Stroheim paid attention to what Griffith and other directors did, and by the time the war was over, he was ready to take a shot at writing and directing his own film. The result was *Blind Husbands* (1919; fig. 225), a movie that displayed in embryonic form all the traits that would make Stroheim a great and very singular filmmaker,

as well as a memorable on-screen presence. In this picture, Stroheim played Lieutenant Eric Von Steuben, an arrogant and immaculately turned out Junker type who attempts to seduce the wife of an American doctor in an Alpine ski resort. The plot is melodramatic, but it's colored by the worldly cynicism that was to be Stroheim's trademark, and full of touches that anticipate the Zola-esque realism found in his later films. The poster for the film, however, is anything but realistic, having only a symbolic relationship with Stroheim's "wonder play" (as the copy describes it). The imagery consists of a drawing of the heads of nineteen blindfolded men against a red background, making this one of the most unusual items in my collection.

His next surviving film was *Foolish Wives* (1922; fig. 227), in which he revisited the theme of *Blind Husbands* but in a more lavish Monte Carlo setting and with himself playing a White Russian officer rather than a Prussian. There were still touches of melodrama, but they were subsidiary to Stroheim's cynical vision of high society, to the realism he brought to his presentation of the story, and to his mastery over the language of the silent film. *Blind Husbands* is one of the greatest masterpieces of early cinema, yet he would surpass this achievement in 1924 with *Greed* (fig. 228), his screen version of Frank Norris's realist novel *McTeague*, the story of a dentist whose wife, played by ZaSu Pitts, wins the lottery and becomes obsessed with money.

In its original form, *Greed* ran for an astonishing ten hours. Under pressure from MGM's front office, Stroheim reluctantly managed to edit it down to four hours before it was taken away from him and cut to under three hours. What we see today is only a vestige of the film Stroheim made, yet its brilliance is quite apparent, and I am very happy to have a lobby card that features the climactic final scene in Death Valley.

ABOVE
225. *Blind Husbands*
U.S. (1919)
Universal
Window card
22 × 14 in.
(55.9 × 35.6 cm)

RIGHT
226. *The Merry Widow*
U.S. (1925)
MGM
Lobby card
11 × 14 in.
(27.9 × 35.6 cm)

227. *Foolish Wives*
U.S. (1922)
Universal
Lobby card
11 × 14 in.
(27.9 × 35.6 cm)

After *Greed*, Stroheim returned to the subject of European high society in films like *The Merry Widow* (fig. 226) and *The Wedding March*. His insistence on realism translated into high budgets, which led to problems with studios and producers, and in 1929 he was fired from *Queen Kelly*—financed by Joseph P. Kennedy, founder of the Kennedy political dynasty, and starring Gloria Swanson. To all intents and purposes that was the end of Stroheim's brilliant career as a director, though his acting career continued and included important roles in two classics, Jean Renoir's 1937 *La Grand Illusion* and Billy Wilder's *Sunset Boulevard* (fig. 17) of 1950. Both these directors were among Stroheim's greatest admirers.

The German Influence

Because there was no spoken dialogue, movies of the silent era were truly international in their appeal, so European directors could become well known in America for films made on the other side of the Atlantic and with foreign stars. F. W. Murnau, for example, attracted a great deal of attention in Hollywood with his 1922 movie *Nosferatu*, an adaptation of Bram Stoker's *Dracula* and one of the most influential films of the German Expressionist movement. He followed this with another great success, *The Last Laugh* (1925), which starred Emil Jannings as a doorman at a very grand hotel who is demoted to working as a bathroom attendant. Like *Nosferatu*, this picture was highly innovative, this time for its use of moving camera shots, often from the viewpoint of the principal character. In 1926 Murnau moved to Hollywood, where he made the third of his classic silent films, *Sunrise* (figs. 126 and 229). Released in 1927, this is the tragic story of a farmer (George O'Brien) who plans to murder his wife (Janet Gaynor) to run off with

The two friends that were!

Erich Von Stroheim's **Greed**

Picture of Real Life.

A *Metro Goldwyn* Picture

MADE IN U. S. A.

a woman from the city (Margaret Livingston). An astonishing film, it builds both on the idea of expressionistic sets that create a subjective viewpoint (as in *Nosferatu*) and fluid camera work (as in *The Last Laugh*).

Like Murnau, Ernst Lubitsch came from Germany, but otherwise they had very little in common. Lubitsch was the son of a Jewish tailor in Berlin, who went into the theater and then into movies, working in Europe until 1922 before moving to Hollywood at the invitation of Mary Pickford. In the silent era he made a number of sophisticated comedies, such as a version of Oscar Wilde's *Lady Windermere's Fan*, but he really came into his own with the arrival of sound, having a great ear for witty dialogue, and a knack for bringing out the chemistry between unlikely pairings such as Maurice Chevalier and Jeanette MacDonald or Greta Garbo

and Melvyn Douglas, a knack that came to be known as "the Lubitsch touch." This was apparent from his first talkie, *The Love Parade*, a 1929 musical starring MacDonald and Chevalier, who were teamed again two years later in Lubitsch's *The Smiling Lieutenant*. The following year he made *Design for Living* (fig. 230) and then one of the great comedies of the pre-Code era, *Trouble in Paradise* (fig. 91), which featured Kay Francis, Miriam Hopkins, and Herbert Marshall in a romantic triangle of sexual innuendo that was guaranteed to tweak the tails of the Catholic Decency League and other advocates of censorship. The film was considered so shocking that it was withdrawn from circulation shortly after the Hays Office came into its own in 1934, and was not seen again until the 1960s.

Trouble in Paradise was a collaboration with writer

Samson Raphaelson, who also worked with Lubitsch on two more classics, the irresistible *The Shop Around the Corner* (1940; figs. 97 and 231) and *Heaven Can Wait* (1943). The former stars James Stewart and Margaret Sullavan as store clerks who bicker their workdays away, not realizing how in love they are, their love being expressed only through letters that purport to come from secret admirers. The latter features Don Ameche as a man presenting himself at the gates of hell, demanding entry on the grounds of having led a dissolute life. Earlier, Lubitsch had collaborated with writers Billy Wilder and Charles Brackett on yet another comedy masterpiece, *Ninotchka* (1939; fig. 132), in which his friend Greta Garbo proved that she did possess a sense of humor.

Like Stroheim, Murnau, and Lubitsch, Billy Wilder was born in a German-speaking part of Europe, what is now Southern Poland. Wilder grew up in Vienna and then moved to Berlin where he began writing screenplays. In 1933, he left for America to escape the Nazis and continued his screenwriting career in Hollywood where he teamed up with Charles Brackett with whom he would pen a dozen scripts, *Ninotchka* being one of their first collaborations. Wilder made his directing debut with the 1942 Ginger Rogers comedy *The Major and the Minor*, then established himself as someone to watch with the proto-noir classic *Double Indemnity* (fig. 232). From there he went on to write and direct (and sometimes produce too) a dazzling list of films that includes *The Lost Weekend*, *A Foreign Affair*, *Sunset Boulevard*, *Sabrina* (fig. 212), *The Seven Year Itch* (fig. 218), *Love in the Afternoon* (fig. 223), *Witness for the Prosecution*, *Some Like It Hot* (figs. 220 and 234), *The Apartment*, *Irma La Douce*, *The Fortune Cookie*, and *One, Two, Three*. (Starting with *Some Like It Hot*, his collaborator was writer-producer I.A.L. Diamond.) His sureness of touch with a wide variety of subjects is impressive. Four decades after the film's

release, the American Film Institute selected *Some Like It Hot* as the greatest American comedy ever made, yet Wilder was just as comfortable with a harrowing story such as *The Lost Weekend* or a romance like *Sabrina*. The catalog of stars he worked with is as dazzling as the catalog of films itself. It includes Barbara Stanwyck, Gloria Swanson, Erich von Stroheim, Humphrey Bogart, William Holden, Audrey Hepburn, Marilyn Monroe, Jack Lemmon, Tony Curtis, Walter Matthau, Gary Cooper, James Cagney, and Shirley MacLaine. He was able to coax wonderful performances out of even difficult stars like Monroe, and he was above all a great storyteller, whose narratives always had an edge that was an intrinsic part of his style.

OPPOSITE
230. *Design for Living*
U.S. (1933)
Paramount
Half-sheet
22 × 28 in.
(55.8 × 71.1 cm)

BELOW
231. *The Shop Around the Corner*
U.S. (1940)
Loew's/MGM
Lobby card
11 × 14 in.
(27.9 × 35.6 cm)

"Are you disappointed.. that your romantic suitor turns out to be just me!"

MARGARET **SULLAVAN** ★ JAMES **STEWART** in the *ERNST LUBITSCH production*
THE SHOP AROUND THE CORNER
A Metro-Goldwyn-Mayer Picture

FRED MacMURRAY   BARBARA STANWYCK
EDWARD G. ROBINSON

DOUBLE INDEMNITY

A Paramount Picture

...PORTER HALL · JEAN HEATHER · BYRON BARR · RICHARD GAINES · JOHN PHILLIBER
Directed by BILLY WILDER   Screenplay by Billy Wilder and Raymond Chandler

Copyright 1944 Paramount Pictures Inc. Country of Origin U.S.A. — 2.

PROPERTY OF NATIONAL SCREEN SERVICE CORP. LICENSED FOR 44/179
DISPLAY ONLY IN CONNECTION WITH THE EXHIBITION OF THIS PICTURE
AT YOUR THEATRE. MUST BE RETURNED IMMEDIATELY THEREAFTER.

ABOVE
232. *Double Indemnity*
U.S. (1944)
Paramount
Lobby card
11 × 14 in.
(27.9 × 35.6 cm)

RIGHT
233. Gary Cooper, Audrey Hepburn, and Maurice Chevalier in *Love in the Afternoon*
U.S. (1957)
Allied Artists
Still
10 × 8 in.
(25.4 × 20.3 cm)

234. *Some Like It Hot*
U.S. (1959)
Ashton/Mirisch/
United Artists
Lobby card
11 × 14 in.
(27.9 × 35.6 cm)

GEORGE BANCROFT IN 'THE DOCKS OF NEW YORK'

ABOVE
235. *The Docks of New York*
U.S. (1928)
Paramount
Lobby card
11 × 14 in.
(27.9 × 35.6 cm)

RIGHT
236. Josef von Sternberg and Marlene Dietrich
U.S. (1931)
Paramount
Publicity still
10 × 8 in.
(25.4 × 20.3 cm)

OPPOSITE
237. *The Blue Angel*
German title:
Der blaue Engel
Germany (1930)
Poster for U.S. release
UFA/Paramount
Lobby card
11 × 14 in.
(27.9 × 35.6 cm)

Josef von Sternberg

Josef von Sternberg was born Jonas Sternberg in Vienna, but grew up partly in New York City, where a job maintaining and repairing film prints led to work at the then-thriving production facility in Fort Lee, New Jersey. By the mid-1920s he was making some interesting silent films, including the 1927 gangster movie *Underworld*, which anticipated the style and mood of Warner Bros. crime movies of the early 1930s. *The Docks of New York* (fig. 234) was a gem. He directed the great German actor Emil Jannings in *The Last Command*, which led to him being invited to Germany to take the helm of UFA's first big sound film, *Der blaue Engel* (*The Blue Angel*; figs. 135 and 237), in which he cast Marlene Dietrich opposite Jannings, who played a schoolteacher reduced to ignominy by Dietrich's seductive cabaret artist.

When Paramount released the film in America, it was a sensation. Dietrich was signed to make movies in Hollywood, and von Sternberg was engaged to direct her in a series that would include *Morocco* (figs. 136 and 177), *Dishonored*, *Shanghai Express* (fig. 137), *Blonde Venus* (figs. 134 and 161), *The Scarlet Empress* (fig. 139), and *The Devil Is a Woman* (fig. 138), all made between 1930 and 1935. It's on these films, along with *The Blue Angel*, that Sternberg's reputation rests, and all are marked by his distinctive visual style. Shooting in the studio rather than on location, he set up each scene with great skill and imagination, planning precise camera angles and lighting as if he had a storyboard in his head. (The storyboard was then unknown.) Sternberg's ability to combine theatricality with cinematography—he loved and understood how to use soft focus as few others

OPPOSITE
240. *You Can't Take It with You*
U.S. (1938)
Columbia
Title card
11 × 14 in.
(27.9 × 35.6 cm)

ABOVE
238. *The Bitter Tea of General Yen*
U.S. (1933)
Columbia
Lobby card
11 × 14 in.
(27.9 × 35.6 cm)

RIGHT
239. *Lost Horizon*
U.S. (1937)
Columbia
Lobby card
11 × 14 in.
(27.9 × 35.6 cm)

Frank Capra's
YOU CAN'T TAKE
IT WITH YOU

with

JEAN ARTHUR * LIONEL BARRYMORE * JAMES STEWART * EDWARD ARNOLD

MISCHA AUER * ANN MILLER

SPRING BYINGTON · SAMUEL S. HINDS · DONALD MEEK · H. B. WARNER

Based on the Pulitzer Prize Play by George S. Kaufman and Moss Hart

Screen play by Robert Riskin · Directed by FRANK CAPRA

A COLUMBIA PICTURE

have—and his ability to construct a movie with great economy of means would win the admiration of a whole generation of filmmakers, and he had a special influence on the film noir directors of the 1940s and '50s.

Frank Capra

Frank Capra was born in Sicily and brought to America as a child. He graduated from the California Institute of Technology before talking his way into movies, becoming a gag man for producers like Mack Sennett, then a comedy director at Columbia during the silent era. With the advent of talkies, he demonstrated that he possessed the common touch that allowed average moviegoers to identify with the characters in his films. His first major hit—and it was enormous—was *It Happened One Night* (fig. 98), which won multiple Oscars following its 1934 release. This was an out-

and-out screwball comedy, but Capra followed it up with a string of movies in which comedy played a subdued second fiddle to themes that were at the same time inspirational and sentimental and that held a great deal of appeal for audiences during the Great Depression and when a new set of emotional stresses were brought on by World War II. These films included *Mr. Deeds Goes to Town* (1936), *Lost Horizon* (1937; fig. 239), *Mr. Smith Goes to Washington* (1939; fig. 158), *Meet John Doe* (1941), and, most remarkable of all, *It's a Wonderful Life* (1946; fig. 241). Some critics felt that these movies were served up with a little too much corn on the side, but another way of viewing it would be to say that Capra always had his finger on the pulse of the audience. He wasn't attempting to innovate, but no one was better at putting over a story or getting the most out of great screen personalities like James Stewart and Gary Cooper.

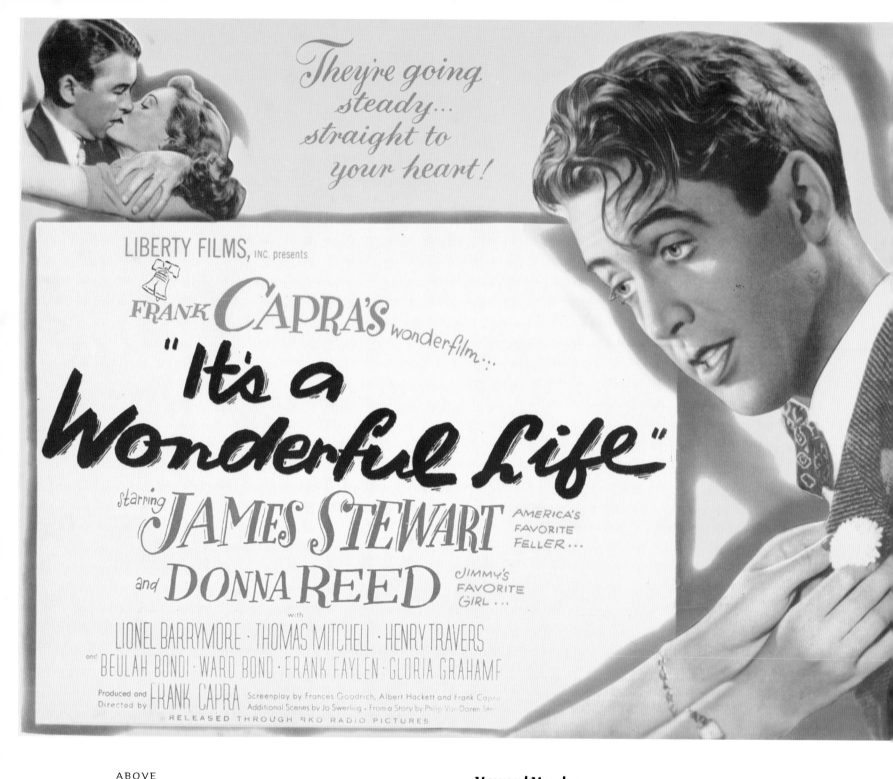

ABOVE
241. *It's a Wonderful Life*
U.S. (1946)
Liberty/RKO
Title card
11 x 14 in.
(27.9 x 35.6 cm)

OPPOSITE
242. *Bringing Up Baby*
U.S. (1938)
RKO
Midget window card
14 x 8 in.
(35.6 x 20.3 cm)

Howard Hawks

The American film industry had its share of native-born directors too, and one of the best was Howard Hawks, born in Indiana but raised partly in southern California within shouting distance of Hollywood. He attended Cornell University and during summer vacations had his first taste of moviemaking at the Famous Players–Lasky studios. During World War I he served in the U.S. Army Air Corps, and for several years after the war lived a daredevil life as, among other things, a pilot and a race car driver before trying his hand at filmmaking once again, directing his first film in 1925 and making several pictures during the silent era before really coming into his own with the arrival of sound. His breakthrough film was the 1932 gangster picture *Scarface* (fig. 145), starring Paul Muni, and he followed it

KATHARINE **HEPBURN**

CARY **GRANT**

in a **HOWARD HAWKS** PRODUCTION

Bringing up Baby

with CHARLIE **RUGGLES**

BARRY FITZGERALD • MAY ROBSON
WALTER CATLETT • FRITZ FELD
DIRECTED BY HOWARD HAWKS

ASSOCIATE PRODUCER CLIFF REID • SCREEN PLAY BY DUDLEY NICHOLS AND HAGAR WILDE

the next year with *The Crowd Roars*, with James Cagney as a race car driver. In 1934 he proved he could do screwball comedy as well as anybody in the form of *Twentieth Century* (figs. 119 and 142), with Carole Lombard and John Barrymore, and in 1938 directed another classic of the genre, *Bringing Up Baby* (figs. 113 and 242), which he followed with a couple more, *His Girl Friday* (1940; figs. 160 and 243) and *Ball of Fire* (1941; fig. 244). In 1944 and 1946 he made two archetypal proto-noirs with Humphrey Bogart and Lauren Bacall, *To Have and Have Not* and *The Big Sleep*, then in 1949 returned to comedy, directing Cary Grant and Ann Sheridan

ABOVE
243. *His Girl Friday*
U.S. (1940)
Columbia
Title card
11 × 14 in.
(27.9 × 35.6 cm)

LEFT
244. Gary Cooper and
Barbara Stanwyck
in *Ball of Fire*
U.S. (1941)
Goldwyn/RKO
Still
10 × 8 in.
(25.4 × 20.3 cm)

in *I Was a Male War Bride* (fig. 245). He also directed some major-league westerns including *Red River*, *The Big Sky*, and *Rio Bravo*, and even took a shot at a musical with Fox's 1953 Marilyn Monroe–Jane Russell romp *Gentlemen Prefer Blondes*.

Whatever the genre, Hawks's muscular and unfussy way with the medium was apparent. He was fond of saying things like, "A good director is someone who doesn't annoy you," yet his signature is to be found everywhere in his films, perhaps because he is known to have put a great deal of effort into rewriting and restructuring the scripts he worked from.

Preston Sturges

Preston Sturges was born in Chicago and while growing up bounced between America and Europe, sometimes traveling with the Isadora Duncan dance company—Duncan was a friend of his mother, whose eccentric behavior included an affair with the notorious satanist Aleister Crowley. Like Howard Hawks, Sturges joined the U.S. Army Air Corps during World War I, and afterward spent several years as a manager at an upscale New York store owned by his

mother's fourth husband. Sturges did not become a professional writer until he was in the early 1930s, when his hit Broadway show, *Strictly Dishonorable* (fig. 277), attracted the attention of Hollywood, at which point he promptly sold the script of *The Power and the Glory* to Fox, who used it as a vehicle for Spencer Tracy. He became the highest-paid hack in Hollywood, taking home $2,500 a week—a fortune during the Great Depression—for working on screenplays that, in his opinion, were misunderstood and mismanaged by inferior directors, if they were produced at all. In 1939, thoroughly frustrated, he went to the Paramount brass and offered to sell them a script—*The Great McGinty*—for one dollar if they would let him direct it. Because the movie could be made without major stars and on a comparatively low budget, he was given the go-ahead.

The plot of *The Great McGinty* was the opposite of an

ABOVE LEFT
245. Cary Grant in *I Was a Male War Bride*
U.S. (1949)
20th Century-Fox
Still
10 × 8 in.
(25.4 × 20.3 cm)

ABOVE RIGHT
246. *The Palm Beach Story*
U.S. (1942)
Paramount
One-sheet
41 × 27 in.
(104.1 × 68.6 cm)

JOEL McCREA ★ VERONICA LAKE

SULLIVAN'S TRAVELS

A PARAMOUNT PICTURE

with
ROBERT WARWICK · WILLIAM DEMAREST
MARGARET HAYES · PORTER HALL
FRANKLIN PANGBORN · ERIC BLORE
Written and
Directed by PRESTON STURGES

uplifting Capra tale, taking on political corruption with wildly inventive enthusiasm in a style that would become recognized as Sturges's unique take on screwball comedy, which might be described as screwball plus satire. It would be the trademark of all his best movies, which include *The Lady Eve* (1941; fig. 157), *Sullivan's Travels* (1941; figs. 200 and 247), and *The Palm Beach Story* (1942; fig. 246), three of my top favorites. *Sullivan's Travels* is about a comedy director who decides he should be making a serious film about the real America, one he plans to call *O Brother, Where Art Thou?*—a title very knowingly borrowed by the Coen brothers more than half a century later. Sturges sends his director, John L. Sullivan—played by Joel McCrea—on a hobo pilgrimage, at the outset of which he meets up with a disillusioned young would-be actress—Veronica Lake.

A striking couple—he six foot four, she barely five feet tall—they encounter real America at uncomfortably close range, inspiring the director to reconsider his low opinion of comedy. "It may not be everything," he says, "but it's better than nothing in this cockeyed caravan, boy." I can go along with that.

Sturges's later films did not always measure up to the high standards he had set for himself in the early 1940s, but the movies he made during that brief prime are amongst the most hilarious ever to come out of Hollywood.

247. *Sullivan's Travels*
U.S. (1941)
Paramount
Lobby card
11 × 14 in.
(27.9 × 35.6 cm)

Alfred Hitchcock

The darling of the auteur critics, and Truffaut in particular, was Alfred Hitchcock. Hitchcock was born in London, and began his career there writing titles for silent movies, and in the mid-1920s he spent some time in Berlin, where he had the opportunity to familiarize himself with German film, and in particular to spend time watching F. W. Murnau at work. Later he would incorporate many of Murnau's techniques into his own films.

Hitchock made his first European picture, *The Pleasure Garden*, at the UFA studios in Germany in 1925. The following year, he made his first thriller—*The Lodger: A Story of the London Fog*—the story of a hunt for a serial killer in which, as in so many Hitchcock films, the wrong man is suspected of the crime and has to prove himself innocent. This movie was a hit and guaranteed his future in the British film industry. After several more silent pictures he made his first sound film, *Blackmail* (1929), which was followed by three early classics of the suspense genre, *The Man Who Knew Too Much* (1934; fig. 248), *The 39 Steps* (1935; fig. 249), and *The Lady Vanishes* (1938; fig. 250).

In 1939, David O. Selznick brought Hitchcock to Hollywood, where his career would go from one success to another for the next three and a half decades. To give any kind of account of this phase of his career would require a chapter to itself, but a very partial listing of his notable films would include *Rebecca* (fig. 251), *Suspicion*, *Shadow of a Doubt*, *Spellbound*, *Notorious* (fig. 252), *Strangers on a Train*, *Dial M for Murder* (fig. 209), *Rear Window*, *To Catch a Thief*, *The Man Who Knew Too Much*, *The Wrong Man*, *Vertigo*, *North by Northwest*, *Psycho*, and *The Birds*. In these films he made brilliant use of established stars like James Stewart and Cary Grant, and introduced new ones like Kim Novak and Tippi Hedren. The movies were all brilliantly crafted—planned down to the last detail with the help of storyboards, and edited with obsessive precision—but beyond that they were marked by an atmosphere of menace that was Hitchcock's signature, one that no one else has ever quite been able to fake.

Hitchcock's subject matter lent itself very well to poster design, and I'm fortunate to have some fine examples in my collection, from one-sheets for *The 39 Steps* and *The Lady Vanishes*, which are strong on period feel, to dramatic lobby cards for *North by Northwest* and *Dial M for Murder*. To see the image of Grace Kelly sprawled on the floor in the latter is to be transported back to the terror at the center of the movie. It's exactly the kind of thing that fuels my passion as a collector.

Great Directors

248. *The Man Who Knew Too Much*
United Kingdom (1934)
Poster for U.S. release
Gaumont British
Insert
36 × 14 in.
(91.4 × 35.6 cm)

THE ARCH CRIMINAL..OF ALL CRIME..OF ALL TIME

NOVA
PILBEAM
PETER
LORRE
LESLIE
BANKS
EDNA
BEST

THE MAN WHO KNEW TOO MUCH

DIRECTED BY
ALFRED HITCHCOCK
A GB PRODUCTION

249. *The 39 Steps*
United Kingdom (1935)
Poster for U.S. release
Gaumont British
One-sheet
41 × 27 in.
(104.1 × 68.6 cm)

Starstruck

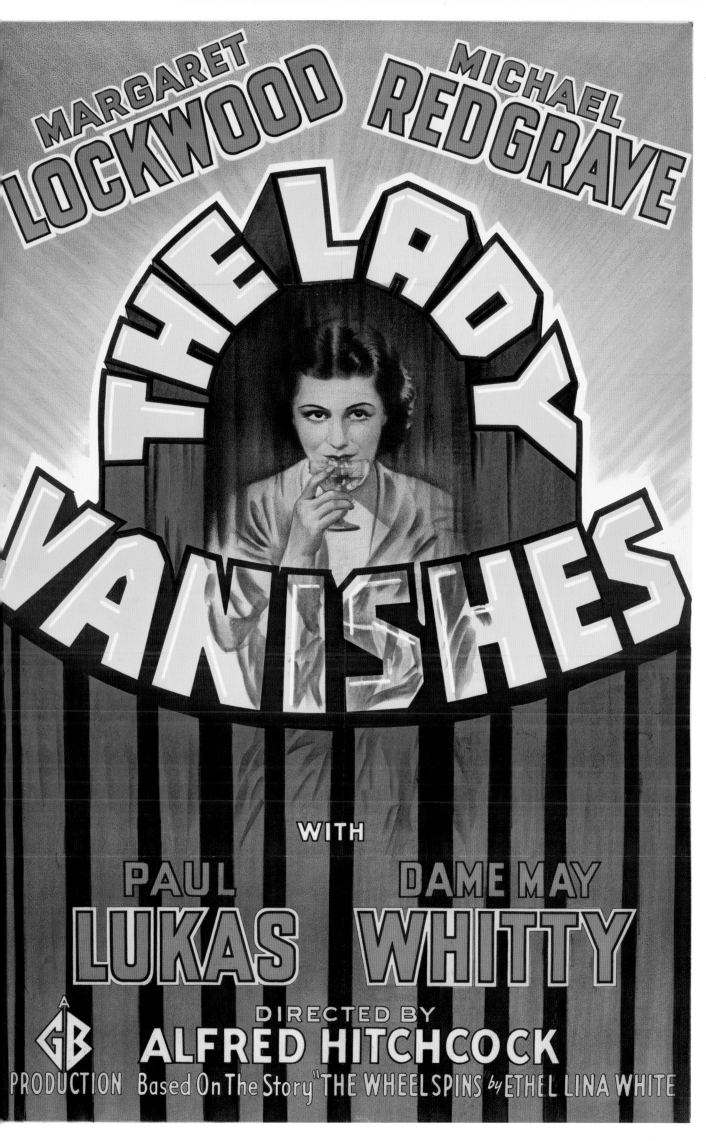

250. *The Lady Vanishes*
United Kingdom (1938)
Poster for U.S. release
Gainsborough/ Gaumont British
One-sheet
41 × 27 in. (104.1 × 68.6 cm)

Selznick International PRESENTS

Rebecca

starring

LAURENCE OLIVIER · JOAN FONTAINE

hero of "Wuthering Heights" · *in her sensational starring debut*

with

GEORGE SANDERS · **JUDITH ANDERSON**

Directed by **ALFRED HITCHCOCK** · *From the best-selling novel by* **DAPHNE DU MAURIER**

Produced by **DAVID O. SELZNICK** *who made "Gone With The Wind"* · *Released thru* **UNITED ARTISTS**

© 1939 by United Artists Corporation — Made in U.S.A.

This advertising material is leased and not sold and is the property of United Artists Corporation, and upon completion of the exhibition for which it has been leased by the exhibitor, it should be returned to the United Artists Corporation.

ABOVE

251. *Rebecca*
U.S. (1940)
Selznick/
United Artists
Lobby card
11 × 14 in.
(27.9 × 35.6 cm)

OPPOSITE

252. *Notorious*
U.S. (1946)
RKO
Title card
11 × 14 in.
(27.9 × 35.6 cm)

Not everything was serene at Mt. Rushmore. (Cary Grant, Eva Marie Saint).

M-G-M Presents "**NORTH BY NORTHWEST**" in VistaVision TECHNICOLOR"

William Wyler

If Hitchcock is the darling of auteur theorists, William Wyler presents them with a puzzle, because he does not possess a signature style as such; rather, he made a career of taking on a wide range of projects and tailoring his approach to the subject matter of each (as opposed to someone like Howard Hawks, who also took on a wide range of projects but had a recognizably consistent style). Yet Wyler is an undeniably great director whose films include such disparate classics as *Wuthering Heights*, *The Little Foxes*, *Jezebel* (fig. 254), *Mrs. Miniver*, *The Heiress*, *Friendly Persuasion*, *Ben-Hur*, and (most astonishingly, perhaps) *The Collector*. And that's without mentioning a trio of movies that have to be on anyone's all-time Hollywood list—*Dodsworth* (fig. 222), *The Best Years of Our Lives* (fig. 118), and *Roman Holiday*.

Wyler was born in Alsace and came to New York to work as a messenger for Universal, owned by a distant cousin, Carl Laemmle. He moved to Hollywood in the early '20s and, after a brief apprenticeship on the Universal lot, began directing low-budget westerns with titles like *Galloping Justice* and *Daze of the West*. In the sound era, he began to make his mark at the helm of films like *The Love Trap* and *Counsellor-at-Law*, but he fully came into his own with the

253. *North by Northwest*
U.S. (1959)
MGM
Lobby card
11 × 14 in.
(27.9 × 35.6 cm)

1936 classic *Dodsworth*. Based on a Sinclair Lewis novel, this movie tells the story of American industrialist Sam Dodsworth (Walter Huston), whose vain and foolish wife Fran (Ruth Chatterton) drags him to Europe, where she takes on airs. She abandons Sam, who she now considers unbearably dull, driving him into the arms of Edith Cortright (Mary Astor), an attractive widow, disillusioned with life, whose acquaintance he had made during the Atlantic crossing. The story could have become banal, but as presented by Wyler and his outstanding cast, it is full of tenderness and melancholy with undertones of tragedy and moments of unforced romance. *Dodsworth* is one of the greatest pictures ever to come out of Hollywood, and one of my absolute favorites.

The Best Years of Our Lives is a 1946 film that follows three World War II servicemen returning to the Midwest to discover that the world they knew has changed while they

were away. It displays much the same blend of tenderness and melancholy as *Dodsworth* and, like the earlier film, is blessed with outstanding performances—this time from Fredric March, Myrna Loy, Dana Andrews, Virginia Mayo, Teresa Wright, Hoagy Carmichael, and, unforgettably, Harold Russell, an actual veteran who had lost both his hands in a training accident.

Released in 1953, *Roman Holiday* is a romantic comedy as refreshing as a *sorbetto al limone* on the Via Flamina. This time the stars are Audrey Hepburn, in her American debut, and Gregory Peck. Although very different from *Dodsworth*, *Roman Holiday* also deals with the uneasy connection between American and European culture, and, light as it is, it too has its share of tenderness and melancholy, raising the possibility that perhaps "Willie" Wyler (as he was universally known) did after all have a signature—the depth of feeling that he brought to every story and every set of characters.

Orson Welles

Then there was Orson Welles! The exclamation mark is permissible, I think, because there never was another director quite like Welles—the man behind what is often considered the greatest movie ever made, who after *Citizen Kane* (figs. 189, 190, and 282) showed a few more flashes of brilliance before seeing his directorial career stymied. The closest comparison would be to Erich von Stroheim, who like Welles fell foul of the Hollywood establishment because of the overreaching ambition of projects that went far beyond the goal of entertainment that has always been the primary raison d'être of the big studios.

Like Stroheim, Welles was his own greatest work of art, a self-invented character so larger than life that he demanded stardom on top of his role as a behind-the-camera genius. Born in Wisconsin and brought up largely in Chicago, he lost his mother at the age of nine, and his father at fifteen. At the age of sixteen, he traveled to Ireland and talked himself into being hired as a member of the company at the famous Gate Theater in Dublin, earning strong reviews for his appearance as the Duke in an adaptation of Lion Feuchtwanger's novel *Jew Süss*. He

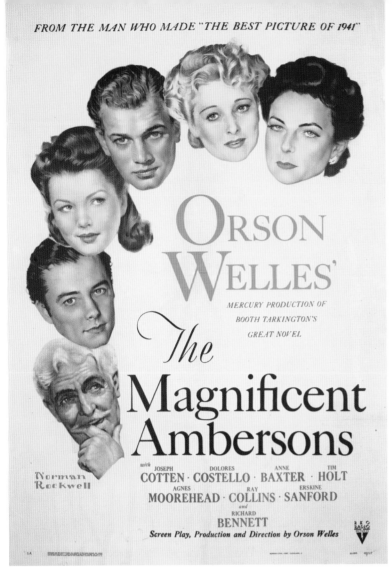

OPPOSITE
255. *The Letter*
U.S. (1940)
Warner Bros.
Title card
11 × 14 in.
(27.9 × 35.6 cm)

LEFT
256. *The Magnificent Ambersons*
U.S. (1942)
Mercury/RKO
One-sheet
41 × 27 in.
(104.1 × 68.6 cm)

ABOVE
257. *The Lady from Shanghai*
U.S. (1948)
Columbia
Lobby card
11 × 14 in.
(27.9 × 35.6 cm)

returned to his prep school in Woodstock, Illinois, where he began work—in collaboration with Roger Hill, one of his teachers—on the Everybody's Shakespeare books, the first of which was published in 1934, before Welles was out of his teens, and immediately became a best seller.

By then he had gravitated to Broadway, and was also performing in radio dramas. At the age of twenty, Welles directed an all-black production of *Macbeth* that was a sensation and brought him national fame. After adventures with the Federal Theater Project—the premiere of one play was aborted when audience and performers were locked out by the National Guard—Welles and John Houseman went on to form the Mercury Theater, which had successes both onstage and on the radio, most notably with the famous adaptation of H. G. Wells's *The War of the Worlds*, which had some listeners believing that Martians had landed in New Jersey.

It was only a matter of time before all this led to Hollywood, and inevitably Welles's arrival there stirred up a storm of publicity and controversy. The controversy would come to a head when the gossip columnist Hedda Hopper saw a sneak preview of *Citizen Kane* and, realizing it was based on events in the life of media tycoon and former presidential candidate William Randolph Hearst, tipped him off. Hearst, incensed, used his newspaper empire to

attempt to suppress the movie, threatening theater chains that he would not accept their advertisements for any movies if they booked *Kane*. Hearst was especially upset by the fact that Kane's mistress, Susan Alexander—presented as a talentless wannabe opera singer—would unjustly be identified by audiences with his real-life mistress, Marion Davies. (According to some sources, Herman J. Mankiewicz, who coauthored the screenplay with Welles, had a bitter grudge against Davies, a former friend who had dumped him—probably at Hearst's behest—because of his heavy drinking.) After many delays, RKO released the film, which, despite glowing reviews, left the moviegoing public cold. Audiences in 1941 were confused by the multiple narrative viewpoints, by the layered sound track (a legacy of Welles's radio experience), and by Gregg Toland's deep-focus cinematography and eccentric-seeming camera angles. It took more than a decade for the film to be fully accepted as the innovative masterpiece it is.

At the age of twenty-six, Orson Welles had peaked. He went on to make other remarkable films, including *The Magnificent Ambersons* (1942; fig. 256)—which was truncated by the studio—*The Lady from Shanghai* (1947; fig. 257), and *Touch of Evil* (1958), but everything he did was bound to be compared with *Citizen Kane*, and certain to suffer from the comparison.

PAGES 232–33
*The Werewolf
of London*
Detail
(See fig. 269 on p. 244)

RIGHT AND DETAIL
OPPPOSITE
258. *The Wizard of Oz*
U.S. (1939)
MGM
Title card
11 × 14 in.
(27.9 × 35.6 cm)

Some collectors acquire poster art by specializing in one film genre to the exclusion of all others. One of the biggest examples of this exclusion is animation—and Disney animation in particular. I am not by any means an animation specialist, but I'm happy to own material from *Snow White and the Seven Dwarfs* (fig. 26), the first great animated feature. Similarly, I am not a great fan of MGM musicals, but who could resist a souvenir of *The Wizard of Oz* (fig. 258)? Horror movies interest me more, and as I wrote earlier, I'm sorry now that I did not invest decades ago in some of the great horror film posters I had a shot at buying. They seemed expensive back then, but what I didn't quite realize at the time is that items from the top horror movie titles—such as the Universal classics of the 1930s—are among the most sought-after in the entire collectible field. The competition to acquire them is fierce, and prices have become astronomical. I may have missed out on some gems, but nonetheless I have managed to assemble a worthwhile sampling of the genre.

Horror Films

Any account of the great horror movies has to begin in Germany with a trio of silent masterpieces—*The Golem* (1920), *The Cabinet of Dr. Caligari* (1920; figs. 259 and 260), and *Nosferatu* (1922). Among my most prized possessions is a poster for the 1921 American release of *Caligari*, Robert Wiene's chilling story of murders in a small mountain village. I also have a pair of rare items from the film that clearly illustrate Wiene's expressionistic style, which proved so influential on

directors from Murnau to Hitchcock to Welles. A little later, at the beginning of the sound era—and before they both moved to America—Fritz Lang directed Peter Lorre in the terrifying story *M* (1931; fig. 261), about the serial crimes of a child murderer.

The first great Hollywood horror film was the 1925 silent version of *The Phantom of the Opera* (fig. 262), from Universal, which starred Lon Chaney and Mary Philben. In the 1930s, Universal began to release a series of horror films, the most famous of which were directed by Tod Browning, James Whale, and Karl Freund. Browning (who also directed the outrageously creepy circus movie *Freaks*) was responsible for *Dracula* (1931; fig. 264), which introduced American movie audiences to Bela Lugosi. That same year, James Whale directed Boris Karloff in *Frankenstein* (figs. 264 and 265), the film that made Karloff a star, and he followed this up with three more masterpieces of the genre—*The Old Dark House* (1932), *The Invisible Man* (1933), and *The Bride of Frankenstein* (fig. 263), which provided Elsa Lanchester with her most iconic role. Better known as a cinematographer (he shot films such as *The Last Laugh*, *Metropolis* [fig. 39], and *Dracula*), Karl Freund drew upon his vast experience of German Expressionist cinema when he directed *The Mummy* (1932), which capitalized on Karloff's huge success in *Frankenstein*. Other notable Universal horror films of the 1930s and early 1940s include *Murders in the Rue Morgue*, *The Raven*, *Werewolf of London* (fig. 268), *The Invisible Ray*, and *The Wolf Man*.

It's fair to say that the most archetypal and sought-after of these Universal movies are *Dracula*, *Frankenstein*, and *The*

with Judy GARLAND • Frank MORGAN • Ray BOLGER • Bert L

THE WIZARD OF

It's METRO-GOLDWYN-MAYER'S TECH

and BILLIE BURKE
MARGARET HAMILTON
CHARLEY GRAPEWIN
AND THE MUNCHKINS

SCREEN PLAY by NOEL LANGLEY, FLORENCE
RYERSON AND EDGAR ALLAN WOOLF
FROM THE BOOK BY L. FRANK BAUM
DIRECTED BY VICTOR FLEMING

A VICTO

Produce

259. *Das Cabinet des Dr. Caligari*
U.S. title:
The Cabinet of Dr. Caligari
Germany (1920)
Poster for U.S. release (1921)
Decla-Bioscop/ Goldwyn
One-sheet
41 × 27 in.
(104.1 × 68.6 cm)

Starstruck

BELOW
261. *M*
Germany (1931)
Nero Film/Paramount
Still
10 × 8 in.
(25.4 × 20.3 cm)

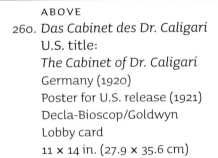

ABOVE
260. *Das Cabinet des Dr. Caligari*
U.S. title:
The Cabinet of Dr. Caligari
Germany (1920)
Poster for U.S. release (1921)
Decla-Bioscop/Goldwyn
Lobby card
11 × 14 in. (27.9 × 35.6 cm)

Bride of Frankenstein, and I'm happy to say that all three are represented in my collection, though I still regret some lost opportunities.

A blockbuster that belongs to a subcategory of the horror genre—the monster genre—but that has to be considered beyond category because of the enormity of its impact is the original 1933 version of *King Kong* (figs. 267 and 268). *Kong* was conceived by Merian C. Cooper—who directed with Ernest B. Schoedsack—and is notable for the stop-action animation of Willis O'Brien (who brought Kong and his fearsome dinosaur costars convincingly to life) and for the special effects photography that allowed the ape to

tickle the understandably hysterical Fay Wray with a finger the size of a tree trunk. Spectacles like the climactic scene when the giant primate climbs the then-brand-new Empire State Building and swats away aircraft like flies, bowled over audiences at the film's opening at Radio City.

This was a movie that had it all, and never has one provided better opportunities for poster artists. I have a pair of lobby cards that capture the excitement of the film, one of which amplifies the visual drama with the assertion that this story—"Unique! Thrilling! Startling!"—is the strangest ever told. For once, no exaggeration was involved.

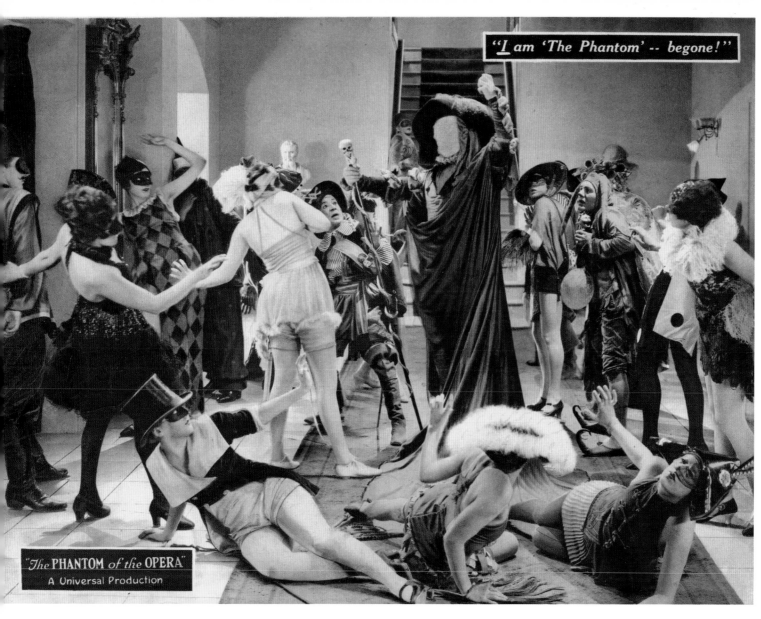

"I am 'The Phantom' -- begone!"

"The PHANTOM of the OPERA"
A Universal Production

LEFT
262. *The Phantom
of the Opera*
U.S. (1925)
Universal
Lobby card
11 × 14 in.
(27.9 × 35.6 cm)

CARL LAEMMLE presents THE MONSTER THRILLER KARLOFF in
The BRIDE OF FRANKENSTEIN
A UNIVERSAL Picture

CARL LAEMMLE presents
DRACULA
UNIVERSAL PICTURE

LEFT
263. *The Bride of
Frankenstein*
U.S. (1935)
Universal
Lobby card
11 × 14 in.
(27.9 × 35.6 cm)

ABOVE AND
DETAIL OPPOSITE
264. *Dracula*
U.S. (1931)
Universal
Lobby card
11 × 14 in.
(27.9 × 35.6 cm)

Classic Films

ABOVE
265. *Frankenstein*
U.S. (1931)
Universal
Title card
11 x 14 in.
(27.9 x 35.6 cm)

RIGHT AND
DETAIL
OPPOSITE
266. *Frankenstein*
U.S. (1931)
Universal
Lobby card
11 x 14 in.
(27.9 x 35.6 cm)

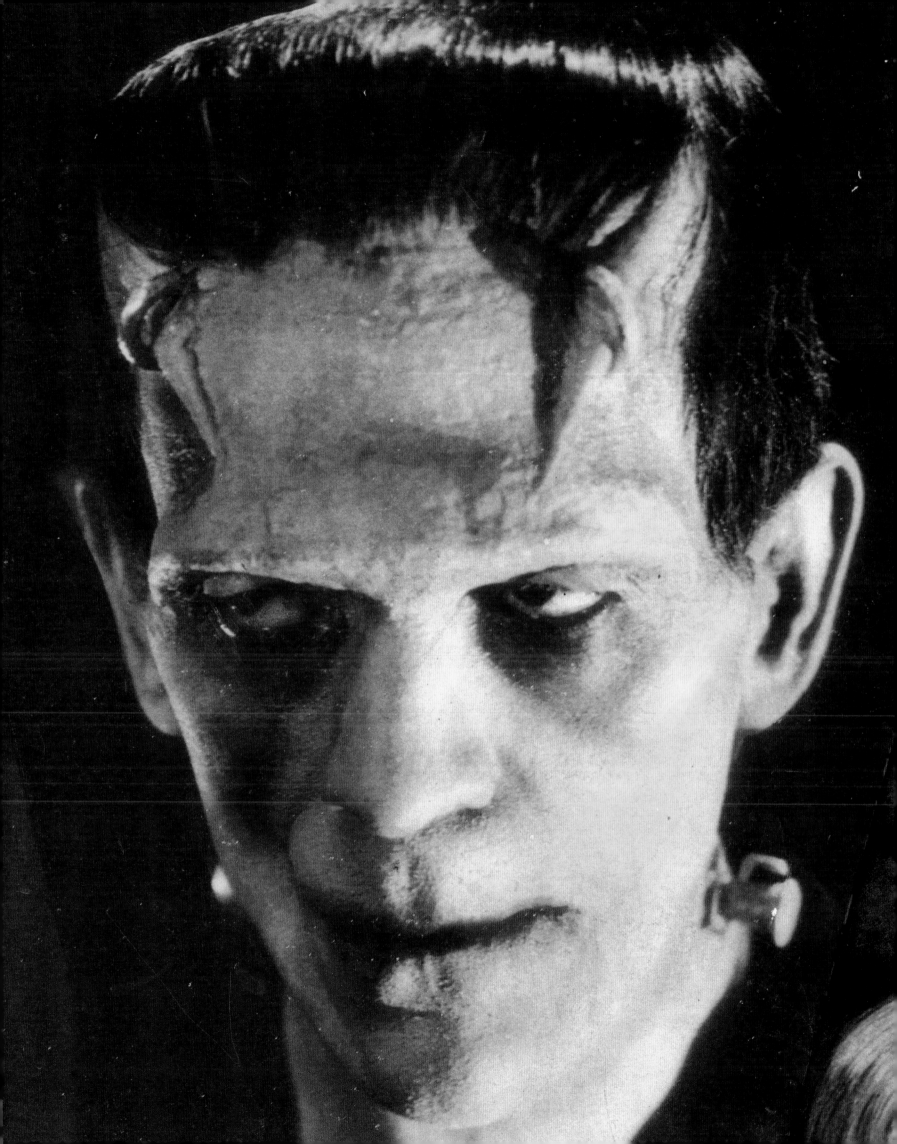

ABOVE
267. *King Kong*
U.S. (1933)
RKO
Lobby card
11 x 14 in.
(27.9 x 35.6 cm)

RIGHT AND
DETAIL OPPOSITE
268. *King Kong*
U.S. (1933)
RKO
Title card
11 x 14 in.
(27.9 x 35.6 cm)

242

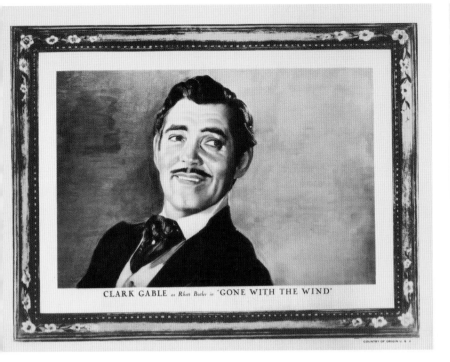

ABOVE
271. *Gone with the Wind*
U.S. (1939)
Selznick/MGM
Lobby card
11 × 14 in.
(27.9 × 35.6 cm)

ABOVE
272. *Gone with the Wind*
U.S. (1939)
Selznick/MGM
Lobby card
11 × 14 in.
(27.9 × 35.6 cm)

Gone with the Wind

Some movies attain a beyond-category greatness because they were planned that way, while others—and this is more interesting, I think—have greatness thrust upon them. *Gone with the Wind* (figs. 163, 271, and 272) is probably the archetypal example of the former. David O. Selznick did everything he possibly could to make it the ultimate block-buster, the whirlwind of publicity that preceded the production being as important to the total phenomenon as the film itself. "Who will play Scarlett? Will it be Bette Davis? Might it be Greer Garson? Could it be Tallulah Bankhead?" Almost every eligible actress in Hollywood was tested for the part, or at least considered for it, before Vivian Leigh was finally given the role. "And what about Rhett Butler? Why has Gary Cooper turned down the part? Will Clark Gable finally take it?" The buildup was relentless, the premiere in Atlanta was spectacular, and the production delivered all the color, action, and glamour that Selznick had promised. On top of that it cost a fortune in Depression dollars—an unheard of $3.9 million—and it ran for four hours complete with overture, intermission, and rousing music to head for the exits by. And when you hit the street, exhausted, you came away with a legendary put-down line to use when the occasion arose.

"Frankly, my dear, I don't give a damn. . . ."
That alone was worth the price of admission.

Casablanca

Perhaps the most outstanding example of a film that had greatness thrust upon it is *Casablanca* (figs. 191, 273, and 274), now considered one of the best movies ever made but at the time looked on as a routine film made at a period when the big studios turned out almost one movie a week. In retrospect, the genesis of *Casablanca* seems almost accidental, though the many changes that occurred during preproduction, and even production, were probably par for the course in Hollywood during the studio period. The most famous story about changes made to the project, the one that asserts that Ronald Reagan was the first choice to play Rick Blaine, is in fact completely untrue, though it does have an explanation. Six months before production began, the Warner Bros. publicity department—always keen to have their contract players' names in the papers—did put out a press release linking the future president and Ann Sheridan with the upcoming project. In fact, *Casablanca* was technically not a Warner Bros. film. The story had been bought for the studio by Hal Wallis when he was head of production, but his status there had changed. He now headed his own independent unit, Hal Wallis Productions, which was contracted to produce movies for Warner Bros. using the studio's actors and crews. From the outset, Wallis insisted on Bogart for the part of Rick, though this was thought something of a risk since he had never played a romantic lead.

There were plenty of other changes, however, usually based on accidents of chance and availability. William Wyler was Wallis's first choice to direct, but he was otherwise committed, so Michael Curtiz was brought in. (His credits included *The Adventures of Robin Hood* [fig. 20] and *Angels with Dirty Faces*, and he would go on to direct *Yankee Doodle Dandy* [fig. 10].) A number of writers were involved in developing the story, which was based on the never-produced play *Everyone Comes to Rick's* by Murray Burnett, a former schoolteacher, and Joan Alison. The first writers to work on the screenplay were the twins Julius and Philip Epstein, who lightened up the dialogue and were responsible for many of the catchy phrases that everybody remembers. ("Of all the

gin joints in all the towns in all the world . . .") They were joined by Howard Koch, credited with giving the movie its political edge. (Later he would be blacklisted.) And, although he received no screen credit, Casey Robinson—who wrote *Dark Victory* (fig. 105) and *Now, Voyager* for Bette Davis— seems to have crafted at least some of the romantically charged scenes between Rick and Ilsa (Ingrid Bergman). Curtiz, of course, worked closely with the writers, and Wallis is known to have had a very hands-on involvement in the production. That, of course, is how most scripts were produced under the studio system, but in this case the different personalities jelled—on paper at least—to produce a near-perfect script. Julius Epstein was quoted in his obituary

as having said that it contained "a great deal of corn, more corn than in the states of Kansas and Iowa combined. But when corn works, there's nothing better."

Another interesting aspect of *Casablanca* is the astonishingly strong European connection. Curtiz was Hungarian, and of the three stars, only Bogart was American, Bergman having been born in Stockholm and Paul Henreid in Trieste. As one goes down the cast list, one finds Peter Lorre (Hungarian by birth and the star of *M*), Conrad Veidt (German, and one of the stars of *The Cabinet of Dr. Caligari*), Claude Rains and Sydney Greenstreet (both English), S. Z. "Cuddles" Sakall (Hungarian), while other cast members hailed from France, Germany, Austria, Denmark, and Russia.

The only thing *Casablanca* has in common with *Gone with the Wind* is that both were scored by yet another European, Max Steiner, born in Vienna. One of the happenstances of the movie involved Steiner. It would be hard to imagine *Casablanca* without the Herman Hupfield song "As Time Goes By," yet in fact Steiner was planning to replace it with one of his own compositions. Luckily, Ingrid Bergman had had her hair cut short for her next role so that some of the scenes in which the song was performed could not be reshot.

"As Time Goes By" is an appropriate theme song for *Casablanca* because time has been very kind to the film's reputation. It was well reviewed when it appeared in 1942, it established Bogart at the top level of stardom, it did good but not exceptional business in its first release, and it won three Academy Awards, including best picture, but nobody called it one of Hollywood's greatest until much later. How did this change in estimation come about? The war years were a time of shifting values, and perhaps it was difficult to see all of *Casablanca*'s merits at the time. In the postwar years, they became more apparent. Although it did not strictly speaking belong to the genre, *Casablanca* helped prepare the way for film noir, and film noir in turn helped prepare the way for a reconsideration of *Casablanca*. In retrospect it seemed very different from other Hollywood movies of World War II because it didn't deal in the same black-and-white certainties. There were as many shades of gray in the plot as in Arthur Edeson's dramatic cinematography. The approval of the *Cahiers du cinéma* crowd helped guarantee the film's cult status, but the importance of the film went beyond that. Seeing *Casablanca*, and identifying with Rick, became a milestone in the education of young American males, and much of that, of course, had to do with Bogart's portrayal, which took screen acting somewhere it had never been before. His Rick cleared the brush for Brando and Dean and Newman and Nicholson and De Niro and the rest.

Here's lookin' at you, kid.

OPPOSITE
273. *Casablanca*
U.S. (1942)
Warner Bros.
Lobby card
11 × 14 in.
(27.9 × 35.6 cm)

BELOW
274. *Casablanca*
U.S. (1942)
Warner Bros.
Midget window card
14 × 8 in.
(35.6 × 20.3 cm)

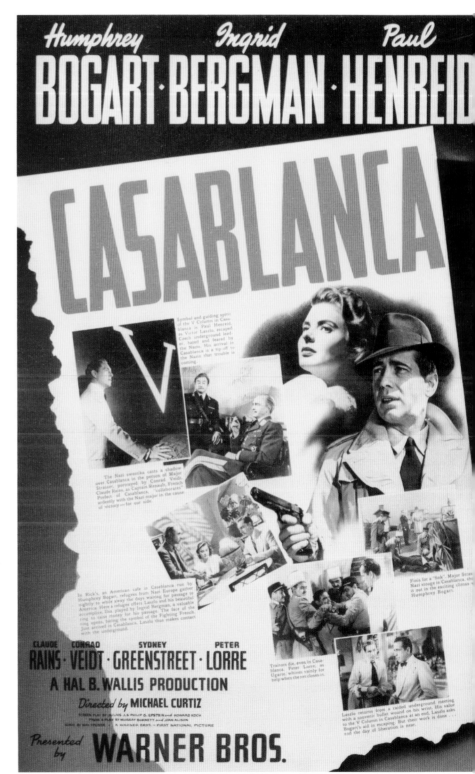

ORABLE

m the BROCK... stage success
by PRESTON STURGES

Paul **LUKAS**

(Courtesy of Paramount Pictures)

SIDNEY FOX
LEWIS STONE
GEORGE MEEKER
WILLIAM RICCIARDI
and SIDNEY TOLER

PAGES 248–49
Strictly Dishonorable
Detail
(See fig. 277 on p. 252)

RIGHT
275. *Manhattan Cocktail*
U.S. (1928)
Paramount
Title card
11 × 14 in.
(27.9 × 35.6 cm)

In my early poster-collecting days, I would sometimes visit a store like Hollywood Poster Exchange and lay out a few dollars for a one-sheet or a lobby card simply because I liked the graphics, without necessarily knowing much about the movie itself, or its stars. As my knowledge grew, my poster hunting became much more systematic, but from time to time I still come across posters that I want in my collection simply because the design is so strong, even though the films they advertise are obscure or forgotten. You would think that such posters would be relatively inexpensive, and sometimes they are, but I'm not the only collector around with an eye for outstanding graphics, so some items can be very expensive even when they are attached to titles that most movie fans would not even recognize.

The classic example of this is a poster I own for a 1933 film titled *The Sin of Nora Moran* (fig. 276). A B thriller, it presents the plight of a young woman who, though innocent, is on death row, scheduled to die in the electric chair. The studio that produced the picture was Majestic, and don't feel too bad if that doesn't ring any bells—it was one of those Poverty Row companies that distributed its pictures wherever it could find an independent theater manager who wasn't too fussy about content. Its specialties were raunch and cheap thrills, and the implementation of the Hays Code effectively put Majestic out of business. As for the movie's star, Zita Johann was a Romanian-born actress who never made the big time, though dedicated horror movie fans may recognize the name as belonging to the beauty who was Boris Karloff's love interest in *The Mummy*. (Later she married John Houseman.) Despite

its titillating title—and unlike some of Majestic's other products—*The Sin of Nora Moran* is not especially salacious. The poster, however, which takes the form of a sophisticated and spectacular piece of pinup art with neoclassical overtones, drips sexual innuendo (and no one seems to have cared that the movie's star was a brunette, not a blond). Combined with its rarity, this overt eroticism has made the *Nora Moran* one-sheet much sought after. It has become so coveted, in fact, that in at least one poll it was voted the greatest film poster of all time.

Not quite as sexy, but still very much in the pre-Code genre, is a one-sheet for a 1931 Universal film called *Strictly Dishonorable* (fig. 277). The most notable thing about this movie is that it was based on a 1929 stage play by Preston Sturges. The poster portrays a young woman—the movie's female star, Sidney Fox—provocatively silhouetted against a red background. Nothing about the image suggests that she is a music student in love with an opera singer, though that is in fact the storyline.

Hollywood Party (fig. 278) is a chaotic 1934 MGM musical, starring Jimmy Durante, that has its devotees but can hardly be considered a classic. What cult fame it enjoys derives from a couple of outstanding moments, one of which is the opening musical number which features a chorus of pre-Code telephone operators in shockingly skimpy costumes. The other is a Technicolor sequence—"The Hot Chocolate Soldiers"—animated by Disney and introduced by Mickey Mouse. The messy scenario also squeezes in guest spots by stars ranging from Laurel and Hardy to Lupe Velez. The title lobby card I own boasts that *Hollywood*

Majestic Pictures *presents*

The SIN of NORA MORAN

with

**ZITA JOHANN • JOHN MILJAN • ALAN DINEHART
CLAIRE DuBREY • PAUL CAVANAGH**

PRESENTED IN
A NEW MARVELOUS SCREEN TECHNIQUE
Directed by PHIL GOLDSTONE

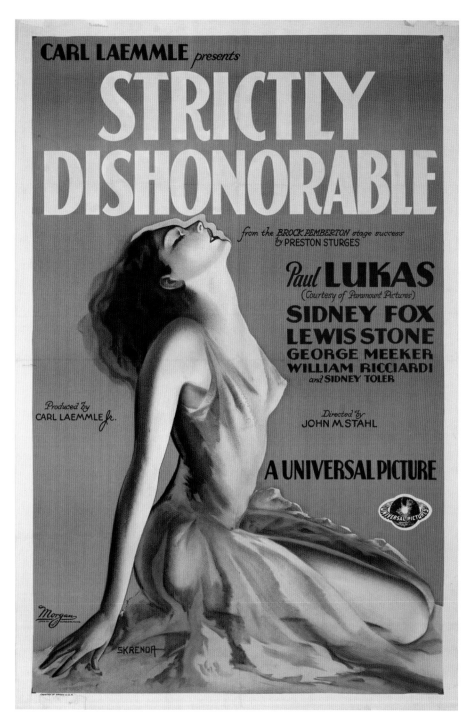

277. *Strictly Dishonorable*
U.S. (1931)
Universal
One-sheet
41 × 27 in.
(104.1 × 68.6 cm)

Party has everything: "Stars! Girls! Music!" Certainly the *poster* has everything—vivid color, jazzy modern lettering, and the photographic image of a showgirl montaged into the ensemble above a sea of skillfully executed caricatures. This is a poster I think anyone would want to own.

I have an equally jazzy poster, all angles and silhouettes, for the silent-screen backstage comedy *Manhattan Cocktail* (fig. 275). The image, in fact, hints at what the New York skyline might have looked like after a couple of speakeasy-era Manhattans made with bootleg bourbon. This movie seems to be lost—sadly, because it was directed by Dorothy Arzner, one of the few women directors of that period.

Many films of the silent era are now largely forgotten even though they were presumably popular when they appeared. Corinne Griffith was a big star in her day—dubbed "The Orchid Lady" because of her stunning beauty—who starred in a string of movies that were scripted to provide her with the opportunity to make as many costume changes as possible. One gathers from the title alone that the 1926 film *Mademoiselle Modiste* (fig. 280) fit nicely into this formula. It was based on a Victor Herbert operetta, and Griffith portrayed Fifi, a charming and of course gorgeous employee of an upscale Parisian dress store who is elevated to the status of modiste by a rich American tourist who takes over the business. The poster from this film is one of the most beautiful and painterly that I own, a stunning portrait of Griffith embodying her archetypal fashion plate persona. It captures her beauty convincingly, and like many silent-era posters makes wonderful use of color, in this case to evoke the fantasy world that was the star's natural habitat.

In a very similar idiom is a poster for *East Is West* (fig. 280), a 1922 release starring Constance Talmadge, another big silent actress, as was her sister Norma. Talmadge was a bubbly blonde with a good feel for comedy, but in this film she was given a black wig and cast as a Chinese girl, Ming Toy. She is about to be sold into slavery but is rescued by a young American and brought to San Francisco, where her freedom is threatened all over again by a Tong leader played by Warner Oland (later famous as the detective Charlie Chan). It turns out that Ming Toy is really Caucasian—stolen from missionary parents if you haven't already guessed—so her Yankee boyfriend is able to save her by marching her down the aisle. The story may be absurd, but I've always loved the poster, with its delicate Asian feel. It now hangs in my daughter's room.

Like Dorothy Arzner, Lois Weber was a member of an elite group of women directors who succeeded in early Hollywood, and she was prolific too, making literally hundreds of films during the silent era. *What Do Men Want?* (1921) seems to have been a routine production about the battle of the sexes, but the charming poster (fig. 279) distills the film's theme into a single image that shows the movie's star—Claire Windsor, another great beauty of the period—mixing a potion from ingredients labeled "Happiness," "Success," "Love," and even "$." Whether or not this has anything to do with anything that actually happens in the film we may never know.

Every poster carries a special meaning for me. If I find a great one-sheet for *Dodsworth* or a pristine set of lobby cards for *A Night at the Opera*, I am connected to a specific experience: where I first saw the film, whom I saw it with, where we had dinner afterward, how we relived the highlights of the movie over pasta and a bottle of Soave in the West Village, or perhaps hot dogs and a Coke on the sidewalk outside Pink's in Hollywood.

Let's not forget that the moviegoing experience is *not* a solitary one. It's about shared pleasures aroused before, during, and after the actual screening of a movie. Even if you go to a movie theater on your own, you share with the audience an emotional ride that can make you laugh or cry. Like another pleasure so often celebrated by Hollywood, movies are about bringing people together in the dark for unadulterated enjoyment.

When it comes to little-known films like *Mademoiselle Modiste* and *The Sin of Nora Moran*, the posters do two things for me in addition to providing pure aesthetic pleasure. They provide a bridge to the entire history of the cinema and Hollywood in particular, a history that

278. *Hollywood Party*
U.S. (1934)
MGM
Title card
11 × 14 in.
(27.9 × 35.6 cm)

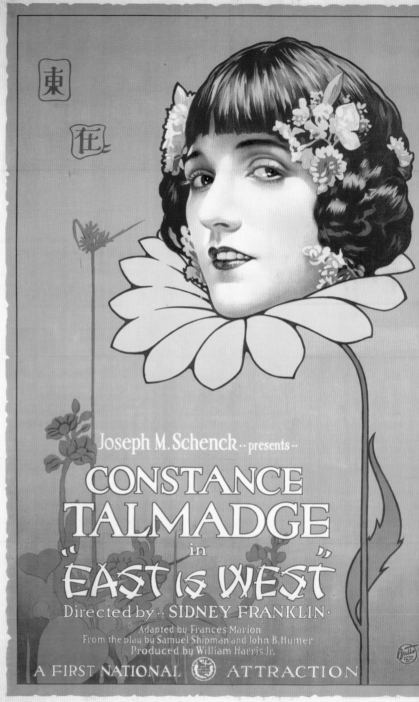

includes flops as well as hits, flash-in-the-pan starlets as well as superstars, Poverty Row back lots as well as major studios, movies seen once and best forgotten as well as classics that can be watched any number of times without their allure wearing thin. And these posters let me imagine myself back in the movie palaces, bijou theaters, and fleapits of yesteryear, sharing in the emotional rush of audiences from the Roaring Twenties, the Great Depression, or the World War II home front—surrounded by strangers whose hearts beat as one with mine, gasping as the villain ties the heroine to the railroad tracks, sharing the thrill and relief as the hero cuts her free.

So bring on Barrymore and Bogart, Garbo and the Gish sisters, Gable and Lombard, Spence and Kate, Fred and Ginger, Pickford and Fairbanks, Jimmy C and Jimmy S,

Laurel and Hardy, Cary Grant and Audrey and all the rest. But don't forget Zita Johann and Claire Windsor. They were part of the story too, and it's a story that's bigger than the biggest stars, the most gifted directors, the most powerful moguls—its magnitude most accurately defined by the millions or billions of people who have sat spellbound in darkness since Thomas Edison's Kinetoscope was unveiled to the public at the Chicago World's Fair of 1893.

Posters are a means of gaining entry to this wonderful, never-finished story. It's been my privilege to build this collection, and it's my pleasure now to share it with you.

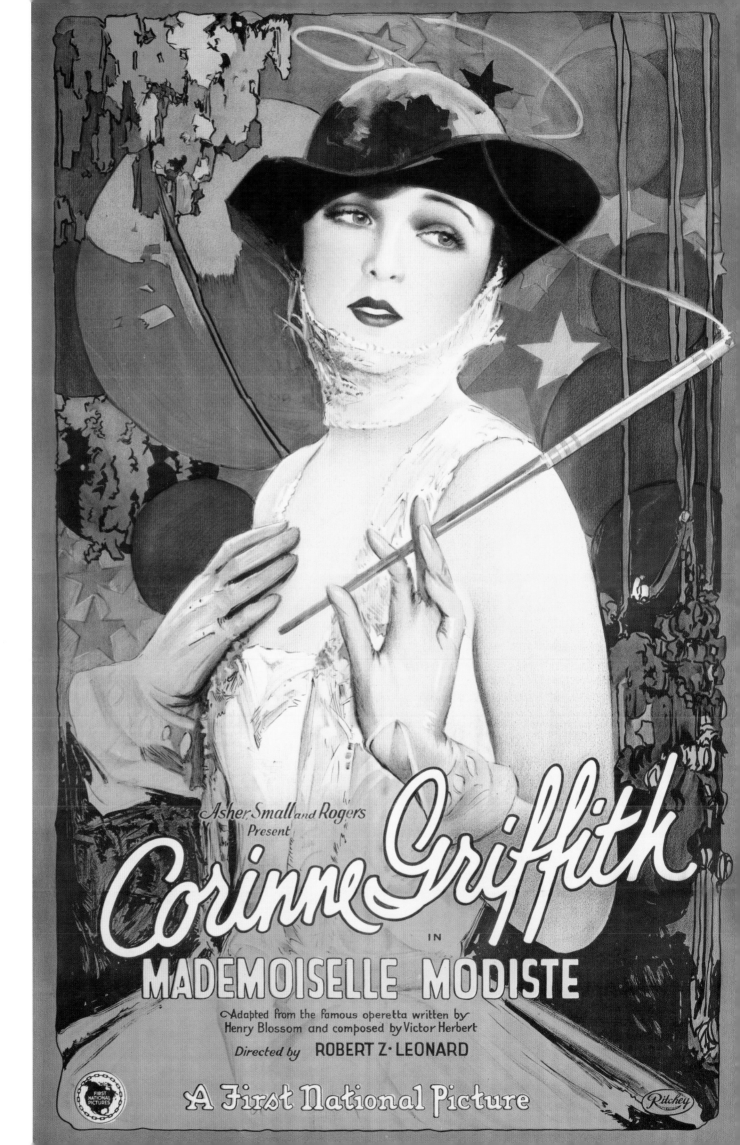

The Mercury Actors

JOSEPH COTTEN

DOROTHY COMINGORE

EVERETT SLOANE

RAY COLLINS

GEORGE COULOURIS

My Fifty Favorite One-Sheets

In some ways, picking my favorite posters is a cruel task, like a parent being asked to pick his favorite child. The fact is, though, that some are rarer and more valuable than others, and I am more attached to some than others. So here is a list of my favorite fifty one-sheets, ordered by figure number and appearance in the book.

3. *Love Before Breakfast*
    This was the first poster I ever purchased. The 1936 film it promotes is forgettable, but the image of Carole Lombard with a black eye was immortalized by the great Walker Evans, who photographed it on a billboard.

4. *Gun Crazy*
    Originally named *Deadly Is the Female*, the poster for this 1949 film noir classic, directed by Joseph H. Lewis, features a sexy Peggy Cummins.

6. *Ziegfeld Follies*
    Another example of a poster by a big-name—Alberto Vargas illustrates his magic for this movie glorification of the American girl in 1946.

7. *The Awful Truth*
    Starred Irene Dunne and Cary Grant in a 1937 screwball comedy. This was one of my first posters, and the film is still one of my favorites. I had a wirehaired terrier as a child, and Mr. Smith, the wirehaired terrier in this movie, is the same dog that played George in *Bringing Up Baby* and Asta in the Thin Man series, which makes him a pretty big star in his own right.

8. *Her Husband's Trademark*
    Another 1922 Swanson vehicle with a charming and sexy poster that catches her in one of her classic "clotheshorse" roles and reminds us that she was one of the very brightest stars in the silent movie firmament.

21. *Beyond the Rocks*
    Based on a melodramatic novel by Elinor Glyn, this 1922 film was an early triumph for Rudolph Valentino, but it was Gloria Swanson who received top billing, reflecting her enormous popularity at the time. This movie was considered lost, but a print was recently found and restored in Holland. The poster features stunning graphics.

33. *The Freshman*
    In this 1925 comedy, Harold Lloyd is a hapless freshman striving to be the most popular student on campus. The graphics for this poster are irresistible.

35. *Stagecoach*
    Made in 1939, which is considered the greatest year in Hollywood history, John Ford's classic western launched John Wayne's stardom. This is the film Orson Welles ran over and over again to learn how to make a great movie before starting on *Citizen Kane*.

45. *Johanna Enlists*
    Fairbanks's future wife Mary Pickford in a 1917 World War I comedy.

53. *The Canary Murder Case*
    This 1929 release was Louise Brooks's last major Hollywood movie; her career was destroyed when she refused to return

from Europe to dub the dialogue. It was important for her costar, William Powell, as it invigorated his career by casting him as a witty and debonair sophisticate, the persona by which he is now remembered.

62. *The Son of the Sheik*
Valentino at his peak, shortly before his sudden death in 1926 at the age of thirty-one.

63. *Sherlock Holmes*
The 1922 edition of the great detective, starring John Barrymore. William Powell made his screen debut in this film.

64. *Babe Comes Home*
A striking 1927 poster for a movie starring Babe Ruth, released in his greatest year, when he caused a sensation by hitting sixty home runs. Larger than life and always hungry for publicity, Babe was no stranger to Hollywood. This is the ultimate "crossover" poster, since it is avidly sought by baseball collectors as well as movie collectors.

65. *The Big Parade*
A rarely seen poster from King Vidor's 1925 classic, which stars John Gilbert and Renée Adorée as star-crossed lovers in World War I France.

67. *Don Juan*
Although this 1926 film starring John Barrymore had no spoken dialogue, it had a synchronized music track and synchronized sound effects, making it the immediate precursor of *The Jazz Singer*.

76. *Peter Pan*
King Vidor's 1924 telling of J. M. Barrie's children's tale, with Betty Bronson refusing to grow up.

80. *Gold Diggers of 1933*
Produced at the lowest point of the Great Depression, this sparkling Busby Berkeley musical showcased the naive appeal of Ruby Keeler and the down-to-earth charm of Dick Powell. The film includes three immortal numbers— "Remember My Forgotten Man," "The Shadow Waltz," and "We're in the Money"—written by Harry Warren and Al Dubin and choreographed and staged by Berkeley.

83. *Ladies They Talk About*
A sexy poster for a provocative pre-Code Barbara Stanwyck movie.

89. *Jewel Robbery*
William Powell and Kay Francis are one of my favorite pairings of the early sound era, and in this 1932 comedy Powell plays the world's greatest jewel thief, who softens up his intended victims with the help of marijuana. How's that for a pre-Code plot device?

101. *Of Human Bondage*
Bette Davis's unhinged performance as a Cockney waitress won her favorable attention in this 1933 movie costarring Leslie Howard.

104. *Marked Woman*
The simplicity of this poster is stunning. The film came out in 1937, when Bette Davis had just returned to the Warner Bros. fold after a fiercely fought lawsuit. Her career was reaching a peak. Humphrey Bogart, who had second billing, was still a few years away from major stardom.

108. *Morning Glory*
Hepburn's third movie, about an aspiring young actress, won her an Academy Award.

109. *A Woman Rebels*
This 1936 movie was a disaster for Katharine Hepburn—her third flop in a row—but you'd never know it from this gorgeous example of poster art.

121. *White Woman*
This time Lombard was cast with Charles Laughton in a 1933 melodrama set on a rubber plantation. The poster's sexy image, with its strong, sensual colors, was Paramount's pre-Code way of playing up her fabulous, fun-loving personality.

124. *What Price Hollywood?*
Released in 1932, and one of the best movies about Hollywood ever made. The poster foresees the headline mania that haunts celebrities to this day.

125. *Seventh Heaven*
A beautiful story directed by Frank Borzage at the end of the silent era. It stars the oft-teamed pair of Janet Gaynor and Charles Farrell, twenty-five years before he became known to another generation as Vernon Albright, the father on *My Little Margie*.

128. *White Shoulders*
I've never seen this 1931 Mary Astor film, but the poster's a beauty—an example of drop-dead design that may or may not have had anything to do with the movie.

136. *Morocco*
This is Marlene Dietrich's first American film, in which she and director Josef von Sternberg take the young and handsome Gary Cooper along on a journey to their exquisite and exotic world of cinematic glamour and intrigue.

141. *A Bill of Divorcement*
This is the only copy of this poster known to exist. The 1932 film was Katharine Hepburn's first.

142. *Twentieth Century*
Another screwball classic, Howard Hawks's fast-talking 1934 theater yarn has Lombard finally finding her rhythm and Barrymore still in control of his vast but quickly disappearing talents.

147 and 148.   *The Cocoanuts* and *Animal Crackers*
The first two Marx Brothers films. I dream of going back to the 1920s to see the boys perform these routines on stage.

160. *His Girl Friday*
Made in 1940, this archetypal hard-nosed, wisecracking Howard Hawks comedy memorably pits newspaper editor Cary Grant against ex-wife and crack reporter Rosalind Russell, who is about to quit to marry Ralph Bellamy.

166. *Captain Blood*
This 1935 film launched Errol Flynn's career as the swashbuckling heir to Douglas Fairbanks.

174. *Private Detective 62*
The poster presents a strong and rather dramatic image, reflecting the fact that in this film William Powell did not have many chances to display the wit and sophistication that marks his roles opposite Kay Francis, Myrna Loy, and Carole Lombard.

176. *My Man Godfrey*
The ultimate screwball comedy paired William Powell and Carole Lombard, five years after their short-lived marriage.

200. *Sullivan's Travels*
Preston Sturges's 1941 parable about Hollywood, with Joel McCrea as a famous director who wants to leave comedy behind and try his hand at more serious fare. His costar is Veronica Lake in her brief prime.

205. *Gilda*
Rita Hayworth at her most fabulous in a sexy 1946 movie tinged with film noir. The famous *Gilda* "B" poster is one of the most sensual and sought-after of all time.

222. *Dodsworth*
As I get older, I appreciate this 1936 William Wyler film more and more. Mary Astor is wonderful as a disillusioned expatriate who falls in love with a drifting ex-auto tycoon whose wife has left him for another man. Based on a Sinclair Lewis novel, this is one of the most successful literary adaptations of all time, and one of my top five films.

249 and 250.   *The 39 Steps* and *The Lady Vanishes*
Classic Hitchcock films from his British period.

254. *Jezebel*
This was Bette Davis's 1938 response to not being awarded the role of Scarlett in *Gone with the Wind*. The image is as strong as any in poster history.

256. *The Magnificent Ambersons*
Orson Welles's 1942 film, which, had it not been butchered by RKO, might have been his second masterpiece. Norman Rockwell did right by him, though, with this striking design, a rare example of a poster by a famous artist.

259. *The Cabinet of Dr. Caligari*
This poster is for Goldwyn's 1921 U.S. release of the German horror classic.

276. *The Sin of Nora Moran*
Another pre-Code gem of a poster that features the raciest graphics of all time.

282. *Citizen Kane*
To me and to many others, this is the greatest film of all time. To think that it was the work of a twenty-five-year-old first-time director boggles the mind.

283. *No Man of Her Own*
Another 1932 film that paired Clark Gable and Carole Lombard four years before they became a couple in real life.

284. *The Thief of Bagdad*
A lovely poster portraying Douglas Fairbanks in his 1924 Arabian Nights fantasy.

A Collector's Guide

POSTER SIZES

With the exception of lobby cards, window cards, and a few other items, the size of American movie posters is described in terms of the dimensions of the basic one-sheet—41 × 27 in. (104.1 × 68.6 cm)—a standard printing format determined by the dimensions of the bed of a commonly used commercial lithography press. Thus a three-sheet is the size of three one-sheets placed side by side.

Lobby Cards
11 × 14 in. (27.9 × 35.6 cm)
As the name implies, these were intended for display in theater lobbies. Produced in sets of eight, they consisted of a title card—which combined credits with imagery—and seven cards illustrating key scenes from the movie. Even in the black-and-white era these were often printed in color.

Jumbo Lobby Cards
14 × 17 in. (35.6 × 43.2 cm)
These were produced by major studios for a few big budget releases, so they tend to be rare. Typically they were printed on high quality stock, either linen-textured or glossy, and a title card was seldom included in the set. Jumbo cards were discontinued during the outbreak of World War II.

Window Cards
22 × 14 in. (55.9 × 35.6 cm)
Intended for display in store windows, these were printed on heavy cardboard stock. At the top of each card is a white strip on which the local theater's name could be printed or, in some cases, written by hand.

Midget Window Cards
14 × 8 in. (35.6 × 20.3 cm)
Miniature cards intended for display in showcases within retail stores.

Jumbo Window Cards
22 × 28 in. (55.9 × 71.1 cm)
Double-sized window cards.

Inserts
36 × 14 in. (91.4 × 35.6 cm)
Tall, narrow posters printed on card stock paper, often used in theater lobbies. Typically these posters were issued folded into thirds.

One-sheets
41 × 27 in. (104.1 × 68.6 cm)
When the term "movie poster" comes up, what most people visualize is the classic one-sheet. Used both in lobbies and outside movie theaters, the one-sheet derived from the classic theater posters employed since the nineteenth century to promote everything from Broadway shows to vaudeville. Usually one-sheets were printed on light paper stock and came folded with one vertical fold and two horizontal folds.

Half-sheets
22 × 28 in. (55.8 × 71.1 cm)
This term has come into use because these posters are approximately half the size of a one-sheet, though originally they were called "displays," the term used to refer to them in the press books—volumes containing illustrations of promotional material circulated to movie theaters when a film was about to be released. These press books are very collectible.

Three-sheets
81 × 41 in. (205.7 × 104.1 cm)
Commonly used outside theaters, the three-sheet was normally printed on three separate sheets which had to be assembled *in situ*, each being carefully aligned with the adjacent sheet or sheets. When found today, three-sheets have usually been mounted together on a linen or heavy paper backing.

Six-sheets
81 × 81 in. (205.7 × 205.7 cm)
Very rare, these large posters were designed for display on small billboards. Like three-sheets, they had to be assembled from separate printed panels.

Twenty-four–sheets
108 × 246 in. (274.3 × 624.8 cm)
Huge posters of this sort were used on standard full-sized billboards. Usually printed in twelve sections, these were installed by billboard professionals working for companies like Foster & Kleiser which dominated outdoor advertising on the West Coast from Hollywood to Seattle. The extreme rarity of these behemoths is due both to their size and to the fact that when a promotion was over they were unceremoniously stripped from their supports.

40 × 60 in. (101.6 × 152.4 cm)
In the 1930s, these unusual-sized posters—usually distributed rolled rather than folded—were printed on light paper stock either using silk screen technology, or the same photo-gelatin process used to produce lobby cards. Examples of these are very rare. Later, offset-lithography was used. These large posters were sometimes mounted on card to be displayed on easels in theater lobbies.

30 × 40 in. (76.2 × 101.6 cm)
Like their 40 × 60 in. (101.6 × 152.4 cm) siblings, these were sent out rolled, but were printed on heavier card stock. They enjoyed popularity with certain studios, being favored over one-sheets by Disney, for example, in the mid-1930s. After World War II, many theater operators preferred them to one-sheets since, being on card, they were more durable. This size is equivalent to the British poster size designated "quad."

Door Panels

60 × 20 in. (152.4 × 50.8 cm)
Printed for major productions, these were usually issued in sets of four or six. They were intended for display on doors inside theaters.

Banners

Produced in many different sizes—up to ten feet in length—these were originally silk-screened onto canvas or heavy fabric. By the 1930s there was a transition to silk screening on card, sometimes with a photograph pasted to the banner.

Subways

54 × 41 in. (137.2 × 104.1 cm)
Now familiar to New York City subway riders and users of other mass transport systems, these are a relatively modern phenomenon not known in the classic period.

British Posters

Posters from overseas are often very handsome. Different countries have their own standard sizes. In the United Kingdom, for example, the most common format is the 30 × 40 in. (76.2 × 101.6 cm) horizontal "quad," which is used more frequently than the local version of the one-sheet (41 × 27 in. [104.1 × 68.6 cm]). The three-sheet is also encountered, as is the "double crown" (30 × 20 in. [76.2 × 50.8 cm]), while the equivalent of the American "subway" is the "British giant fly" (65 × 40 in. [165.1 × 101.6 cm]), which will be familiar to anyone who has been in a London Tube station. Larger still is the "billboard" (90 × 80 in. [228.6 × 203.2 cm]).

CONDITION

Descriptions of the condition of a poster are somewhat determined by subjective factors. For example, one collector might accept a certain level of restoration in a poster described as "fine" while another might find it excessive. Similarly, one auction house might interpret "near mint" slightly differently from another. In general the wide expertise now existing in the field ensures that deliberate misrepresentation is not common.

Mint

An exceptional example in the condition in which it was distributed to theaters, with no fading of color or other defects. Since the majority of posters were folded when distributed, evidence of the folds is not considered a fault.

Near Mint

Similar to "mint" but with very minor defects such as slight wear on the fold lines or pinholes at the corners. The color should still have its original sparkle, but minimal, discreet restoration may be acceptable.

Fine

The wear on the fold lines may be more extensive and there might be some minor tears or a frayed edge. The color should still be strong, though a little more restoration is acceptable.

Very Good

Superficially similar to "fine" but displaying more wear and tear on close inspection, and possibly more evidence of restoration.

Good

This describes an imperfect but acceptable example, especially if the poster is rare. There may be some foxing (reddish-brown age spots), slight paper discoloration, paper loss, and significant wear and tear, especially to fold lines and edges, but the image remains readable and the color reasonably strong.

Fair

Differs from "good" in that paper damage may encroach on the imagery. There may be significant tears and/or evidence of amateur restoration (such as traces of scotch tape). Such a poster, if it has significance for the collector, is a candidate for professional restoration.

Poor

Beyond hope—unless the poster is extremely rare or has special meaning for the collector.

Acknowledgments

To my family and friends for their love and support through all these years. To my pal James Delson, for his hours and hours of interviews that pulled stories and feelings out of me for the introduction and star profiles. To Patricia Morrisroe, a real writer, who encouraged me with her editing and years of friendship. To Robert Osborne of Turner Classic Movies who saw my collection and pushed me to go to Abbeville and pursue creating this book. To everyone who ever worked at my Motion Picture Arts Gallery, especially Joe Burtis who after all these years still guides me through the treacherous collecting seas. To all the other dealers and collectors who share my passion for film art. I learned from you all and enriched many of you as well. To Robert Abrams for seeing the art in film posters for a second time and giving this book life. To Susan Costello and, especially, my editor, Michaelann Millrood, who nurtured a novice to produce this culmination of forty years of collecting. To David Graveen and Annette Daniels who were always supportive, and whose photographic taste and excellence opened up my collection for everyone to enjoy. To Gil Wang for his constancy and caring as he poured over endless documents and who has always had my back. To Susan, Steffi, and Alan who didn't live to see this book but who gave me love and affection which fueled me along the way. To my parents, Jack and Pearl Resnick, who gave me the means and freedom to follow my passions. So many people helped me to this point, The Knights of the Green Felt Table, Aaron Stern, my friends—past and present—at the Film Society of Lincoln Center, Christopher Finch, James Card, Kevin Brownlow, Karl Katz, Jeany Wolf, Kent Jones, and everyone else who interacted with me along this quest experiencing movie magic.

Bibliography

Allen, Richard, and Stephen Rebello. *Reel Art*. New York: Abbeville Press, 1988.

Basinger, Jeanine J. *Silent Stars*. New York: Alfred A. Knopf, 1999.

Chierichetti, Davis and Steve Schapiro. *The Movie Poster Book*. New York: Penguin Group, 1979.

Fahey, David, and Linda Rich. *Masters of Starlight*. New York: Ballantine Books, 1987.

Griffith, Richard. *The Movie Stars*. Garden City: Doubleday and Company, 1970.

Jaccard, Roland. *Louise Brooks—Portrait of an Anti-Star*. New York: Zoetrope, 1986.

Katz, Ephraim. *The Film Encyclopedia*. New York: Harper Collins Publishers, 1998.

Kerr, Walter. *The Silent Clowns*. New York: Alfred A Knopf, 1975.

Kobal, John. *Hollywood: The Years Of Innocence*. New York: Abbeville Press, 1985.

Lawton, Richard. *Grand Illusions*. New York: McGraw Hill Book Company, 1973.

Monaco, James. *The Encyclopedia of Film*. New York: Putnam Publishing, 1991.

Paris, Barry. *Louise Brooks*. New York: Alfred A. Knopf, 1989.

Peary, Danny, ed. *Close-Ups: The Movie Star Book*. New York: Simon and Schuster, 1978.

Scorcese, Martin. *A Personal Journey with Martin Scorcese Through American Movies*. New York: Miramax Books/ Hyperion, 1997.

Thomson, David. *The New Biographical Dictionary of Film*. New York: Alfred A. Knopf, 2002.

Trent, Paul. *The Image Makers*. New York: McGraw Hill Book Company, 1972.

Vieira, Mark A. *Hollywood Portraits: Classic Scene Stills 1929–41*. Greenwich: Portland House, 1988.

Vieira, Mark A. *Sin in Soft Focus*. New York: Harry N. Abrams, 1999.

Woody, Jack. *Lost Hollywood*. Altadena: Twin Palms Publishers, 1987.

Index